GW01191955

Work Organi_____
Labour & Globalisation

Volume 3, Number 1, Summer, 2009

Published by Analytica Publications Ltd.
46 Ferntower Road, London N5 2JH, UK
www.analyticapublications.co.uk
phone: +44 (0)20 7226 8411
fax: +44 (0) 7226 0813
email orders@analyticapublications.co.uk
(for subscriptions and editorial queries)

in the UK in association with Merlin Press Ltd.
96 Monnow Street,Monmouth NP25 3EQ, UK
www.merlinpress.co.uk
phone: +44 (0)1600 775663
fax: +44 (0)1600 775663
email: orders@merlinpress.co.uk

Printed and bound in the UK by Lightningsource UK Ltd.
6 Precedent Drive
Rooksley
Milton Keynes
MK13 8PR, UK

Edited by Ursula Huws
Designed by Andrew Haig Associates

ISBN: 978 0 85036 700 3
ISSN: 1745-641X

© Analytica Publications, 2009

Working at the interface:
call-centre labour in a global economy

edited by Ursula Huws

About this journal

The globalisation of world trade in combination with the use of information and communications technologies is bringing into being a new international division of labour, not just in manufacturing industry, as in the past, but also in work involving the processing of information.

Organisational restructuring shatters the unity of the traditional workplace, both contractually and spatially, dispersing work across the globe in ever-more attenuated value chains.

A new 'cybertariat' is in the making, sharing common labour processes, but working in remote offices and call centres which may be continents apart and occupying very different cultural and economic places in local economies.

The implications of this are far-reaching, both for policy and for scholarship. The dynamics of this new global division of labour cannot be captured adequately within the framework of any single academic discipline. On the contrary they can only be understood in the light of a combination of insights from fields including political economy, the sociology of work, organisational theory, economic geography, development studies, industrial relations, comparative social policy, communications studies, technology policy and gender studies.

Work Organisation, Labour and Globalisation aims to:

- bring together insights from all these fields to create a single authoritative source of information on the new global division of labour, combining theoretical analysis with the results of empirical research in a way that is accessible both to the research community and to policy makers.
- Provide a single home for articles that specifically address issues relating to the changing international division of labour and the restructuring of work in a global knowledge-based economy.
- Bring together the results of empirical research, both qualitative and quantitative, with theoretical analyses in order to inform the development of new interdisciplinary approaches to the study of the restructuring of work, organisation and labour in a global context.
- Be global in scope, with a particular emphasis on attracting contributions from developing countries as well as from Europe, North America and other developed regions.
- Encourage a dialogue between university-based researchers and their counterparts in international and national government agencies, independent research institutes, trade unions and civil society as well as policy makers. Subject to the requirements of scholarly peer review, the journal is open to submissions from contributors working outside the academic sphere and encourages an accessible style of writing in order to facilitate this goal.
- Complement, rather than compete with existing discipline-based journals.
- Bring to the attention of English-speaking readers relevant articles originally published in other languages.

Each issue addresses a specific theme and is also published independently as a book. The editor welcomes comments, criticisms, contributions and suggestions for future themes. For further information, visit the website: http://www.analyticapublications.co.uk

Editorial board

Contents

Working at the interface:

call-centre labour in a global economy

Ursula Huws

Ursula Huws *is Director of Analytica and Professor of international labour studies at London Metropolitan University and the in London, UK.*

ABSTRACT

Introducing this volume, this paper describes the contradictory nature of many aspects of call-centre work, drawing on the results of the EC-funded STILE project to demonstrate the difficulties of classifying call-centre workers. The lack of a clear objective 'place' in the technical division of labour and the social order for this transient and poorly-defined workforce is mirrored by a subjective failure, on the part of call-centre workers, to identify themselves as such. This makes it difficult to develop stable collective occupational identities that could form a basis for organisation and representation. Such conflicts are exacerbated by call-centre workers' position 'at the interface' between companies and their customers and between the local and the global. Many are also having to deal with the difficult transition from other types of work to call-centre work as the process of 'callcenterisation' sweeps through the public sector as well as private companies. The paper concludes by noting that, despite many similarities between call centres across the globe, national industrial relations systems and other aspects of particular locations still make a significant difference to the working conditions of call-centre workers.

Call-centre workers occupy a central – and emotionally-charged – position in the public imagination. In their capacities as consumers, there must be few people who have not been exasperated by their encounters with call centres. These often start with the sinking discovery that a phone number leads, not directly to a virtual version of a shop assistant or a counter clerk but to a menu of numbered options within which further menus may be nested. Then, having negotiated a way through this virtual labyrinth, there is the experience of waiting whilst recorded messages are played, informing customers how busy the agents are and urging them to visit the company's website or call back later. The message that callers are an expensive nuisance is transmitted before they have even spoken to anyone. Those who survive this experience, which may involve many minutes listening to recorded music jarringly interrupted by looped messages, may finally be rewarded with the chance to speak to a real person, but only after they have been warned that 'your call may be recorded for training purposes' and put through an extensive interrogation, involving the recall of passwords or 'memorable words', confirmation of zip code, mother's maiden name, order number or other information to establish their identity 'for your own protection'. If, after all this, it turns out that they have been routed to the wrong team, or the query is unanswerable, patience is liable to snap.

Such experiences make it abundantly clear that much call-centre work is highly Taylorised. The proof of this is in the way that this Taylorisation is transmitted to the consumer. The script that dictates what the call-centre worker must say, and in what sequence, also, by definition, dictates the timing and structure of the conversation from the point of view of the customers, who must fit their responses into the narrow range of options predicted by the programme (Huws, 2003). The exasperation of the call-centre customer is a measure of the misfit between these predicted options and the complex reality of the problem that led to the phone call in the first place.

Of course there are many situations where all goes smoothly. A few bad call-centre experiences provide a strong incentive to customers to become self-servicing, substituting their own unpaid time and self-developed skills for those of paid service workers, and learning to obtain what they want by using a corporate website or, at least, being well-prepared to select the correct numerical options and feed the call-centre worker with the right responses in the appropriate jargon so that the encounter can be a simple and constructive one. But, where the problem is intractable, the relationship between the customer and the call-centre worker becomes complex and contradictory. Losing one's temper, whilst often an understandable reaction, is rarely productive. Not only are most customers inhibited from doing so by norms of good manners (although these may be undermined by racism); they are usually aware that whatever temporary satisfaction may be obtained from expressing their rage will be cancelled out by the realisation that the problem will remain unfixed if they do so. A much more likely outcome is that the customer tries to suppress his or her annoyance in order to enlist the collaboration of the call-centre agent into a joint effort to solve the problem.

The tension produced by this effort to reconcile contradictory impulses mirrors the tension experienced by the call-centre worker at the other end of the phone line, who is similarly trying to reconcile the need to bring the conversation to a successful outcome with the need to meet tight time targets. Hovering in the background is a shared awareness that there are many other callers waiting in line and that the call is probably being monitored. Call-centre customer and call-centre worker are trapped together in a shared virtual space, under the same surveillance, constrained by the logic of the same computer programmes and equally helpless to change the rules of the encounter which is a cause of stress for both. Whether any given interaction will reach a productive conclusion, with a moment of temporary solidarity between them, or dissolve into failure, resentment and antagonism, is not always immediately clear, lending drama to the encounter.

Much will depend on the communication skills of the two protagonists, whether empathy can be established, the degree of latitude granted to the call-centre worker to deviate from the script, and a host of other factors, many of which are explored in this volume.

The knowledge of call centres that is obtained by people in their capacities as users of their services is, increasingly, tempered by another sort of knowledge, that comes from direct experience of working in them, or the indirect experience that comes from having a friend or family member who has worked in a call centre.

There can be few occupations whose members are distributed so widely across the class spectrum as call-centre workers. As formerly stable public sector bureaucratic organisations evolve towards call-centre models, workers who saw themselves as skilled public servants find themselves transformed into call-centre workers. Other specialists with expert knowledge in fields as diverse as IT and medicine may also work in call-centre environments. At the other extreme are very routine jobs, such as directory enquiries, or verifying details for database maintenance, increasingly carried out in outsourced call centres operating in a global labour market that bears many of the hallmarks of a secondary labour market (Doeringer & Piore,1971). The use of a contingent workforce, largely female, often part-time, on a variety of casual contracts makes this segment of the call-centre workforce similar to other forms of low-paid service work (Paul & Huws, 2002). In between are a wide range of jobs, often requiring good educational qualifications and language skills but nevertheless pressurised, repetitive and lacking in career prospects. These are filled by people from a range of different backgrounds, many of whom are students or recent graduates 'just passing through' the industry as a short-term means of generating an income.

It is not surprising, then, that when the British National Statistics Office created the new occupational category 'call-centre worker' in its 2000 revision of the occupational classification, SOC2000, very few respondents in the survey actually stated that this was their occupation. In Spring 2003, the UK Labour Force Survey recorded numbers in this category that grossed up to only 81,000 nationally, although it was known from other sources (such as industry estimates derived from shipments of workstations) that there were at the time almost as many call-centre workers as this in a single British city such as Manchester or Liverpool, with the total number of call-centre workers in the UK estimated conservatively at well over one million in that year (Paul & Huws, 2003:11).

It seems likely that many call-centre workers do not think of themselves as such. If asked, they might say something like 'This is just a job I am doing until I graduate', or 'until I get my novel published', or 'until my children start secondary school', or 'until I get a job as an actor', or 'until my husband recovers from his surgery and is able to return to work', or 'until I decide to stop travelling and settle down'. They may well retain a sense that their primary identity is something quite different – student, artist, engineer, teacher, musician or housekeeper and parent.

The diversity of this workforce, its transience, and the relative newness of this kind of work suggest that no coherent collective occupational identity has yet emerged, creating challenges not just for the individuals concerned, and the trade unions that might wish to recruit them, but also for the agencies that collect the statistics on which public policies relating to call centres might be based. In 2003-4, the STILE[1] project, in an attempt to find out where workers in the 'new economy' might be found in the official employment statistics, collected 150 job descriptions and asked experienced coders from the national statistics offices of four European countries to code them according to the International Standard Classification of Occupations (ISCO), as they would when recording the results of a survey such as the European Community Labour Force Survey. A sample of the results relating to call-centre jobs is shown in Table 1. As can be seen, not only was there considerable disagreement between these coders about

---

1   STILE stands for Statistical Indicators on the Labour market in the eEconomy. This international project, funded by the European Commission under its 6th Framework Programme from 2001 to 2004, carried out research in eight EU Member States. For further information, visit: http://www.stile.be/

how to classify any given job. There was not even a common understanding of where to place them at the single-digit level which assigns each occupation to a one of nine larger groups, designated by the first number of the code.

Table 1: Coding of call-centre occupations in four European countries

Job title	Job description	ISCO code / description			
		Hungary	Ireland	Netherlands	UK
Call centre agent – travel sales	I work in a call centre handling calls from US members regarding timeshare properties. I provide information on travel requirements and sell them travel and insurance products, working to meet sales targets.	341 Finance and sales associate professionals	911 street vendors and related workers	422 Client information clerks	911 street vendors and related workers
Customer relations team leader	I head up the 'win back' team for the call centre of a financial services company. I coach and motivate a team of agents trying to persuade customers to return to our service.	123 Other departmental managers	419 Other office clerks	122 Production and operations department managers	422 Client information clerks
Team leader in sales call centre	As a team leader I supervise the shift arrangements for the team, and monitor attendance, holidays etc. We work in a sales call centre. I have to ensure my team meets targets and goals. I handle time-consuming customer contacts, and coach and develop team members as well as arranging necessary training with the training manager.	343 Administrative associate professionals	419 Other office clerks	122 Production and operations department managers	911 street vendors and related workers
Contact centre team leader	As a team leader in a contact centre I carry out monitoring of calls to assess quality levels and use software to predict call loads and arrange staffing levels. I train new recruits and existing staff. I work to maintain motivation of the agents and to improve customer satisfaction. The centre handles holiday reservations.	343 Administrative associate professionals	419 Other office clerks	122 Production and operations department managers	422 Client information clerks
Online marketing account manager	I am responsible for selling online marketing services to business customers in Ireland, the UK and the US. The services include search engine optimisation, banner advertising, email marketing and consultancy services on design and revenue generation options.	241 Business professionals	123 Other departmental managers	522 shop salespersons and demonstrators	123 Other departmental managers

source: Huws and Van der Hallen, 2004

In just this small group of five call-centre job descriptions, we can see that no fewer than six of the nine groups were regarded as appropriate for classifying them by expert coders in at least one country (Huws & Van der Hallen, 2004). These include 'managers' (numbers starting with 1), 'professionals' (starting with 2), 'technicians; (starting with 3), 'clerks' (starting with 4), 'service and sales workers' (starting with 5) and 'elementary occupations' (starting with 9). From the entire spectrum of occupations, only the categories 'agricultural workers', 'craft workers', and 'machine operators' are missing!

There is, in short, considerable confusion about the 'place' of call-centre workers in the technical division of labour, and hence in the social hierarchy. Are they unskilled service workers, clerical workers, sales workers, professionals, technicians or on the lower rungs of a managerial ladder? With which other occupational groups do their interests lie? This confusion about their objective position mirrors the subjective reluctance of call-centre workers to 'place' themselves as such and is reinforced by the feeling that their traditional occupational identities are disintegrating expressed by workers whose jobs have undergone restructuring to transform them into call centres (Schönauer, 2008, Huws & Dahlmann, forthcoming). This in turn has implications for their ability to develop the sorts of collective occupational identities that facilitate trade union organisation and form the building blocks of class consciousness (Huws, 2006).

With no clear sectoral identity, call-centre workers often fall outside the scope of national social dialogue representation and regulations and lack formalised certification of skills and institutionalised qualification trajectories[2]. The lack of clarity about where they belong often also extends to a lack of clarity about who is actually responsible for their working conditions. It is not unusual in an outsourced call centre to have one company responsible for facilities management, another for recruiting the workers, a third for training them and a fourth for provision and maintenance of technical equipment (Paul & Huws, 2004). With many aspects of the work process, including scripts and computer programmes, determined by client companies, rather than the outsourced call centre company which is the nominal employer of the workforce, who then is legally responsible if a worker develops work-related injuries?

There is also ambivalence among policy-makers about call centres. Should they be regarded as gateways to the global knowledge economy, providing a form of fast-track development for lagging regions? Or are they just electronic sweatshops, providing only routine dead-end jobs that do little to enhance a region's skill-base?

Call centres also represent something of a conundrum for researchers. In many ways, they fit the model of 'post-industrial' workplaces: the work is white-collar, requiring considerable amounts of knowledge to perform; it relies crucially on information and communications technology; the services it provides are immaterial; as long as the right infrastructure is in place, it can be located just about anywhere in the world; and, unlike Fordist production industries, it caters individually to each client in a form of mass customisation (Pine II, 1992). Yet it exhibits many of the features commonly supposed to epitomise 'industrial' Fordist production, including Taylorist management and a work-pace determined by machines and their programmes. Call-centre workers have been studied from several different perspectives, including gender studies (e.g. Belt, Richardson

---

2   I am grateful to Monique Ramioul for drawing this point to my attention.

& Webster, 2000; 2002; Glucksmann, 2004), ethnicity and imperialism (e.g Mirchandani, 2004), labour process theory and labour sociology more generally (e.g. Bain & Taylor, 2000; Callaghan &Thompson, 2002; Wickham & Collins, 2004) and industrial relations (e.g. Taylor & Bain, 1999; Rainnie & Drummond, 2006).

This collection of papers adds to this body of work. It has been given the title 'working at the interface' because this sums up the multifaceted nature of call-centre work and the multiple tensions that shape the workers' everyday experiences

The first interface is between the call centre, or its corporate clients, and their customers. The call-centre worker is, quite literally, the public face of most companies – the primary channel by which its customers communicate with it. Several of the papers in this collection explore what this means, both physically and mentally, for the working experience of call-centre workers. Simone Wolff, in her case study of the telemarketing unit of a telecommunications company in Brazil, describes the process whereby the agents' tacit knowledge, and the information gleaned by them during the course of their conversations with customers, is captured and embedded in the software as part of a continuous process of fine-tuning the programme and developing ever-more sophisticated ways of targeting the company's marketing strategy. The agents are thus expected to make creative inputs whilst simultaneously being tightly controlled and required to stick precisely to their scripts. The tension between trying to develop a friendly relationship with the customer and make a sale, whilst not deviating from the programmed text is a major source of stress. Päivi Korvajärvi explores the way in which the voice of the worker becomes a crucial working tool in call centres, with its characteristics consciously used to sell particular kinds of products and services. Whilst masculine voices are regarded as attractive in their own right, feminine voices are associated with certain kinds of products and services so that gendered characteristics actually become embedded in the commodified products. The physical strains that result from using the voice all day, as well as the emotional impact of acting as a shock-absorber between the service provider and the public, are described in several papers, including another study of telemarketing agents in Brazil, by Claudia Mazzei Noguiera and a study of public sector call-centre agents in Canada, by Norene Pupo and Andrea Noack.

The second interface is that between the local and the global. Although (as Ursula Holtgrewe, Jessica Longen, Hannelore Mottweiler and Annika Schönauer demonstrate in their analysis of the results of the Global Call Center Industry Project) the majority of call centres around the world still serve national markets, there are, nevertheless, large, and growing numbers of call-centre workers who spend their working hours speaking to customers in other countries or continents. This adds an extra dimension of difficulty to the already demanding challenge of communicating with customers whilst simultaneously meeting tightly-defined performance targets. Premilla d'Cruz and Ernesto Noronha describe the stresses this induces in international call centres in India, whilst Vassil Kirov and Kapka Mircheva give an account of the rapid evolution of international call centres in Bulgaria. In global call centres, many of the problems found in national call centres are exacerbated, with workers having to communicate in foreign languages, accommodate their speech and comprehension to differences of accent and culture, observe foreign holidays, adapt their body clocks to foreign time structures, and, in some cases, adopt false names and disguise their location as well as putting up with racist abuse.

A third interface that has to be negotiated by call-centre workers is that between the sphere of production and that of reproduction, in other words between their paid work and their family lives. Kirov and Mircheva show how the flexible working hours offered by call centres in Bulgaria make them especially attractive to students who want to combine paid work with study. Noguiera focuses on the relationship between paid work and the sexual division of labour in the home in her study of women telemarketing workers in Brazil, demonstrating that the company's strategy of creating part-time work for these workers supports a traditional gender division of labour.

As if mediating conflicts in these dimensions of their lives is not enough, many call-centre workers are also having to cope with major upheavals in other aspects of their work and identity as a result of the ongoing organisational restructuring in which call centres play a crucial role. What might be called the process of 'callcenterisation' destabilises many features of work that were formerly taken for granted. In this collection, two contributions look in depth at restructuring in the telecommunications industry. Wolff describes how even a state-owned telecommunications company was obliged, in order to survive in the new competitive market that emerged after privatisation in Brazil, to shift its focus from providing a public service to aggressively marketing a range of new products and services via an outsourced unit. In the process, its workforce found their roles and their work processes radically altered. Enda Brophy depicts a similar process of restructuring and creeping callcenterisation in a Canadian telecommunications company and recounts the story of how the workforce responded by organising a strike, the analysis of which offers a number of lessons on trade union organisation in call centres.

Two other contributions chart the callcenterisation process in the public sector. Pupo and Noack look at the introduction of 'one stop shops' in Canadian government services and the damaging impact of this on the quality of these services as well as on the working conditions and career prospects of the public servants who have found themselves transformed into call-centre agents. Pia Bramming, Ole Sørensen and Peter Hasle examine the introduction of a call-centre model into the administration of the tax system in Denmark, which accompanied a major restructuring involving the centralisation of functions that had formerly been dispersed geographically and administratively across multiple authorities and locations. This case study shows that, in a context of good industrial relations, and in an environment which is not fiercely competitive, it is possible to bring about significant improvements in working conditions.

This conclusion supports the evidence from Holtgrewe, Longen, Mottweiler and Schönauer that, despite the many similarities between call centres around the world, their specific location still does make a real difference. The evidence from the Global Call Center Industry Survey demonstrates significant variations in employment conditions between countries with different types of industrial relations systems. Their case study of a global electronics company also provides evidence that companies select locations for international call centres on the basis of specific local competitive advantages. Kirov and Mircheva also show how Bulgaria has managed to attract international call centres largely on the basis of the high education and language skills of its young workers, but also because costs are lower than in Western Europe. In India, as d'Cruz and Noronha explain, companies in the international outsourced call-centre sector are well aware that their competitive advantages may be threatened by other, cheaper locations and put considerable effort into inculcating their workers with a sense of loyalty to the industry as a whole and suspicion of trade unions as agencies whose activities could threaten these competitive advantages. Brophy demonstrates that call-centre workers are capable of organising in trade unions and have achieved some limited success by doing so in Canada and, as we have noted, there are examples of good practice, like the Danish case presented by Bramming, Sørensen and Hasle. The extent to which such examples can be followed elsewhere is an open question, but one which we hope will be addressed in future issues of this journal.

© *Ursula Huws, 2009.*

REFERENCES

Bain, P., & P. Taylor (2000) 'Entrapped by the 'electronic panopticon? Worker resistance in the call centre', *New Technology, Work, and Employment*, Vol 15, No 1:2-18

Belt, V., R. Richardson & J. Webster (2000) 'Women's Work in the Information Economy: The case of telephone call centres', *Information, Communication & Society* Vol 3, No 3:366-385

Belt, V., R. Richardson & J. Webster (2002) 'Women, Social Skill and Interactive Service Work in Telephone Call Centres', *New Technology Work and Employment,* Vol 17, No 1:20-34

Callaghan G. & Thompson P. (2002) 'We recruit attitude: the selection and shaping of call centre labour', *Journal of Management Studies*, Vol 39, No 2:233-254

Doeringer, P. B. & M. J. Piore. (1971) *Internal labour markets and manpower analysis*, Lexington: Lexington Books

Glucksmann, M. (2004) 'Call configurations: varieties of call centre and divisions of labour', *Work, employment and society* Vol 18, No 4:795-811.

Huws U. & P. Van der Hallen (2004) *Opening the Black Box: Classification and Coding of Sectors and Occupations in the eEconomy*, Leuven: Hooger Institut Voor der Arbeid

Huws, U. & S. Dahlmann (Forthcoming) Global Restructuring of Value Chains and Class Issues, in N. Pupo & M. Thomas, editors. *Interrogating the New Economy: Restructuring Work in the 21st Century*. Toronto: UTP Higher Education.

Huws, U. (2003) 'Who's waiting? the contestation of time', in U. Huws *The Making of a Cybertariat: virtual work in a real world,* New York: Monthly Review Press:177-186

Huws, U. (2006) 'What will we do? The destruction of occupational identities in the Knowledge-based Economy', *Monthly Review*, Vol 57, No 8

Mirchandani, K. (2004) Practices of Global Capital: Gaps, Cracks and Ironies in Transnational Call Centres in India. *Global Networks,* Vol 4, No 4:355-373.

Paul,J. & U. Huws (2002) *How can we help? Good Practice in Call Centre Employment*, Brussels: European Trade Union Confederation

Pine II, J. (1992), Mass Customization: The New Frontier in Business Competition, Boston, Mass.: Harvard Business School

Rainne, A. & G. Drummond (2006) 'Community unionism in a regional call centre: The organizer's perspective', in J. Burgess & J. Connell (eds) *Developments in the call centre industry: Analysis, changes and challenges*, New York: Routledge:136-151

Schönauer, A. (2008), 'Reorganising the front line: the case of public call centre services' in U.Huws & C. Hermann (eds) *The New Gold Rush: the new multinationals and the commodification of public services, Work Organisation, Labour and Globalisation,* Vol 2 No 2:131-147

Taylor, P. & P. Bain 1999. '"An assembly line in the head": Work and employee relations in the call centre', *Industrial Relations Journal*, Vol 30, No 2:101-117

Wickham J. & G. Collins (2004), 'The call centre: a nursery for new forms of work organisation?', *Service Industries Journal*, Vol 24, No 2:1-18.

Global or embedded service work?

the (limited) transnationalisation of the call-centre industry

Ursula Holtgrewe, Jessica Longen, Hannelore Mottweiler and Annika Schönauer

Ursula Holtgrewe *is a senior researcher at the Working Life Research Centre (FORBA) in Vienna, Austria.*
Jessica Longen *is a postgraduate student in sociology at Darmstadt Technical University, Germany.*
Hannelore Mottweiler *is a research associate in the department of sociology at Duisburg-Essen University, Germany*
Annika Schönauer *is a researcher at the Working Life Research Centre (FORBA) in Vienna, Austria.*

ABSTRACT

This paper explores the amount of 'real' internationalisation in the call centre industry and looks at its effects on work organisation from two angles. First, we analyse the data from the Global Call Center Industry Project, with regard to the amount of internationalisation and the profiles of call centres serving an international market. Then, these industry-wide findings are confronted with a case study of the customer service operation of a US-based electronics multinational. Overall, while global business service providers exist and shape the perception of the industry to a considerable extent, internationalisation is chiefly limited to younger, larger subcontracting companies with standardised work, although national patterns vary. While some services in some segments have certainly been internationalised (for example airline travel reservations and IT helplines), language and cultural proximity continue to matter.

Introduction

Call centres are frequently cited as prime examples of a global restructuring of service work in which work may be shifted across locations and organisations in real time. Globalisation theorists (Rugman, 2001) regard service work as more locally bound than manufacturing, because it is performed and consumed simultaneously, involves customer participation and collaboration, and hence allows only limited increases in productivity. However, the use of call centres enabled by connected telecommunications and computer technology means that 'the physical separation of the worker from the workplace and the customer is now possible' (Burgess & Connell, 2006). Services that do not depend on face-to-face contact may now be treated in similar ways to manufacturing processes and, since their products are immaterial, even without some of the logistical complications that exist in manufacturing.

Call-centre operations may be routed through networks in which individual sites are connected by phone and data lines that cross organisational and national boundaries. This opens up a wide range of strategic options for companies and their managers. Their service units may be outsourced, sold off, relocated, or shifted to greenfield sites outside the purview of established industry boundaries and collective agreements. They may also be relocated to lower-cost countries ('offshoring' or 'nearshoring' within the region), either by using subsidiaries or external subcontractors. On the other hand, institutionalists have argued that sweeping technological possibilities do not determine the actual development of industrial restructuring and that institutional configurations continue to shape company strategies, which may use potentially global possibilities in regional and path-dependent patterns.

Call centres represent a generic, ICT-enabled mode of restructuring the organisation of services across industries and sectors. Thus, they provide a liminal case to pursue the extent to which services are being restructured on a 'global' scale, and whether it is actual organisations or rather organisational blueprints that are moving across national borders.

Such blueprints, in our case, specifically consist of the standardisation of interactive work on the one hand and a changing use of employee skills on the other. The interpretation and explication of knowledge and information in databases and the scripting of interactions are both a prerequisite and an outcome of service restructuring through call centres. However, conducting customer interactions remotely requires workers to bring considerable cognitive and communicative capabilities to a standardised and regimented form of work.

This paper explores the amount of 'real' internationalisation in the call-centre industry and looks at the profile of internationalised call centres from two angles. First, we analyse data from the Global Call Center Industry Project, which shows that the industry is internationalised only to a limited extent. Call centres catering to an international market are concentrated among subcontractors with standardised and regimented work, although there is some variation between countries. The findings on the industry-wide picture are then confronted with a case study of the customer service operation of a US-based electronics multinational. This study shows how transnational relocation strategies 'work' in between technological and 'global' possibilities and actual practice. Moving between industry-level analysis and case study evidence, the paper aims to contribute to a multi-layered picture of an industry that neither underrates critical and pioneering developments that are not yet widespread nor overrates their impact.

Transnational restructuring of service work)

Globalisation and transnational restructuring of services

The transnationalisation and restructuring of work and organisation has been discussed in a range of debates from the 'global' level to the role of regions and localised arrangements. Comprehensive surveys on European outsourcing are only now being conducted (Nielsen, 2007). Most studies at the organisational level address multinational corporations' (MNC) strategies and patterns of transnationalisation (Morgan, 2005; Ghoshal & Bartlett, 2005; 2006). Recently, under the heading of 'global value chains', the analysis of restructuring has moved beyond the scope of individual organisations (Faust, Voskamp & Wittke, 2004; Gereffi, Humphrey & Sturgeon, 2005) or production networks (Dicken, 2004).

However, most analyses at the organisational or value-chain level still focus on manufacturing sectors such as electronics, cars or clothing. Service restructuring has only recently come to the fore, with most emphasis on business process outsourcing and IT services (Dossani & Kenney, 2003; Miozzo & Grimshaw, 2005). Few studies that also involve services address the actual effects of these changes on employment relations and the quality of work (Huws & Flecker, 2004; Marchington, 2005; Flecker, Holtgrewe, Schönauer, Dunkel & Meil, 2008).

Theoretical approaches to transnational restructuring can be grouped simplistically into arguments focusing on the 'disembedding' of organisations and value chains from their surrounding institutional and social environment and arguments insisting on their 'embeddedness' (for a more comprehensive overview see Morgan, 2005; Geppert & Williams, 2006).

'Disembedding' approaches argue that companies are becoming 'stateless' (Ohmae, 1990) or that their structures and strategies are converging on the Anglo-American business model. There is broad agreement on the driving factors of global disembedding processes, especially with regard to service restructuring: the wide diffusion of information and communication technologies, the pressure of financial markets and investors on short-term growth, and the political deregulation of critical sectors such as telecommunications and financial services.

With regard to service restructuring, the varied prognoses of further and intensified outsourcing also work within this framework. For a few years now, consultancies and call-centre service providers have somewhat self-interestedly been predicting that service offshoring in Europe is about to expand outside English-speaking countries (e.g. Datamonitor 2003; Competence Call Center 2006). In 2006, an industry website run by a recruiting agency touted an explosion of offshoring of non-English-speaking work by 2011 along lines of old colonial ties and current economic proximity. In the view of this agency, clients will increasingly pursue multi-site/multi-country/multi-vendor solutions in order to have service providers compete with one another within a single contract.[1] Competence Call Center, an Austrian-based service provider with recent acquisitions of call centres in Slovakia, reported in 2006 that in a survey of 300 industry experts in Austria, Germany and Switzerland, three-quarters of respondents regarded Slovakia, Poland and Romania as important offshoring locations in the present or the future and 83% regarded offshoring to non-EU countries as a current or future trend. These prognoses tend to be based on and extrapolate growth rates from existing outsourcing and offshoring cases, although their empircal basis is unclear. They can be read as 'advocacy statements' or performative texts that seek to generate the structures they forecast and present them as inevitable (for a critical analysis with a focus on US-based prognoses see Srivastava & Theodore, 2006).

Arguments focusing on 'embeddedness' are represented by research along the lines of 'societal effects' (2000), national business systems (Whitley, 1999) and 'varieties of

---

1   http://www.call centres.com/articles/5yearson.htm

capitalism' (2001). In these views, specific institutional configurations both constrain and enable specific company strategies. MNCs will carry these patterns with them as 'country-of-origin' effects, but will embed them with the respective host country's environment as well (Harzing & Sorge, 2003). Current empirical studies of service sector outsourcing mostly confirm its regional and embedded character. In its 2003 employer survey, the EMERGENCE project (Huws, 2003) found that 34.5% of employers who outsourced some service business function kept outsourced services within their region, 18.3% outsourced within their country and 5.3% used providers or subunits outside national borders.

On an empirically grounded level, the many studies of work practices and managerial control in Indian call centres show the very negotiation of global and local logics and the dialectic of disembedding/embeddedness in action. They point out the cultural gaps and tensions that Indian customer service representatives (CSRs) face (Taylor & Bain, 2006), as call centres in India put effort into training on 'accent neutralisation' and immersion into a US-American cultural environment. This research provides ample illustration of post-colonial cultural imperialism (Mirchandani, 2004), but it also shows how intricate and culturally complex the offshoring of customer service work actually is and how much translation and legitimation work is shifted onto both agents and customers. Conversely, perceptions of cultural proximity may influence company decisions to 'nearshore' work or relocate within the region rather than further abroad.

Call centres and service restructuring

Since the 1990s the use of call centres for customer contact has spread across countries and economic sectors beyond the traditional telephone services such as directory enquiries or mail order. Anglo-American companies, and among them those in the financial and telecommunications sectors, were at the forefront of this expansion. They were also the first industries to offshore customer-contact operations to locations such as India or the Philippines. At a more local or regional level, small businesses, public sector and non-profit organisations have restructured customer services in many countries. Technologies such as automated call distribution, call monitoring, customer relationship management and standardisation of interactions enable this development, and so does management knowledge. However, both are diffusing through multinational consultancies and technology providers as well as through small businesses and individuals who may be more locally based.

There is considerable evidence that call centres are neither a global nor a truly international phenomenon, and that in terms of employment structure and working conditions they are embedded within their national institutional contexts (Shire, Mottweiler, Schönauer & Valverde, 2009). The initial report on the Global Call Center Industry Project survey summarises the situation: 'we find that the call-centre sector looks quite similar across countries in terms of its markets, service offerings, and organisational features. But beyond these similarities, we find that call-centre workplaces take on the character of their own countries and regions, based on distinct laws, customs, institutions, and norms. The 'globalisation' of call-centre activities has a remarkably national face' (Holman, Batt and Holtgrewe 2007: V).

There is a wide consensus that lower cost is a central motive for international relocation in labour-intensive services specifically, and that outsourced and offshored services are connected to a standardisation of work and an intensification of monitoring (Marchington, 2005; Doellgast & Greer, 2007; Flecker, Holtgrewe, Schönauer, Dunkel & Meil, 2008; Batt, Holman & Holtgrewe, 2009). The obvious principal-agent reasoning is that companies hiring a subcontractor will need to specify their demands and monitor that service provider's performance in more detail than that of an internal unit. In turn, they are more likely to outsource work that lends itself to this kind of monitoring.

Traditionally, within 'old' industrialised countries such standardisation is associated with low-skilled work or actual deskilling along the lines of a 'low road' of cost-cutting service restructuring (Batt & Moynihan, 2004). However, this association may be broken where wage differentials between originating and destination countries are substantial. Then, more highly skilled labour forces may become affordable for clients even for lower-skilled jobs. This is one of the reasons why Indian call centres mostly tend to hire youngish college graduates for tightly regimented and standardised work with little discretion and learning opportunities (Batt, Doellgast & Kwon, 2006; Taylor & Bain, 2006). A skilled workforce offers offshored companies or subsidiaries the theoretical possibility of taking over more complex or value-added work ('moving up the value chain') at prices that are still competitive (Dossani & Kenney, 2003), as can be observed in software and IT services. However, Batt, Doellgast and Kwon (2006) argue that, with this prevalent combination of highly educated agents and highly standardised and regimented jobs, call centres in India may be locking themselves into a low-road configuration and effectively blocking themselves from pursuing a path of professionalised, higher value-added service work – for which they have the labour force but not the work organisation.

An industry overview

We now turn to an examination of the extent of internationalisation of call centres across different countries and the differences in the profiles of international and national call centres. The key questions are which types of call-centre operations lend themselves to internationalisation, and to what extent the profile of India as an offshoring destination with well-educated agents doing tightly standardised work is also found in other countries in the sample. We present an analysis of the data gathered by the 'Global Call Center Industry Project'[2].

On average only 13% of call centres in the Global Call Center Industry Project's survey served an international market, as can be seen in Table 1.

---

2   The Global Call Centre Industry Report (Holman, Batt and Holtgrewe 2007) covered almost 2,500 centres in 17 countries.. Taken together, the centres in the survey employed a total of 475,000 people. The survey was translated and administered to senior call-centre managers by national teams who also selected the samples from industry databases, call-centre association member lists, regional-development-agency sources and trade press subscriber lists. The report thus does not claim representativeness but it does represent the best possible effort to move beyond selected case studies and gain an overview of the industry. For further details see Batt, Holman and Holtgrewe 2009.

Table 1: Call centres serving an international or domestic market

Country	Domestic market		International market	
	% *	N**	% *	N**
Austria	85.4	82	14.6	14
Brazil	97.4	111	2.6	3
Canada	64.9	248	35.1	134
Denmark	96.6	112	3.4	4
France	89.5	188	10.5	22
Germany	86.2	131	13.8	21
India	26.7	16	73.3	44
Ireland	62.8	27	37.2	16
Israel	92.5	74	7.5	6
Japan	94.8	145	5.2	8
Korea	99.2	120	0.8	1
Poland	96.0	72	4.0	3
South Africa	91.4	53	8.6	5
Spain	84.4	92	15.6	17
Sweden	90.6	126	9.4	13
UK	86.7	143	13.3	22
US	98.6	434	1.4	6
All	**86.8**	**2,226**	**13.2**	**339**

* % of Call centres serving domestic vs. international market

** Valid number of observations

Source: GCC data, analysis by the authors, 2009

Higher proportions only occur in English-speaking countries that are known as offshoring destinations for both the US and the UK, that is in India (with 73.3%), Canada (with 35.1%) and Ireland (with 37.2%) of internationalised call centres in the sample[3]. Some countries, such as South Africa or Poland, that we originally expected to be outsourcing destinations did not figure as such in the sample.

Call centre profiles

In order to identify different types of call centre, and find out which types of call centres are more prone to internationalisation we conducted a k-means cluster analysis. To reduce the number of variables and to control for multicollinearity we conducted a principal component analysis (PCA) before running the cluster analysis. Five components with eigen value higher than one were extracted using orthogonal varimax rotation with Kaiser-normalisation. More details on the variables that were included and thhe PCA outcomes

---

3   Any deviations in the figures provided here from the Global Call Center Industry Report result from improvements in the dataset since publication of the report.

can be found in the appendix to this article. For the K-means cluster analysis we included the five PCA components as variables.[4] Four call-centre clusters emerged that are roughly in line with existing typologies that distinguish between in-house and outsourced, higher- and lower-skill call centres (Brasse, Engelbach, Schietinger & Schmitz, 2002).

Table 2: Descriptive statistics by cluster

Cluster	1	2	3	4
	'young standardised sub-contractors'	'large old in-house telcos'	'old standardised high-volume call centres'	'skilled inbound in-house call centres'
In-house	24.4%	76.5%	52.8%	89.0%
Subcontractor	75.6%	23.5%	47.2%	11.0%
Inbound	30.2%	95.2%	83.0%	97.0%
Outbound	69.8%	4.8%	17.0%	3.0%
Telecoms sector	13.8%	91.5%	45.3%	0.0%
Education till 16	35.8%	33.6%	35.8%	32.3%
Education till 18	45.5%	47.9%	58.5%	45.5%
University degree	17.1%	17.8%	5.7%	20.8%
Age (mean)	7.6	14.3	17.1	10.5
Size (mean)	191.4	235.4	126.4	133.7
Call duration (sec)	337.8	373.1	113.1	221.6
Days initial training (mean)	9.7	17.8	11.3	16.3
Extent ot script use (mean)	3.51	2.26	3.04	2.06
performance monitoring (mean)	69.3	52.1	77.9	60.2
Internationalisation	24.0%	8.6%	5.8%	11.0%
Mean annual earnings (f-t core workers in US$)	18,566.52	26,176.98	23,075.44	26,212.23

Source: GCC data, analysis by the authors, 2009

Cluster 1 contains medium-sized subcontractor call centres with a high proportion of outbound calls, little skill investment, and a high degree of monitoring and script use. However, call volume here is slightly lower than average. On average these centres are 7.5 years old. Agents working in call centres in this cluster earn an average $18,566.52 US a year – significantly less than in other clusters. We call them the 'young standardised subcontractors'.

---

4   In line with the number of principal components we conducted the analysis for five clusters. The results showed one outlier cluster with seven cases which was excluded from the analysis (for more information see appendix). The lower N compared to the original dataset is due to missing values.

Cluster 2 has large, old (14 years on average) in-house call centres that handle mostly inbound calls, with the majority in the telecommunications industry. They are concentrated in the USA.[5] Here, skill investment is above average but monitoring and script use, as well as call volume, are below average. Agents earn an average $26,176.98 US. We call them the 'large old in-house telcos'.

The small but distinct *Cluster 3* has both in-house and subcontracting call centres that are small, old (on average 17 years old) and handle a high volume of calls with high script use and monitoring and little training. Agents here earn $23,075.44 US per year on average. They are called the 'small standardised high-volume' call centres.

Cluster 4 is an in-house-inbound cluster covering non-telecommunications call centres of average age, with a high proportion of graduates, a lot of initial training, little script use and average monitoring, and with call duration below average. Annual pay amounts to an average $26,212.23 US. We named the centres in this cluster the 'skilled inbound in-house' call centres.

We derived three hypotheses in relation to these clusters.

First, we expected that call centres catering to an international market would be larger, possibly younger and more likely to be outsourced service providers than in-house units. They would also be more likely to offer outbound services and thus would be concentrated among the 'young standardised subcontractors'.

Second, we also expected nationally distinct patterns of internationalisation. Since offshoring has taken place earlier in the English-speaking countries, we expected more variation among international call centres in these. In particular, we expected to find notable proportions of the 'skilled inbound in-house' type. Conversely, in Germany and Austria we expected that internationalisation would be more restricted to subcontractors.

Finally, in lower-wage countries such as India, we expected that it would also be more likely that international operators would be found, and that this would also mean high proportions of 'skilled inbound in-house' call centres handling less standardised calls.

Profiles of internationalisation

The following analysis investigates patterns of internationalisation in selected countries. We selected the countries with the largest proportion of international call centres, i.e. Canada, Ireland and India, and, as a comparison, the UK – where call centres may also cater to international English-speaking markets – and the German-speaking countries, Austria and Germany. There is anecdotal evidence that Austrian international call centres cater to a German market, and the difference in wages may render such a relocation attractive. On the other hand, serving the Austrian market from low-wage locations in Germany is less of an option, because managers report that Austrian customers are not sympathetic to (northern and eastern) German accents.

---

5   Indeed, telecommunications call centres were oversampled in the USA (Batt, Holman & Holtgrewe, 2009).

Table 3: Distribution of domestic and international call centres by country and cluster

Country	Type	Cluster 1 'young standardised sub-contractors' %	Cluster 2 'large old in-house telcos' %	Cluster 3 'old standardised high-volume call centres' %	Cluster 4 'skilled inbound in-house call centres' %	N
Austria	Domestic	44.4	11.1	0.0	44.4	63
	International	80.0	10.0	0.0	10.0	10
	All	49.3	11.0	0.0	39.7	73
Germany	Domestic	38.2	22.1	7.4	32.4	68
	International	81.8	9.1	0.0	9.1	11
	All	44.3	20.3	6.3	29.1	77
Canada	Domestic	18.4	20.1	5.6	55.9	179
	International	49.5	18.2	2.0	30.3	99
	All	29.9	19.2	4.3	46.6	278
India	Domestic	50.0	21.4	7.1	21.4	14
	International	59.3	22.2	0.0	18.5	27
	All	56.1	22.0	2.4	19.5	41
Ireland	Domestic	21.7	8.7	4.3	65.2	23
	International	14.3	21.4	0.0	64.3	14
	All	18.9	13.5	2.7	64.9	37
All	Domestic	21.4	28.1	3.6	46.9	1359
	International	43.8	17.1	1.4	37.6	210
	All	24.4	26.6	3.3	45.6	1569

Source: GCC data, analysis by the authors, 2009

While we are not discussing the variation in country profiles overall in this paper, the distribution of international call centres by country confirms our first two hypotheses to some extent. As we expected in hypothesis 1, most call centres catering to an international market are found among the 'young standardised subcontractors'. In line with hypothesis 2, in Austria and Germany this effect is stronger than in English-speaking countries. Here, internationalisation is found in young standardised subcontractors in 80% of the cases. Telecommunications companies and 'small old high-volume' subcontractors have internationalised to a negligible extent.

However, more than a third of international call centres are 'skilled in-house' operations. Contrary to hypothesis 3, this is not the case in India. India has the majority of international call centres in the 'young standardised subcontractors' cluster, although this finding should not be overrated due to the small cell sizes. Ireland, however, well known for its internationalised call-centre market as well, has nearly two thirds of these call centres in the 'skilled in-house-inbound' cluster and surprisingly few 'young standardised subcontractors'.

Thus, the data from the Global Call Center Industry Project do not support a conclusion that there is a general trend towards the offshoring of call-centre services. This trend is chiefly restricted to the English-speaking world. India, Ireland and Canada, especially, provide offshoring or nearshoring destinations for call-centre services, and Ireland emerges with a distinct profile of 'skilled in-house-inbound' offshoring. Elsewhere, outsourcing mostly takes place within the same region or country and exerts its well-known negative impacts on the quality of jobs (Holman, Batt & Holtgrewe, 2007) and workers' interest representation (Doellgast, Holtgrewe & Deery, 2009) at that level. The Irish profile suggests that relocations and/or consolidations of English-speaking transnational 'in-house-inbound' services aim less for lowest-wage regions but more for some cultural proximity. It also suggests that India's prospects (or those of other more remote offshoring destinations) for attracting this higher-skilled type of work and shifting to a 'higher road' of service provision will remain extremely limited. Most offshoring appears to occur through a route of outsourcing and standardisation.

Outsourcing at a global and regional level: The example of the customer service centres of ABC Electronics (Germany)

ABC Electronics (the name is a pseudonym) is the German-speaking IT support hotline of a large, US-based multinational electronics company that vertically integrates manufacturing, distribution through online or telephone ordering and customer service. Its call centres thus fit into cluster 4 of the previous analysis, representing the relative minority of in-house inbound call centres with skilled agents and little standardisation of calls. Although in the sample internationalisation of such call centres is below average, this case study illustrates the offshoring strategy of a MNC with a 'global' product range and the way this strategy is locally shaped by the interaction of its adaptation to regional markets with a globally enforced form of work organisation emanating from the company's headquarters.

Worldwide, ABC Electronics has nearly 90,000 employees. In the USA, the company is known for its low prices and its strategy of offshoring service centres as well as production plants to low-wage countries. Although, in the past, the company's location and organisation of work was driven by expansion, in recent years, plans for internal restructuring have included a 10% reduction of the workforce, which will not only affect customer service staff but also employees at plants, retail stores and other departments. In the next section we will focus on the restructuring processes that affect staff in call-centre locations.

Against the global trend of workforce reduction, the company's call-centre service in Europe was still being expanded until 2007. In 2005 a new location was opened in Scotland and by the end of 2007 about 850 new jobs had been created there. However, most of the newly created service jobs have gone to offshore locations that serve the English-speaking market, like the Philippines and India, while locations in Canada and the USA have been closed down. ABC Electronics has recently consolidated its service centres in Canada, El Salvador, the Philippines and India into a single business unit, which it aims to sell.

Service for German-speaking customers is provided at three different locations. Sales and marketing are located in West Germany whilst service and support centres have been established in East Germany and in Slovakia. The East German centre caters to business customers; Slovakia serves the mass market. Both locations were chosen because of low labour costs (and low rents), the availability of the necessary ICT infrastructure and an employer-friendly labour market. Managers consider employees' skills, especially the language skills of Slovakian customer service representatives (CSRs), to be good.

The East German location came into service at the end of 2005 employing 300 CSRs. In 2007 the total number of employees increased to almost 700, of whom 270 worked in support, and at the time of our research there were plans to further expand employment at the location. The majority of the other workers provide sales services, which were shifted to East Germany from the West German location. Even though most employees have completed vocational training as technicians or IT specialists, wages are low, due to the high unemployment rate in eastern Germany (with 15.2% in the region compared to 8.1% in all of Germany in December 2007). Most of the employees work full-time; the percentage of women and students employed is negligible.

Observation of work in the East German support centre for business customers shows it to be quite different from other German call centres, even technical support hotlines. Employees who are not engaged in a call gather together to discuss technical problems rather than working at their desks. Although work is very fragmented, calls are not standardised and there is little time pressure, although agents' calls and computer activity are comprehensively monitored. The low standardisation of the calls is best explained by the specialisation in business customer service and not least by the nature of the tasks themselves. The strategy of customer segmentation with different centres serving business and mass-market customers is pursued globally by ABC Electronics.

The Slovakian support centre is located close to a city near the Austrian border that hosts other call centres serving the German-speaking market. It started as a general German-speaking customer-service location in 1997. In 2002 the location was transformed into a business centre for the regions of Europe, the Middle East and Africa, with 800 new jobs. In 2003, all German-speaking mass-market support services were transferred there. At the time of our research, the centre had 2,000 employees, although not all served support functions.

In spite of serving different customer segments, the East German and Slovakian call centres are connected by VoIP and 'classic' telephone lines. Though it would be technically possible to shift calls between the two locations at peak times, the company prefers to shift calls between hotlines serving the same customer segment even if this means having customers change to speaking English. Generally, this organisation of the service is centrally decided by the US headquarter which also develops and administers hardware, software and training materials centrally. It also permits only very little and short-term use of external contractors. At the regional level, service centre management thus has little discretion. Local managers consider it important to maintain contact with local or regional institutions (e.g. data protection officers, vocational training institutions, chambers of commerce etc.), but these contacts do not lead to any differentiation in management practices.

Here, ABC emerges as a multinational with a low-cost orientation in terms of location that still responds to different markets differently. The expansion of its market in non-English-speaking Europe has led to a growth in its customer service operations that runs counter to the consolidation and offshoring on the English-speaking side. However, the low-wage operations do not prevent (or may even allow) considerable workplace discretion in line with the demands of a technical support helpline that caters to business customers in East Germany.[6]

However, even in this case, the logic of cost-cutting does not fully explain the structure of ABC's offshoring. The company obviously takes customers' institutionalised expectations and notions of quality into account but does so selectively. Originally, all German customers received support from the Slovakian location and only later did business customer support move to East Germany. Business customer support has thus been adapted to contain an element of conspicuous consumption that goes beyond effective communication. By assigning better-paid native speakers with high discretion to business customers, the company appears to be investing in the relationship. But surprisingly this investment comes with bureaucratic limitations, because German-language services are only available during (extended) office hours both for business and individual customers. The more standardised mass market, in which, however, customers bring a more limited level of complexity to the interaction, has to accept foreign accents.

Discussion and Conclusion

This paper has connected an analysis of the most comprehensive dataset on the call-centre industry that is currently available with an analysis of a case study that explores the transnational aspect of outsourcing. Overall, while global business service providers exist and shape the perception of the industry to a considerable extent, internationalisation is mostly associated with outsourcing and larger, younger subcontractors. Where higher-skilled 'in-house inbound' work is concerned, cost-cutting calculations so far appear to be tempered by notions of cultural proximity. While some services in some segments have certainly been internationalised (for example airline travel reservations or IT helplines), national and regional specifics continue to play a part. Even in the English-speaking world, a considerable part of transnationalisation takes the form of 'nearshoring' to countries that are spatially and culturally close to the USA and the UK – especially when higher-skilled in-house work is concerned. This also suggests that, at the moment, the options for more distant offshoring destinations to 'move up the value chain' and attract higher-skilled in-house call centres appear very limited indeed unless subcontractors evolve in that direction.

Language, the use of native speakers and (anticipated) customer acceptance of foreign accents clearly structures transnationalisation. This is shown both by the prevalence of 'nearshoring' and also by the investment of Indian call centres in the language and cultural adaptation skills of their agents. The case of ABC Electronics is also illustrative. In spite of the multinational's centralised low-cost approach aiming at consolidation and possible outsourcing of call-centre operations, it makes concessions to the requirements

---

6   As interview and observation access had not been granted in Slovakia at the time of writing this paper, we have no evidence that standardisation in the mass-market centre is higher there, but it is certainly very likely.

of an expanding European market – and, where German-speaking business customers are concerned, it uses native speakers in a low-cost region within the country. The need to 'embed' customer service within its market environment is thus answered selectively for a particular market with higher value-added. On the mass market, the effort of translation and creating understanding is left to the intercultural competencies of Slovak agents on the one hand and German consumers on the other.

With regard to the predictions cited at the beginning of this paper, the prognosis of an explosion of non-English language offshoring into central and eastern Europe and the Mediterranean rim may be overstated. The industry in these regions is clearly expanding (Holtgrewe, 2009), and the Datamonitor prediction of 5% of European call-centre agents working in nearshored call centres is roughly in line with the GCC data. However, a considerable part of the East European expansion is aimed at local or regional markets there (for instance in the financial sector, which we do not expect to offshore customer service soon). It is not easy to forecast what kind of specialisations and types of value chain and networks will emerge, but institutional actors such as unions and consumer-interest groups and policymakers would be well advised to develop European strategies that go beyond immediately addressing visible job relocations.

However, the Global Call Center Industry Project has not provided data on outsourcing patterns that would involve ownership structures, internal and external competition, multilingualism and entire national and transnational outsourcing configurations. Data analysis of the impact of internationalisation on the quality of work has been limited by low cell sizes. Nor has the case study explored the genesis of decisions to relocate or outsource work very deeply. The importance of (networked) outsourcing only came into focus through the project's results and the significant differences between outsourced and in-house call centres. Certain European offshoring destinations such as Poland have only emerged as such since 2004, somewhat later than the project predicted, and they have not yet been investigated by much independent research. There is obviously considerable work still to be done on multinationals with different countries of origin and language backgrounds, on the multinational strategies of call-centre and BPO service providers, on smaller businesses for whom international markets may come into focus if customer service can be outsourced, and on the role both of global and local consultancies and (on the employee side of relocation) on the role of migrant and multilingual employees in call-centre services.

© *Ursula Holtgrewe, Jessica Longen, Hannelore Mottweiler and Annika Schönauer, 2009*

ACKNOWLEDGEMENTS

Research specifically for this paper was funded by Hans-Böckler-Stiftung, Jubiläumsfonds der Österreichischen Nationalbank and FWF Austria. A previous version was presented at the International Labour Process Conference, April 6-8, 2009 in Edinburgh. We thank all colleagues involved with the Global Call Center Industry Project who contributed to the international dataset (www.globalcallcenter.org), and specifically Rose Batt, Alfons Bauernfeind, Jörg Flecker, David Holman, Ursula Huws, Karen A. Shire and our interviewees. We also thank David Westacott for swift and painstaking copy-editing. As usual, all remaining faults are ours.

APPENDIX
Table 4: Variables used in this paper

Variable	Definition	Coding
	Organisational variables	
Ownership*	Call centre organised as in-house centre providing services to own company or as a sub-contractor providing services to other companies	In-house = 1 Subcontractor=0
Call type: Inbound*	call-centre primarily deals with inbound or outbound calls	Inbound =1 Outbound = 0
Sector*	Dummy variables reflecting the sector served by the call centre. The two primary sector variables used were telecommunications and financial services.	Yes =1 No = 0
Age*	Age of call centre in years	
Size*	Total number of employees in the call centre	
	Work organisation variables	
Initial training*	number of days initial training a core employee receives in the first year	
Performance monitoring*	percentage of core employees' work activity monitored continuously throughout the day regardless of whether the information is used or not	
Call duration*	average length of the typical call handled by core employees	
Number of calls per day*	average number of calls a typical agents handles per day)	
Script use*	a) call-centre agents use scripted texts to handle customer calls b) extent of script use on a five item scale	a) yes=1 no=0 b) not at all=1 a great deal=5
	Agent characteristics	
Education level	typical educational level of core employees a) no formal qualifications b) education up to the age of 16* c) education up to the age of 18* d) university education or equivalent	a) yes=1 no=0 b) yes=1 no=0 c) yes=1 no=0 d) yes=1 no=0
	Job characteristics	
Annual earnings	annual earnings of the typical full-time core employee in US $ before deductions and taxes, including wages, earnings, bonuses, commissions, profit sharing, and overtime pay; excluding benefits	

* these variables were also used in the PCA[7].

---

[7]   Normally PCA analysis requires variables with scale level, but it is also possible to conduct PCAs with ordinal and dummy variables although this may create a problem of overly extended datasets and difficulty in interpreting the results (Krzanowski, 1984). In such cases a correspondence analysis may be more robust.

Table 5: Results of principal component analysis:

Rotated Component Matrix

		Component				
		1	2	3	4	5
Age	Young, big subcontractor with high standardisation & high work control	-.479				
Ownership (In-house)		-.657				
Performance monitoring		.412				
Extent to which core empls use scripts		.649				
Size		.560			.460	
Call type (Inbound)	(Big) Inbound call centre with high skill investment				.662	
Initial training					.662	
Average duration of a call	Low call duration, high call volume					-.733
Average number calls per day						.705
Education till age of 16	(Low) education level		.905			
Education till age of 18			-.912			
Sector: Financial services	Sector: Telecommunication services			-.761		
Sector: Telecommunication				.799		

The Barlett's test was significant and the KMO score is 0.559.

Table 6: Standardised means of factors for the final cluster centres

	Cluster 1	Cluster 2	Cluster 3	Cluster 4
PCA factor 1 - Big standardised outbound subcontractor	,830	-,266	,135	-,359
PCA factor 2 - Low education	,013	-,022	-,344	,0164
PCA factor 3 - Telecommunication services	-,166	1,151	1,051	-,669
PCA factor 4 - Inbound services with high skill investment	-1,063	,364	-,592	,349
PCA factor 5 - low call duration & high call volume	-,196	-,360	2,934	,116
Number	391	422	53	730

However, as we are basically using PCA analysis to eliminate multicollinearity and call centre typologies are created in the ensuing k- means cluster analysis PCA seems appropriate.

REFERENCES

Maurice, M. & A. Sorge (eds) (2000) *Embedding Organizations: Societal Analysis of Actors, Organizations, and Socio-Economic Context*, Amsterdam, Philadelphia, PA: John Benjamins

Hall, P.A. & D. Soskice (eds) (2001) *Varieties of Capitalism: The Institutional Foundations of Comparative Advantage*, Oxford: Oxford University Press

Mense-Petermann, U. & G. Wagner (eds) (2006) *Transnationale Konzerne. Ein neuer Organisationstyp?*, Wiesbaden: Westdeutscher Verlag

Batt, R., V. Doellgast & H. Kwon (2006) 'Service Management and Employment Systems in U.S. and Indian Call Centers' in S.M. Collins & L. Brainard (eds) *Brookings Trade Forum 2005: Offshoring White-Collar Work – The Issues and Implications*, Washington D.C.: The Brookings Institute:335-372

Batt, R., D. Holman & U. Holtgrewe (2009) 'The Globalization of Service Work: Comparative Institutional Perspectives on Call Centers. Introduction to the ILRR special issue', *Industrial & Labor Relations Review*, Vol 62, No 4:453-488

Batt, R. & L.M. Moynihan (2004) 'The Viability of Alternative Call Centre Production Models' in S.J. Deery & N. Kinnie (eds) *Call Centres and Human Resource Management,* Houndmills, New York: Palgrave:25-53

Brasse, C., et al. (2002) 'AKL-Typologie. Ein empirischer Ansatz zur Typologisierung von Call Centern', Dortmund: Gesellschaft für Arbeitsschutz- und Humanisierungsforschung

Burgess, J. & J. Connell (2006) 'Developments in the Call Centre Sector: An Overview' in J. Burgess & J. Connell (eds) *Development in the Call Centre Industry: Analysis, Changes and Challenges,* New York, London: Routledge:1-19

Dicken, P. (2004) 'Tangled Webs: Transnational Production Networks and Regional Integration', SPACES Working Paper 2005-04, Marburg: University of Marburg

Doellgast, V. & I. Greer (2007) 'Vertical Disintegration and the Disorganization of German Industrial Relations', *British Journal of Industrial Relations*, Vol 45, No 1:55-76

Doellgast, V., U. Holtgrewe & S.J. Deery (2009) 'The Effects of National Institutions and Collective Bargaining Arrangements on Job Quality in Frontline Service Workplaces. Submitted to Industrial & Labor Relations Review', *Industrial & Labor Relations Review*, Vol 62, No 4:489-509

Dossani, R. & M. Kenney (2003) 'Went for Cost, Stayed for Quality? Moving the Back Office to India', BRIE Working Paper No 156, July 25, Berkeley, CA: Berkeley Roundtable on the International Economy

Faust, M., U. Voskamp & V. Wittke (2004) 'Globalisation and the Future of National Systems: Exploring Patterns of Industrial Reorganisation and Relocation in an Enlarged Europe' in M. Faust, U. Voskamp, & V. Wittke (eds) *European Industrial Restructuring in a Global Economy: Fragmentation and Relocation of Value Chains*, Göttingen: SOFI

Flecker, J., et al. (2008) 'Restructuring across Value Chains and Changes in Work and Employment: Case Study Evidence from the Clothing, Food, IT and Public Sector', WORKS WP 10 Deliverable 10.1

Geppert, M. & K. Williams (2006) 'Global, National and Local Practices in Multinational Corporations: Towards a Sociopolitical Framework', *International Journal of Human Resource Management*, Vol 17, No 1:49-69

Gereffi, G., J. Humphrey & T. Sturgeon (2005) 'The Governance of Global Value Chains', *Review of International Political Economy*, Vol 12, No 1:78-104

Ghoshal, S. & C.A. Bartlett (2005) 'The Multinational Corporation as an Inter-Organizational Network' in S. Ghoshal & D.E. Westney (eds) *Organization Theory and the Multinational Corporation,* Basingstoke: Palgrave:68-92

Harzing, A.W. & A. Sorge (2003) 'The Relative Impact of Country of Origin and Universal Contingencies on Internationalization Strategies and Corporate Control in Multinational Enterprises: Worldwide and European Perspectives', Organization Studies, Vol 24, No 2:187-214

Holman, D., R. Batt & U. Holtgrewe (2007) *The Global Call Center Report: International Perspectives on Management and Employment. A Report of the Global Call Center Research Network,* Sheffield: Institute of Work Psychology

Holtgrewe, U. (2009) 'Callcenter: Nicht Ganz Global, aber Hochflexibel. Ein Internationaler Überblick' in E. Ahlers & A. Ziegler (eds) Beschäftigte in der Globalisierungsfalle?, Wiesbaden: Nomos

Huws, U. (2003) 'When Work Takes Flight', Research Results from the EMERGENCE Project, IES-report 397:Institute for Employment Studies

Huws, U. & J. Flecker (2004) 'Asian Emergence: The World's Back Office?' IES Report 419: Institute for Employment Studies

Krzanowski, W.J. (1984) 'Principal Components Analysis in the Presence of Group Structure', Applied Statistics, Vol 33, No 2:164-168

Marchington, M., et al. (eds) (2005) Fragmenting Work. Blurring Organizational Boundaries and Disordering Hierarchies, Oxford: Oxford University Press

Miozzo, M. & D. Grimshaw (2005) 'Does EDS Add Value? The Expansion of IT Outsourcing and the Nature and Role of Computer Service Firms', Paper Presented at the DRUID 10th Anniversary Summer Conference 2005 on Dynamics of Industry and Innovation: Organizations, Networks and Systems Copenhagen, Denmark, June 27-29

Mirchandani, K. (2004) 'Practices of Global Capital: Gaps, Cracks and Ironies in Transnational Call Centres in India', Global Networks-a Journal of Transnational Affairs, Vol 4, No 4:355-373

Morgan, G. (2005) 'Understanding Multinational Corporations' in S. Ackroyd, et al. (eds) The Oxford Handbook of Work and Organization, Oxford: Oxford University Press:554-576

Nielsen, P.B. (2007) 'International Sourcing-Measurement Issues. The Economic and Social Impacts of Broadband Communications: From ICT Measurement to Policy Implications. Contribution to Joint WPIIS-WPIE Workshop, London May 2007'

Ohmae, K. (1990) The Borderless World: Power and Strategy in the Interlinked World Economy, London: Harper Collins

Rugman, A. (2001) The End of Globalization: Why Global Strategy is a Myth and How to Profit from the Realities of Regional Markets, New York: AMACOM

Shire, K.A., et al. (2009) 'Temporary Work in Coordinated Market Economies: Evidence from Front-Line Service Workplaces. Forthcoming', Industrial & Labor Relations Review, Vol 62, No 4

Srivastava, S. & N. Theodore (2006) 'Offshoring Call Centres: The View from Wall Street' in J. Burgess & J. Connell (eds) Development in the Call Centre Industry: Analysis, Changes and Challenges, New York, London: Routledge:19-35

Taylor, P. & P. Bain (2006) 'Work Organisation and Employee Relations in Indian Call Centres' in J. Burgess & J. Connell (eds) Development in the Call Centre Industry: Analysis, Changes and Challenges New York, London: Routledge:36-57

Whitley, R. (1999) Divergent Capitalisms: The Social Structuring and Change of Business Systems, Oxford: Oxford University Press

Experiencing depersonalised bullying:
a study of Indian call-centre agents

Premilla D'Cruz and Ernesto Noronha

Premilla D'Cruz *is an Associate Professor in Organisational Behaviour at the Indian Institute of Management in Ahmedabad, India*
Ernesto Noronha *is also an Associate Professor in Organisational Behaviour at the Indian Institute of Management in Ahmedabad, India*

ABSTRACT
This article uses the concept of depersonalized bullying to explain the way in which call-centre agents employed in international call centres in Mumbai and Bangalore, India experience their work as an oppressive regime. The characteristics of this bullying regime can be attributed to the service level agreement between employers and clients which determines organisational practices. Call-centre agents' professional identities and material gains facilitate their acceptance of their tough work conditions, causing them to participate in their own oppression. As well as clarifying the concept of depersonalised bullying, the article highlights the critical role of capitalist labour relations in workplace bullying, allowing for a contextualised and politicised understanding to emerge.

The organisation-workplace bullying interface

Workplace bullying is defined as subtle and/or obvious negative behaviours embodying aggression and hostility, characterised by repetition and persistence, displayed by an individual and/or group to another individual and/or group in the context of an existing or evolving unequal power relationship (Adapted from Einarsen, Hoel, Zapf & Cooper, 2003; Hoel & Beale, 2006; Tracy, Lutgen-Sandvik & Alberts, 2006). Research in the field has focused on the interpersonal dimension (Einarsen, Hoel, Zapf & Cooper, 2003; Liefooghe & Mackenzie Davey, 2001), and hence it is not surprising that the engagement of the organisational framework in the understanding of workplace bullying has largely been confined to socio-relational conceptualisations (Keashly & Harvey, 2006) emphasising that various work conditions operate as environmental factors that give rise to interpersonal bullying (Hoel & Salin, 2003). Hoel and Beale's (2006) appeal to expand the field to include contextualised and politicised understandings of workplace bullying bring into play the notion of depersonalised bullying (Liefooghe & Mackenzie Davey, 2001), highlighting socio-structural dimensions (Keashly & Harvey, 2006).

Hoel and Beale (2006) maintain that there are various forms and degrees of oppression, exploitation and control in the workplace that constitute an inevitable feature of capitalist labour relations and that provide critical insights into workplace bullying. In a capitalist labour market, employed work has the purpose of profit making which can only be sustained through continuous exploitation. Management enforced compliance with employer-oriented norms of workplace behaviour is central to the shared experience of employment, and disciplinary sanctions to enforce the rules of the workplace remain central to the employment relationship. Bullying forms part of the day-to-day routine of managing labour and is endemic in labour management practices associated with making a profit. Conceptualisations of bullying at work, therefore, need to go beyond the interpersonal and socio-relational realm to embrace the organisational level of analysis (Ironside & Seifert, 2003).

Liefooghe and Mackenzie Davey's (2001) research is the only empirical work so far on the concept of depersonalised bullying. Drawing on participants' subjectivity, they demonstrate that the organisation itself is the bully, with bullying being attributed to the organisation and its practices. Bullying is institutionalised, with subordination not being related to personality clashes between individuals but to a more Taylorised approach based on impersonal laws applied to supervisors and subordinates (Liefooghe & Mackenzie Davey, 2001).

Through our empirical research on the subjective work experiences of Indian call-centre agents employed in international facing call centres in Mumbai and Bangalore, India, we further the substantive area. This paper highlights the complex aetiology, manifestations and implications of depersonalised bullying and describes and explains employees' responses to their experiences. It engages the extra-organisational business context and the organisational control process and its reliance on inclusivist and exclusivist HRM (human resource management) strategies as well as the roles of agents, supervisors and managers in its analysis. Through the findings, the concept of depersonalised bullying is clarified, allowing for a definition to be developed.

The call-centre industry in India

The call-centre industry in India is located within the country's emerging ITES-BPO (Information Technology Enabled Services-Business Process Outsourcing) sector whose major constituent is global offshoring operations. While the Philippines, South Africa, Latin American and Eastern Europe states are emerging locations, India remains the pre-eminent site for offshored business activities, accounting for 46% of all global offshoring (NASSCOM/National Association of Software and Service Companies-McKinsey, 2005) and offering 'an unbeatable mix of low costs, deep technical and language skills, mature vendors and supportive government policies' (Walker & Gott in NASSCOM, 2007: 29). While the key catalyst for this has been globalisation, aided by India's liberalisation and various central and state government initiatives (NASSCOM, 2006), India provides significant labour cost arbitrage. The large English-speaking and technical talent pool available in India is a critical component of this process (NASSCOM, 2006).

While call centres account for about 60-65% and back offices for about 35-40% of the services provided (Taylor & Bain, 2006), certain key service categories, namely finance and accounting, customer interaction and human resource administration, account for 89% of industry revenues. Services are housed in MNC (multinational corporation) captive, MNC third party, Indian third party (all of which are international facing, i.e., serving overseas clients and customers[1]) and domestic service provider organisations (NASSCOM, 2005), located principally in Tier 1 but now expanding to Tier 2 and 3 cities (NASSCOM, 2005 & 2006). Though there has been considerable diversification in the range of processes delivered from India and there certainly has been growth in higher-value and professional knowledge process outsourcing (KPO), the evidence strongly suggests that, in overall terms, the ITES-BPO industry in India still tends to provide largely standardised and routinised services of low complexity, emphasising mass production and customer service (Taylor & Bain 2006), in keeping with the mass customised model (Batt & Moynihan, 2002; Frenkel, Korczynski, Shire & Tam, 1998).

Direct employment in India's ITES-BPO sector was calculated at 553,000 in the financial year 2006-2007 (NASSCOM, 2007), the sector having become an important avenue for employment, especially for the country's youth. While this workforce is covered by a variety of labour laws promulgated in various Indian states as well as central legislation, the popular notion held in Indian society (and maintained and promoted by ITES-BPO employers, aided by government apathy) is that the labour legislation and related institutional measures do not apply to this sector (See Noronha & D'Cruz, 2009, for a detailed discussion). This augments India's attractiveness as a global offshoring destination. As Taylor and Bain (2005) maintain, India remains attractive to companies who wish to capitalise on the possibilities for flexible labour utilisation and the absence of trade unions in the Indian call-centre sector.

Though the recent rise in labour costs is being offset by declining telecom costs, lower depreciation and other infrastructure costs, improvements in productivity and utilisation and scale economies, the attempt to sustain the long term viability of India's cost advantage has resulted in the adoption of process excellence tactics and a range of other strategies. These include increasing company size and facilities that enable an increased volume of processes to be handled, as well as strategies to increase productivity through reengineering and optimal use of equipment and labour that make it possible to maximise efficiency (NASSCOM, 2006).

Methodology

This paper draws on a study whose aim was to explore employees' subjective experiences of work in international facing call centres in Mumbai and Bangalore, India. Keeping in mind the objective of the study, a phenomenological approach was considered to be appropriate, and van Manen's (1998) hermeneutic phenomenology was adopted to explore the essence of participants' lived experience. Following van Manen's (1998) approach, conversational interviews were used to gather experiential narrative material. Though the interviews were unstructured, they were guided by the fundamental question that prompted the research. Yet this focus did not preclude exploring other issues that emerged during the interview, since we were aware that

---

1   The reader must note the distinction between clients and customers. Clients are the entities seeking services from Indian/India-based service providers while customers are the clients' service recipients who by virtue of being served by the agents/employees of the service provider are also referred to by the latter as customers.

these could generate important insights into the phenomenon under study. Informed consent, voluntary participation and confidentiality marked the ethical protocol of the inquiry.

With most organisations being unwilling to permit us access to their employees or the operations floor (only one call centre in Mumbai gave us access to a few of their employees and this was negotiated through personal contacts), we resorted to snowball sampling initiated via personal contacts. All interviews, held at the convenience of the participants, were conducted in English and lasted between one and two and a half hours. Interviews were recorded on audio-cassettes with the permission of the participants. No participants objected to the use of the recorder once its advantage of accuracy was spelled out to them, and its presence did not appear to hinder their responses. During the interview, observations about the participants were made and written up after the session ended. Data recorded on the audio-cassettes were later transcribed verbatim by the research staff. The quotations in this article are drawn from these transcripts.

Fifty nine agents, 34 from Mumbai and 25 from Bangalore, employed in international facing call centres participated in the study. Thirty nine worked in inbound processes, 12 in outbound processes and eight in both inbound and outbound processes. There were 29 women and 30 men whose ages ranged from 20 to 55 years, with the largest number in the 22-25 year age group. Forty participants were unmarried and forty were graduates. The average monthly salary of participants was approximately Rs. (Indian Rupees) 12,900, based on a range of Rs. 8,000 to Rs. 25,000. All the participants were employed by either MNC captive, MNC third party or Indian third party organisations and served overseas clients and customers. None of the participants were members of trade unions.

Thematic analyses were undertaken, including sententious and selective approaches, following van Manen (1998). In the sententious approach, each transcript was read as a whole to capture the core or essential meaning of participants' experiences. In the selective thematic analyses, categories, patterns and themes that contributed to the core theme were identified. That is, each transcript was read repeatedly and significant statements relating to and illustrating the various dimensions of the core theme were identified and demarcated. These were read and reread to formulate conceptual meanings and explore the essential qualities of the experiences described, and themes were identified in the process. The essential elements of agents' experiences were embodied in the core theme of 'being professional'[2].

---

2   The core theme that captured the essence of agents' experiences was 'being professional'. The notion of professionalism embraced agents' identity, altering their self-concept and enhancing their self-esteem. According to agents, professionals possess superior cognitive abilities, advanced qualifications and a sense of responsibility and commitment to work. They prioritise work over personal needs and pleasure, behaving in a dignified and restrained manner and performing optimally and rationally while on the job. Professionals comply with job and organisational requirements, absorbing emergent strain. Under such circumstances, not only do agents perceive gains accruing from their job as consistent with the notion of professionalism but also transactional psychological contracts of employment as means of discipline are similarly justified. Though resistance is displayed by some agents occasionally, this is described as a temporary outlet to ease job-related strain, co-existing with professional identity – it is not an indicator of anti-work or anti-employer sentiment. Indeed, agents' professional identity precludes engagement with collectivisation attempts which are seen both as inconsistent with the essential features of professionalism and as redundant in instances where employers

A second important theme closely linked to the core theme that emerged during the analysis process was that of an oppressive work regime. Participants repeatedly used this term to describe their work context. We used Miles and Huberman's (1994) data analysis techniques to explore this theme further. That is, through the use of various tools such as charts, matrices, event lists, causal networks and memos (Miles & Huberman, 1994), we identified related themes, categories and patterns emerging from the data. Linkages between these themes, patterns and categories were examined, and interpretations were made (Patton, 1990) in order to understand participants' references to and experiences of the oppressive work regime.

Figure 1: The oppressive work regime

Extra-organisational business context influences service level agreements/SLAs

Occasional individualised resistance of a few (risk of being caught)

Sense of oppression

SLAs determine organisational practices via work systems, job design elements, customer service requirements and technobureaucratic controls
Supervisors and managers implement SLAs

Agents' ambivalence

Victim status = partial

Perception of material gains

Role of professional identity

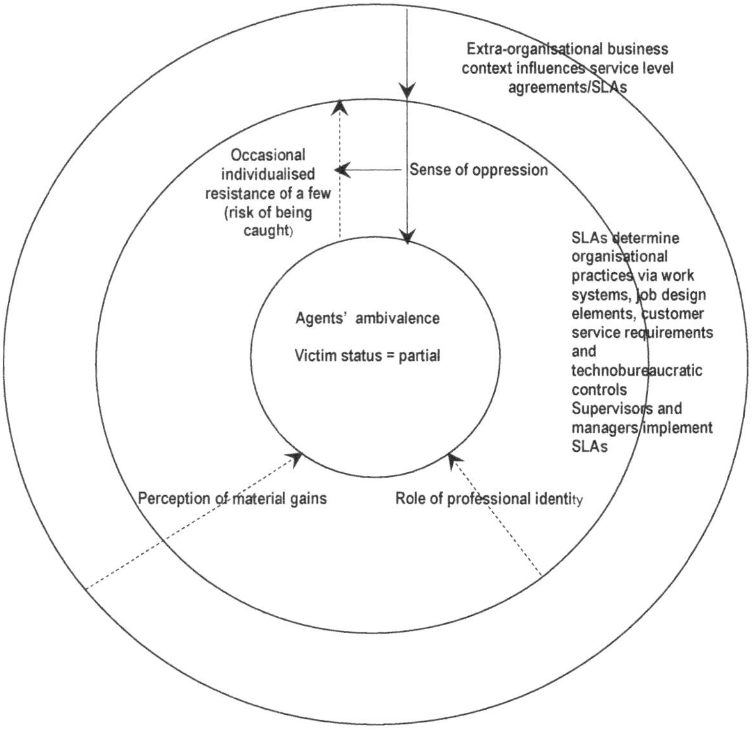

Findings

The participants' description of the oppressive work regime is depicted schematically in Figure 1. Their concept of the oppressive work regime embraced the organisational context, stemming essentially from the SLA (service level agreement) the employer organisation had entered into with the client. These SLAs determined organisational

protect employee interests (Noronha & D'Cruz, 2009).

practices in terms of work systems, job design, customer service requirements and techno-bureaucratic controls. The employer organisation's implementation of the SLAs contributed directly to the oppressive work regime. That is, supervisors and managers (henceforth also referred to as superiors) engaged in overt and covert aggressive behaviours to ensure the fulfilment of the SLAs. Participants' narratives highlighted the role of macroeconomic, extra-organisational factors in determining the SLAs and the organisational context. While participants acknowledged their tough work conditions, their professional identity and the material gains from their jobs facilitated acceptance of these, causing them to participate in their own oppression. In recognition of their ambivalence, participants' victim status can, at best, be termed partial. Nonetheless, the presence of occasional individualised acts of resistance as a means of coping with work-related strain, in spite of the risks involved, was described.

The dynamics of the oppressive work regime

Participants described their work environment as oppressive but attributed this to the SLAs that their employers had entered into with their clients. The SLA is a formalised agreement, either temporal or project-based, between the participants' employer organisations (the offshored Indian/India-based service providers) and the overseas client to deliver stipulated services to the clients' customers who were also located overseas. SLAs lay down the process and outcome requirements of each particular service, the fulfilment of which is critical to the continuity and/or renewal of the contractual relationship between the two parties. With competitive advantage being the key focus, employer organisations diligently implement their clients' expectations. SLAs thus form the basis for organisational practices, setting the work context for the call-centre agents. Indeed, according to our informants, supervisors and managers resorted to intimidatory tactics to ensure the fulfilment of the SLAs. Participants, while acknowledging how SLAs impacted them, emphasised that their employer organisations were merely enacting the SLAs – that is, superiors at various levels of the organisational hierarchy had no choice but to ensure that SLAs were met and their aggressive behaviour in this regard was involuntary and impersonal – and hence no particular person in the workplace was considered to be responsible for the oppression that they experienced.

Agents maintained that the dynamics of doing business in a globalised world played an important role. Clients were relocating their operations to low cost developing countries to maximise revenues, minimise costs and maintain competitive advantage, and their choice of country and of service provider as well as the nature of SLAs were in keeping with these ends. If service provider organisations were unable to comply with the SLAs and provide a conducive set-up for business to flourish, the clients would switch their business to other organisations. Moreover, if the business context in the country did not facilitate clients' success, they would relocate to other, more attractive destinations. Under such circumstances, employer organisations took pains to ensure the appropriate extra-organisational and intra-organisational business environments and to fulfil their SLAs. Delivering on these counts, in their view, was necessary for the continued success of India's ITES-BPO sector and the competitive position of their organisations.

Finally, everything boils down to the SLAs. They [SLAs] dictate the shifts, the targets, the quality, the customer interaction. And they [employer organisation] naturally have to execute it – because if not, the process will go elsewhere. So they [employer organisation] don't bother one way or the other – just deliver ruthlessly.

The team leader and the operations manager often just scream to get the work done. But it is for the [employer] organisation's good. They have no choice. Clients' expectations have to be met. If you do badly, they will humiliate you privately and publicly for days on end. Someone or the other is always being pulled up on the call floor. So that uncomfortable atmosphere is always there – and it is quite stressful. But it is not personal, they are just getting the work done.

In order to meet clients' requirements, employer organisations created 8-9 hour shifts with two 15-minutes breaks, one 30-minute one and 5-day work weeks. Shifts were developed to match the time zones of customers located in the USA, UK, Canada and Australia. This not only meant that agents had to work during the Indian night but also that they had to undergo periodic changes in their work timings as the shifts rotated fortnightly or monthly. Participants worked in teams, headed by a team leader (TL), and were required to report half an hour before their assigned shift for team meetings. During these meetings, TLs indicated the daily requirements, proposed updates, provided individual and team feedback and attempted to energise the team, as well as checking the functioning of equipment. Attendance was recorded via log-in and log-out data. Participants mentioned how such strict observation of time meant that they could not log out of their systems or leave their seats even to go to the restroom (if it was an emergency, they had to seek permission from the team leader to do so).

What makes matters worse is the early reporting – we have to come well in advance before the shift. So that eats into one's personal time. It is so tough. And leaving one's seat during the shift – it is impossible. Because it will be tracked and you will be thrown out. Whether you are unwell or you want to go to the bathroom, you have to sit until the TL allows you to get up.

Participants had to meet targets, the specific nature of which were linked to the particular processes they were working on. Whereas inbound call-centre agents had to take the maximum number of calls possible in a shift, for outbound call-centre agents, targets were fixed in terms of completion of specific number of units pertaining to the particular process being performed. Agents were always encouraged to achieve beyond their specified targets, and being able to do so augmented their incentives and added to their visibility and opportunities for growth. Inability to reach the assigned target resulted in the employee being sent for retraining, which essentially meant notice of dismissal. In addition, agents had to maintain specific time limits for the actual call (also known as AHT/average handling time of the call) and for call wrap-up while also having to pick up calls within a certain number of rings (call waiting time) and being unable to drop calls, alter their position in the call queue or leave calls incomplete (call abandonment rates).

The focus is on targets and superiors' non-verbal signs tell you how you are doing. Sometimes, they are so subtle but the message is clear. Some of my friends get scared, in fact.

During phases when call volumes were high or targets were not being met, agents were made to stretch their working time so that they had to forfeit or shorten breaks, work beyond their shift hours or come into work on days that were designated as their weekly holidays or on public holidays. It is relevant to mention here that the public holidays (both national holidays and festivals) observed in the call centres were not Indian holidays but those of the customer group being served. Moreover, quite often, agents received no overtime for the extra work put in. It was generally those failing to meet targets or put in the required log-in hours who were asked to work on holidays.

> *There is no choice – if they say to stretch, we have to stretch. It could be during the shift, during the week, during the weekend. Or it could be on holidays also. If you don't meet the target, you are in trouble and there is no escape – either retraining or dismissal. So one is always tense.*

Emotional labour remains central to task performance in call centres[3]. There is a strong emphasis on communicating effectively with customers. This encompasses clarity and accuracy of communication, adherence to scripts, avoiding providing wrong information and misleading customers, politeness, cordiality, sensitivity and patience (particularly with irate customers). All this has to be accomplished in a virtual context, concomitant with other process requirements, in real time. The agents we interviewed had been trained to believe that since customers could decipher their moods, the espousal and display of a positive frame of mind was important in order to induce a similar demeanour in customers, to enhance the perceived quality of the service interaction and to leave behind a favourable impression about the client company. To this end, agents were encouraged to empathise with and absorb customers' reactions, apologising to them for any perceived or attributed problem or inconvenience even if it was not their fault. At the same time, maintaining objectivity was emphasised. Agents were not allowed to develop personal relationships with customers or display any partiality towards them. Agents thus had to engage with customers closely enough to perform effective emotional labour, ensure customer satisfaction and promote client interests while simultaneously meeting other qualitative and quantitative performance criteria; failure to do so invited punishment.

For Indian agents working in international facing call centres, training in emotional labour skills went beyond the scope of customer interaction and satisfaction to embrace cultural, linguistic and geographical dimensions linked to the lives of the overseas customers. Cultural training included exposure to various facets of customers' society including its geographical location, political boundaries, time zone, climate, history, demographics and way of life. While agents' fluency with English and neutral accents were checked at the time of recruitment, linguistic training emphasised the adoption of accents appropriate to specific customer groups and familiarity with local speech such as the slang and colloquialisms of the customer group being served. Agents also took on Western names as pseudonyms and engaged in locational masking[4]. These latter four

---

3   For a detailed discussion of emotional labour in India's international facing call centres, see D'Cruz and Noronha (2008) and Noronha and D'Cruz (2009).
4   Locational masking, a term coined by Mirchandani (2003), entails refusal to divulge the geographical location of the offshored call centre and the agent. Non-disclosure agreements between employer organisations and clients forbid agents from revealing their identity and the location of their call centre, and hence they are trained to

requirements were laid down by client companies within the SLAs to ensure that their customers remained comfortable and willing to divulge personal information during service interactions, and retained an illusion of continuity with the company's previous quality standards even after the migration of services via offshoring.

Agents accepted these cultural and linguistic requirements, the adoption of pseudonyms and locational masking as part of their jobs, maintaining that these facilitated customer ease and service interactions and protected them from customer abuse on racial grounds. But locational masking precipitated stress. Participants who were required to claim that they were based overseas needed to know enough about their purported location to be able to answer customer queries. While organisations took care of this via cultural training and provision of current and updated information about the customers' location on the call floor, some participants did admit to uneasiness. According to them, since they could not anticipate all the questions customers could pose, it was possible that they may be at a loss at some point in time.

I find changing my identity very upsetting. Some of my colleagues also say the same. But what to do? Clients' demands have to be met. Saying you are in the customers' location is the worst because you can get caught – but here also, the SLA has to be followed. It is very stifling.

Appropriate handling of irate and abusive customers formed part of the SLAs. Some customers displayed racial and ethnic animosity ranging from subtle comments and sarcasm to explicit comments and cursing. It was not uncommon for customers to refuse to speak to, transact with or buy anything from Indian agents. Quite often, agents had to face the ignominy of customers hanging up. Customers displayed scepticism and cynicism about Indians' ability to help them out, given that India is a developing country. Moreover, they harboured discomfort and distrust about sharing personal and sensitive information with people from another country, particularly in matters relating to their finances and social security. There were also frequent reports of instances of customers expressing anger over the general offshoring trend and holding agents responsible for the unemployment situation in their own countries.

Though customer reactions evoked disappointment, distress and helplessness in agents, customer abuse had to be handled with professional finesse. Even hints of a negative backlash against a customer (whether through an impolite response in English, abuse in an Indian language, non-verbal cues or cutting off the call) would invite termination of employment. Agents accepted their employers' organisational directives about customer abuse, recognising the role of client requirements, and the need for organisational survival and process retention in this.

Customer abuse can just take you off-balance for the whole shift. Sometimes, I feel like screaming back. After all, every human being has basic dignity so why should we put up with these insults because of the colour of our skin?

---

avoid answering such questions from customers. In response to customer queries, agents were trained to say that they were headquartered in the clients' or customers' country. If quizzed further, they either refused to disclose any more information about their location, citing security reasons, or they would mention that they were located in Asia. Only if the customer persisted or if customer inquiries narrowed down to the specific place from where they were calling, would agents divulge the truth or allow the customer to hang up.

But then, I cannot – I would lose my job and the process will go back and everyone will lose their jobs. The SLAs are very clear about these things and they [employer organisation] maintain it carefully.

Participants' narratives alluded to numerous monitoring and surveillance mechanisms employed by call-centre organisations. Apart from technology-based systems directly related to task performance[5], agents spoke about the presence of security personnel who conducted random checks of their person and their belongings prior to them entering their offices. Lockers were provided by the employer within the office premises but outside the call floor for agents to store their belongings during the shift. Agents were not permitted to carry anything (including a piece of paper, a purse, a mobile phone, water or eatables) into or out of the call floor, and security personnel manning the electronically-operated doors at the entrance to the call floor ensured that they complied. All materials required for task performance were provided inside the call floor, as also were drinking water and sometimes tea and coffee. Such practices were described as part of the client's specifications to maximise the security of the process and the protection of customers' interests.

Technology dominated these participants' work context and work experience. Automated call distribution (ACD) systems were the means through which calls were distributed and queue numbers and waiting times were displayed. With ACD technology systematising control, management could set and measure daily output without the need for constant and direct control while agents experienced restricted autonomy. Agents from inbound call centres recounted being confronted with prominent digital displays which emphasise the number of stacked calls waiting to be answered. Predictive dialling (PD) in outbound call centres ensured that customer calls were diverted automatically to agents who were currently not engaged on another call. Not surprisingly, then, on days when the call flow was very high, agents had to take back-to-back calls. During such times, they enjoyed neither breathing space nor breaks.

In addition to targets, agents' work is regulated by numerous quality and quantity parameters, and technology facilitates their monitoring and measurement. The ACD system throws up a range of statistics, and various 'hard' or quantitative measures are

---

5   Call-centre technology includes automatic call distribution (ACD) and predictive dialing (PD) systems. The ACD system automatically processes incoming telephone calls and distributes them to agents' headsets while simultaneously generating a constant stream of up to 200 sets of statistics about the activities it coordinates, including call volume, duration, wrap times, wait times and abandonment rates at the call centre, the team and the individual agent levels. Not only does the ACD system set the pace of work and monitor performance, but managers and supervisors can also view these statistics, as they are generated in real time, on their desktop computers, and can track each employee's activities throughout the day. Aggregate information from the ACD can also be made available to everyone in the call centre, via displays on large electronic display boards throughout the office. Often ACD systems are connected to one or more databases using computer telephony integration (CTI) software, which allows for customer records to appear on the agent's screen at the same time that the call comes through on the headset. In addition, some ACD systems also incorporate interactive voice response (IVR) technology that may be used to obtain preliminary customer information before a call is connected to an agent (Adapted from McPhail, 2002). Predictive dialing (PD) technology is used in outbound call centres to telephone large pre-programmed lists of customers. Predictive dialing involves programming a database of customers into a computer which then `telephones' them, via multiple-dialing, in a predetermined order. It is generally used in conjunction with an ACD system which, when a potential customer answers a call, automatically transfers it to an agent. If the centre also has CTI, the customer's details will simultaneously appear on the agent's screen. If a number is engaged or rings a certain number of times without an answer the computer moves on to the next number (Adapted from McPhail, 2002).

collected routinely and regularly for each call-centre agent individually and for each work team collectively. These include call waiting time, average call handling time (AHT), call wrap-up time and call abandonment rates. 'Call barging' (where TLs, quality analysts and other superiors – and in some cases, even clients - listen in simultaneously but remotely on live calls to evaluate agents' performance) and 'side-jacking' (where TLs, quality analysts and other superiors physically sit next to agents and listen to and evaluate their calls) also form part of performance management. In addition, since all calls are recorded and stored in archives, calls can be retrieved at any time and analysed for the purposes of evaluation and appraisal. It was not uncommon for recorded calls to be randomly pulled out by analysts in the quality department and examined in terms of call opening and closing, customer interaction including sensitivity, politeness, warmth, understanding customer needs and handling irate customers, adherence to the script, fluency in the English language, understanding of the product/service/process, use of a neutral accent, maintenance of prescribed procedures including assistance offered and information provided, accuracy of documentation, and other parameters specified by the client.

One is on the edge all the time – everything is monitored from the time you step into the call floor till the time your shift is over. So how many calls, how long each call lasted, how you spoke, what you spoke, how long was the interval between calls…it never ends, day after day. I feel tense and anxious all the time. And they keep records too. If you make a mistake, Quality will just scream at you. It has happened to some of my friends – it made them so disturbed. But then one has to deliver or else get out.

The use of call-centre technology as a monitoring and measurement device did not spell the end of human supervision. TLs, stationed at a central point on the call floor, were always in a position to oversee the operations and keep an eye on the agents, in addition to having a master screen on their computers which tracked and highlighted in real time the ongoing work of each individual agent in the team. It was not uncommon for superiors, including TLs, project managers and operations managers, to privately or publicly pull up agents either individually or in groups. Agents spoke of their supervisors and managers striding up and down the call floor, reprimanding or egging on their team. Experiences of being individually identified and publicly pulled up for poor performance in front of team members were reported. Private dressing downs of individual agents and of entire teams were also described. Though agents admitted that such experiences were harsh, and both hurt and humiliated them, they maintained that it was their responsibility to perform and deliver and that superiors were merely doing their jobs.

The TL or the operations manager will stand behind you. If you are not performing, he will scold loudly. It is very humiliating. Everyone is quite sincere in doing their job – so when these shouts happen, we feel that we are useless. Of course, they [the TL and operations manager] are just doing their job but still it is difficult for us also. Insults from customer, yelling from boss,' targets', 'quality'…'perform', 'deliver' - it gets overwhelming.

The demands associated with call-centre work precipitate strain in the agents. Temporal adjustments due to shift-based work wrought havoc on their biological clocks, resulting in increased susceptibility to illness. Though most agents' bodies adapted with time, for a few, health problems persisted. It is worth noting however that those whose bodies had adjusted to nocturnal schedules found themselves physically compelled to maintain the same schedule on their weekly and public holidays. Aggravating this predicament was agents' inability to leave their seats during the shift. Uninterrupted call flows, apart from entailing incessant listening and talking which lead to oral and aural complications, necessitated continuous use of various kinds of technology, resulting in sensory-motor problems linked to the visual and auditory systems and repetitive strain injury (RSI). The sedentary nature of the job, coupled with the almost complete absence of any significant chance for locomotion during the shift, caused stiffness, cramps and backaches. Reducing or eliminating breaks interfered with agents' eating habits. Where breaks were permitted, long queues in the cafeteria forced them to choose fast food or skip their meal altogether in order to be back in time to log in, affecting their nutritional intake. Extension of the work day and the work week also exacerbated health problems. Commuting to and from work also played a part. Though employer organisations provided agents with transport, not only were the distances covered long, but the practice of pooling agents living in spatially proximate localities into a single travel group also extended travel time. The state of India's urban infrastructure added to the problem. Strain on the agents was also exacerbated by their superiors' aggressive and hostile behaviour, aimed at ensuring the realisation of the SLAs.

With agents working during the afternoon, evening or at night (and having little opportunity to be connected with their extra-organisational social networks during work time) and sleeping during the day, as well as the mismatch between Indian public holidays and agents' public holidays (determined by the customer group being served), work-life balance was severely disrupted. Agents reported problems related to spending time with family members, keeping in touch with relatives and friends and completing personal chores and household duties. Organisational demands for team outings, team get-togethers and office gatherings, conducted with a view to developing and reinforcing team bonding and organisational commitment, further hampered work-life balance. Declining these organisational invitations resulted in disapproval from TLs and other superiors and was perceived as a lack of compliance and commitment which affected agents' career prospects.

The job really pays but it has its costs too. Health, family life, social life…everything suffers. One cannot even eat a meal in peace at work, because the break is too short, the queue is too long. But what I feel is that it is in the way we go about it – because of the SLAs, all this is happening. Our bosses also have no choice. Or lose the process.

The experience of physical and mental strain, under the circumstances, was inevitable. Health problems such as loss of appetite, changes in body weight, stomach acidity, nausea, constipation, colds and coughs, diabetes, blood pressure, insomnia, chronic fatigue and drowsiness, anxiety, depression, irritability and cognitive disruptions were commonly reported. While participants pointed out that they attempted to cope with physical strain and ill-health through medical intervention and maximisation of rest and sleep, sick leave to recover from illness was not easily granted. The emphasis on mass customised production meant that employers laid down strict guidelines about granting leave. While agents with less than 6 months tenure with the organisation were not eligible for any kind of leave, agents whose tenure went beyond 6 months were expected to plan for and inform managers about their leave requirements well in advance. Taking leave without prior consent was considered to be an unauthorised absence. Employers went to the extent of blocking the bank salary accounts of those who absented themselves and refused to provide references for those who finally decide to quit because of the situation. Requests for leave with no notice even during instances of ill health were examined in the light of expected and/or ongoing call volume and targets, and were granted or denied accordingly. In other words, when the call volume and targets were high, agents were expected to report for duty no matter how ill they were. Agents who absented themselves, whether with or without intimation, were either warned or dismissed. In some organisations, the management kept a strict watch on people taking sick leave, going to the extent of checking out their homes or regular haunts as well as verifying medical certificates that were submitted.

My friend was so unwell on the shift itself. Still, they [TL and operations manager] did not permit him to take leave. So he did not turn up the next day. They called him on his mobile and said, 'No need to come back at all.', and put some one else in his place. There is no humanity in the call centres. I have heard similar stories from many of my friends.

Work systems, job design elements, customer service requirements and techno-bureaucratic controls all combine together to contribute to an oppressive work regime for agents. Though on the one hand, participants' tasks lacked variety, complexity and autonomy, resulting in a routinised monotony, on the other hand, stringent quality and quantity performance parameters enforced via technology-based monitoring and surveillance ensured that the agents met the expectations of their employers and their clients, facing disciplinary measures, under a transactional psychological contract of employment, if they failed to do so. The agents interviewed in our survey maintained that their experience of oppression essentially emerged from the SLAs. Superiors' aggressive behaviours added to this but, in the participants' view, their superiors at various levels in the employer organisation were only implementing the SLAs that were so critical to retaining or renewing their contracts for particular process and thus for organisation success. They were therefore not held personally responsible for the oppressive work environment. It is relevant to add here that the process excellence agendas currently being adopted in the Indian ITES-BPO sector will exacerbate agents' experience of oppression still further.

The participants' descriptions of the work regimes made it very explicit that they regarded these regimes as oppressive. In this regard, their subjective experiences go beyond those observations about work conditions in international call centres in India by Poster (2007), Ramesh (2004) and Taylor and Bain (2005), justifying the use of the concept of depersonalised bullying (Liefooghe & Mackenzie Davey, 2001). In bringing out its relevance in the contemporary capitalist labour process (Hoel & Beale, 2006; Ironside & Seifert, 2003), these participant narratives allow for a contextualised and politicised understanding of this concept (Hoel & Beale, 2006).

Participating in one's own oppression

Whilst taking a firm stand that the work environment is oppressive, participants nevertheless displayed acceptance of it. Two sets of factors accounted for this contradictory response to the oppressive work environment: participants' professional identity; and the material gains associated with their employment in the ITES-BPO sector.

Participants reiterated that, since they were professionals, they could cope with this oppressive work regime. According to them, professionals possess superior cognitive abilities, advanced qualifications and a sense of responsibility and commitment to work. They prioritise work over personal needs and pleasure, behaving in a dignified and restrained manner and performing optimally and rationally while on the job. Professionals comply with the requirements of the job and the organisation, absorbing any strain that results. The notion of professionalism embraced agents' identity, and functioned in a pervasive manner to discipline them on the job. A vivid picture of the context surrounding their professional identity emerged from these narratives. Organisations cultivate the notion of professionalism in their employees through induction training, on-going socialisation, performance evaluation mechanisms and other elements of organisational design. Indeed, interviews that we conducted with call-centre managers[6] confirmed that employer organisations inculcate the professional identity in their agents with a view to gaining their compliance and commitment to the realisation of the organisation's agenda. That professional identity is greatly valued as a symbol of social status and upward mobility in the Indian context facilitates this process.

Agents' professional identity precluded engagement with collectivisation attempts which are seen as inconsistent with the essential features of professionalism. Moreover, participants considered that collectivisation is redundant in situations where employers protect their employees' interests, particularly through career development and employee redressal opportunities.

Agents pointed out the various avenues their employers provided for career advancement. Many organisations had tie-ups with educational institutions for business administration and management courses, and those who took advantage of this opportunity were usually fully or partially funded by their employers. Similarly, agents reported that their employers had created avenues for vertical movement. Staff were notified of promotion opportunities through internal job postings (IJPs) circulated every quarter. It was emphasised by the organisations that career development was determined by performance and not by socio-demographic factors, seniority or intra-organisational social networks, with an emphasis on merit and objectivity. Furthermore, movement was fast-paced in that, for top performers, the

---

6   We attempted to deepen our understanding of the core theme and its constituents through in-depth interviews conducted with 40 call-centre managers in Bangalore and Mumbai employed by MNC captive, MNC third party and Indian third party call-centre organisations. Transcripts derived from the interview data (that were audio recorded with permission), were analysed using Miles and Huberman's (1994) techniques, and major themes with related secondary themes, categories and patterns were developed and interpretations were made (Patton, 1990).These managerial views supported our core theme. Moreover, while acknowledging call-centre organisations' reliance on the notion of professionalism, managers pointed out contradictions between employers' conceptualisation of professionalism as communicated to employees and the actual operationalisation of professionalism within the organisation (See Noronha & D'Cruz, 2009).

transition from an entry level post to a junior level supervisory post could occur within a year of joining the organisation.

Numerous avenues existed for redressing grievances. Agents informed us that, in keeping with a professional style of management, openness of communication in terms of content, form, style and route were valued. Therefore, in addition to periodic employee satisfaction surveys, 'skip-level meetings'[7] and open forums with superiors, employees with grievances were free to approach anyone in the organisation from the CEO (chief executive officer) down to the TL or someone in between via email, letters, telephone conversations or face-to-face meetings. It was strongly emphasised that the professional atmosphere in the organisation precluded the victimisation of complainants.

Agents expressed the opinion that collectivisation in the Indian ITES-BPO sector would not augur well for its continuity and growth. Currently, overseas clients appreciated India as an offshoring destination not just because of the superior workforce but also because of the macroeconomic business environment of the country. Collectivist activities would pose a serious hindrance to this, resulting in a relocation of activities to other places in South and South-East Asia and South America. Such a development would have micro-level consequences for agents because their employment prospects would be severely and adversely affected.

It suits their employers very well that their employees take this position. From agents' narratives and managerial interviews, it appeared that companies take pains to nurture this stand. Cultivating agents' professional identity is an important step in this direction. The organisations then build on agents' self-concept, highlighting the disconnect between professionalism and collectivisation, which is strongly associated with blue-collar work in the popular mind in the Indian context. Providing avenues for grievances legitimises the employers' claims, promoting the view that trade unions are redundant. That employer organisations do not recognise unions further complicates the agents' perspective. They had been told by their employers that associating with unions could result in dismissal from their jobs. Finally, the organisations' insistence that trade unions would hamper the growth of the Indian ITES-BPO sector, with implications for employment opportunities, sealed the agents' opinions on the matter.

The material gains associated with agent-level jobs in international facing call centres in India play an important role in influencing participants' responses to the oppressive work regime. Personal remuneration and organisational facilities work to strengthen their compliance with and commitment to work-related demands. Participants were well aware that such returns were not available in other sectors of the economy and hence reasoned that it was in their interests to meet work requirements in order to ensure the continuity of the ITES-BPO sector.

The participant narratives underscored the extent to which the ITES-BPO sector, especially global offshoring, had altered India's job market. Employees in this sector, particularly those working for MNC captives, MNC third party and Indian third party organisations, received attractive pay packages, performance incentives in financial and

---

7   A 'skip-level meeting' is a type of structured interview carried out by someone who is not the immediate line manager of the interviewee, either from the HRM department or a manager at least one level removed from the situation, designed to gain an insight into how the organisation is perceived from below.

material forms as well as various allowances and facilities such as food allowance, night shift allowance, transport facilities and medical/health services.

Given the limited employment opportunities for those with a liberal arts or science degree as well as the poor returns at the entry level in many technical and professional fields, it is not surprising that the ITES-BPO sector is widely regarded as the most viable means currently available for achieving a decent quality of life. Those who had prior work experience in other sectors, which paid meagrely, compared the returns received from each sector, highlighting in the process the reasons why the ITES-BPO sector was so much sought after in spite of the challenges it presented. Participants emphasised the sense of independence and self-reliance that their income allowed them, demonstrating changes in their self-concept.

Job titles also played a role. Terms such as 'customer care officer', 'call-centre executive', 'customer care executive', 'contact centre representative' and 'customer support executive' by which centre tasks were designated invoked images of white-collar, professional work and upward mobility, enhancing agents' self-esteem. Participants often also experienced status enhancement by association with overseas clients and customers and employment with MNC organisations, as well as through opportunities to visit clients' locations in foreign countries for training purposes, where applicable. The comparative opulence of the physical infrastructure and material artefacts of the employing organisations also augmented participants' sense of gain.

Professional identity and material gains influence participants' acceptance of their oppressive work environment. Displaying ambivalence, agents participate in their own oppression and hence their victim status is partial.

Developing employee loyalty to and identification with the employer organisation, making employees completely dependent on the employer organisation for the protection of their interests, refusal to recognise trade unions and collectivist endeavours and privileging transactional psychological contracts of employment illustrate the engagement of the HRM strategies described by Peetz (2002) as 'inclusivist' and 'exclusivist', adopted as a means of facilitating the organisational control process. Socio-ideological control via the identity regulation process (Alvesson, 2001; Alvesson & Willmott, 2002) serves as the primary organisational control mechanism, paving the way for participants' acceptance of the oppressive work regime and other inclusivist and exclusivist HRM strategies. In this manner, employees' idiosyncratic behaviour is circumscribed and conformity is ensured in a manner that serves the organisational agenda (Hatch & Cunliffe, 2006).

Courting further oppression

Some of our participants pointed out that a few agents need periodically to find outlets to cope with work-related strain. Extending the call wrap-up time during which relevant information from the phone conversation is keyed into the system, altering their position in the call distribution queue by pressing the release button on their phone, entering wrong customer email addresses into the system if the call did not proceed satisfactorily (so that feedback cannot be obtained from that particular customer), extending restroom breaks, unnecessarily transferring customers' calls and delaying the disconnection of calls were some of the ways in which a few agents gained some breathing space. Customer abuse was sometimes dealt with either by placing the phone in mute mode and cursing the customer aloud in the presence of team members or by pressing the mute button and enabling the loudspeaker so that the team could collectively listen to, make fun of and enjoy the customer's tirade.

Agents were able to decipher when their calls were being monitored either because of a tell-tale echoing or beeping sound that accompanied such activity or from the call monitoring data sheet, and they would take special care to ensure that their performance was optimal during those times. Sometimes, agents collaborated to help ease the strain for other members of their team. That is, when agents filled in for TLs who, for some reason, could not monitor calls, they would manipulate the entire system by asking their team members to give a list of calls on which they had performed well.

While similar activities have been labelled as resistance in other studies (Bain & Taylor, 2000; Knights & McCabe, 1998; Mullholland, 1999 & 2002; Sturdy & Fineman, 2001; Taylor & Bain, 1999), our participants maintained that such behaviour on the part of agents, which is occasional and individualised, does not harbour any anti-work or anti-employer sentiment but simply serves to release pressure. Agents engage in these activities in spite of their sense of professionalism while also knowing full well that if their employers discovertheir behaviour, they will be dismissed.

Discussion

Our findings shed light on the concept of depersonalised bullying, helping to clarify its definition. We define depersonalised bullying as the routine subjugation, both covert and overt, of employees by contextual, structural and process-related elements of organisational design, which are implemented as required by supervisors and managers. Organisational agendas, influenced by extra-organisational demands and intra-organisational aspirations, coalesce to determine the intra-organisational environment influencing management ideology and organisational culture. These are manifested via organisational policies, practices, structures, technology, controls and leadership styles. Together, these elements of organisational design subjugate employees, ensuring their deference to organisational expectations. Supervisors and managers whose responsibilities lie in ensuring organisational effectiveness, implement organisational requirements across the workforce, resorting both to subtle and obvious aggression and hostility. While supervisors and managers neither single out nor target any particular employee nor harbour any intention other than the realisation of organisational imperatives, employees report an experience of physiological and psychological strain stemming both from work pressures and from negative behaviours. Depersonalised bullying contrasts with interpersonal bullying where targets are singled out and malicious personalised intentions are nurtured and manifested. It is the presence of negative behaviours that distinguishes depersonalised bullying from the generalised form of capitalist oppression, (neo) Taylorised work organisation and organisational control described in labour process theory. Of course it is still possible that interpersonal bullying could also occur in depersonalised bullying contexts.

These findings reinforce the emerging view within the bullying literature that changes in the business environment world-wide are bringing about concomitant changes in the nature of work systems, organisational design and job processes, with implications for employer-employee relations (Einarsen, Hoel, Zapf & Cooper, 2005; Hoel & Salin, 2003). With these developments necessitating increasing levels of organisational control in order to realise organisational effectiveness and competitive advantage (Einarsen, Hoel, Zapf & Cooper, 2005; Hoel & Salin, 2003; Lewis & Rayner, 2003) such that the achievement of goals justifies the means, organisations are not just providing a fertile ground for bullying (Einarsen, Hoel, Zapf & Cooper, 2005; Hoel & Salin, 2003), but are in danger of themselves becoming bullies (Hoel & Beale, 2006). Ironside and Seifert (2003) emphasise that contemporary changes in the business world are fuelling the emergence of an intimidatory style of management which is in turn leading to a rise of bullying in organisations.

Inevitably, this raises the issue of organisational power. It is important to recognise that the issue of power remains central to the bullying debate, with an imbalance of power between the two parties being emphasised (Einarsen, Hoel, Zapf & Cooper, 2003; Keashly & Jagatic, 2003). Yet the issue of power in the context of workplace bullying remains to be explored (Keashly & Jagatic, 2003; Liefooghe & Mackenzie Davey, 2001). In the literature on interpersonal bullying, some allusions to power relations have been made (See Einarsen, Hoel, Zapf & Cooper, 2003; Liefooghe & Mackenzie Davey, 2001), though the implicit connotation in the discussion at this level is that the power utilised in bullying is illegitimate power, located in the individual's aggressive nature (Liefooghe & Mackenzie Davey, 2001). It is precisely this argument that is currently challenged when notions of organisational-level power are called into play. Given the nature of the labour process in a capitalist set-up, accentuated by the influences of globalisation and offshoring, the line between legitimate and illegitimate power becomes increasingly blurred and needs to be clarified. As Alvesson and Deetz (1996) point out, power is fundamental to the functioning of the organisation and hence power imbalances and the inequalities they give rise to are inevitable. Because power is essential for understanding the relationship between organisations and their employees, the routine subjugation of employees through organisational practices may in itself be seen as constituting bullying, though organisations present these controls as being in the overall interests of employees. Such an analysis presents organisational interests as conflicting with the interests of individual employees, with the power imbalance between the organisation and the individual employees inevitably meaning that organisations are perceived as bullies (Liefooghe & Mackenzie Davey, 2001). The debate is succinctly summarised by Hoel and Salin (2003:205) who state that 'bullying may stem not so much from abusive or illegitimate use of power as from power which is considered legitimate, and tightly related to the labour process and managerial prerogative to manage'.

That the utilitarian instrumentalism of the hard HRM model is being camouflaged within the developmental humanism of the soft HRM model (Legge, 2006) aided by the organisational control process (Noronha & D'Cruz, 2009) and inclusivist and exclusivist strategies (Peetz, 2002), cannot be denied. Not surprisingly, unitarist ideologies are promoted within the organisation in such a way that employees' compliance, identification and commitment are strong, critical detachment is weak and organisational control is legitimised. Clearly, HRM operates as one-sided managerialism where employers' interests are represented, rather than as true unitarism which engages employers and employees together in the employment relationship. Indeed, the absence of discursive and pluralist ideologies limit the alternatives available to agents both in terms of world views and actions (Lewis & Rayner, 2003). Overall, employees' opportunities to resist and challenge managerial actions are becoming more limited in the contemporary context (Hoel & Salin, 2003), increasing their power deficit (Einarsen, Hoel, Zapf & Cooper, 2005). That the fear of harsh personal consequences further restricts employees' choices must be recognised (Ironside & Seifert, 2003), particularly in the Indian context where similar employment opportunities enabling a decent standard of living outside the ITES-BPO sector are virtually non-existent. Yet, such developments underscore Ironside and Seifert's (2003) and Hoel and Beale's (2006) position that solutions to workplace bullying lie in pluralist approaches through collectivist endeavours. Ironside and Seifert (2003) cite evidence to support their view that improvements in working conditions, including freedom from bullying, are unlikely to come from management initiatives, and that the best route is from pressures within the workplace through the mobilisation of the countervailing power of workers, usually in the form of trade union organisation. Bullying is less likely to occur and is more likely to be tackled when it does occur if there is a strong and well organised trade union presence at the workplace.

Overall, the study findings take forward the perspective currently emerging within the organisation-workplace bullying debate that the organisation itself is the bully, fine-tuning contemporary depersonalised conceptualisations that draw on an organisational level of analysis (Hoel & Beale, 2006; Ironside & Seifert, 2003; Liefooghe & Mackenzie Davey, 2001). Participants' references to an oppressive work regime strengthen Hoel and Beale's (2006) thesis that victimisation refers to one end of the bullying continuum where individuals are singled out, while oppressive work regimes refer to the other end where everyone is subject to the same experience, emphasising that bullying is an umbrella concept (Einarsen, 1999; Rayner, Sheehan & Barker, 1999) whose scope is still being discovered.

© *Premilla D'Cruz and Ernesto Noronha, 2009*

REFERENCES

Alvesson, M. (2001) 'Knowledge work: Ambiguity, image and identity', *Human Relations,* Vol 54:863-886

Alvesson, M. & S. Deetz (1996) 'Critical theory and post-modernism' in S.R. Clegg & C. Hardy (eds) *Studying organisations,* London: Sage:191–217

Alvesson, M. & H. Willmott (2002) 'Identity regulation as organisational control: Producing the appropriate individual', *Journal of Management Studies*, Vol 39:619-644

Bain, P. & P. Taylor (2000) 'Entrapped by the "electronic panopticon"? Worker resistance in the call centre', *New Technology, Work and Employment,* Vol 15:2-18

Batt, R. & L. Moynihan (2002) 'The viability of alternative call centre models', *Human Resource Management Journal,* Vol 12:14-34

D'Cruz, P. & E. Noronha (2008) 'Doing emotional labour: The experiences of Indian call centre agents', *Global Business Review,* Vol 9:131-147

Einarsen, S. (1999) 'The nature and causes of bullying', *International Journal of Manpower,* Vol 20:16-27

Einarsen, S., H. Hoel, D. Zapf & C.L. Cooper (2003) 'The concept of bullying at work: The European tradition' in S. Einarsen, H. Hoel, D. Zapf & C. L. Cooper (eds) *Bullying and emotional abuse in the workplace,* London and New York: Taylor & Francis:3-30

Einarsen, S., H. Hoel, D. Zapf & C.L. Cooper (2005) 'Workplace bullying: Individual pathology or organisational culture?' in V. Bowie, B.S. Fisher & C.L. Cooper (eds) *Workplace violence: Issues, trends, strategies,* Devon: Willian:229-247

Frenkel, S., M. Korczynski, K. Shire & M. Tam (1998) 'Beyond bureaucracy: Work organisation in call centres', *International Journal of Human Resource Management,* Vol 9:957-979

Hatch, M.J. & A.L. Cunliffe (2006) *Organisation theory: Modern, symbolic, and postmodern perspectives,* New York: Oxford University Press

Hoel, H. & D. Beale (2006) 'Workplace bullying, psychological perspectives and industrial relations: Towards a contextualised and interdisciplinary approach', *British Journal of Industrial Relations,* Vol 44:239-262

Hoel, H. & D. Salin (2003) 'Organisational antecedents of workplace bullying' in S. Einarsen, H. Hoel, D. Zapf & C. L. Cooper (eds) *Bullying and emotional abuse in the workplace,* London and New York: Taylor & Francis:203-218

Ironside, M. & R. Seifert (2003) 'Tackling bullying in the workplace: The collective dimension', in S. Einarsen, H. Hoel, D. Zapf & C. L. Cooper (eds) *Bullying and emotional abuse in the workplace,* London and New York: Taylor & Francis:383-398

Keashly, L. & S. Harvey (2006) 'Workplace emotional abuse' in E.K. Kelloway, J. Barling & J.J. Hurrell (eds) *Handbook of workplace violence,* California: Sage:95-120

Keashly, L. & K. Jagatic (2003) 'By any other name: American perspectives on workplace bullying' in S. Einarsen, H. Hoel, D. Zapf & C. L. Cooper (eds) *Bullying and emotional abuse in the workplace,* London and New York: Taylor & Francis:31-61

Knights, D. & D. McCabe (1998) 'What happens when the phone goes wild?: Staff, stress and spaces for escape in a BPR telephone banking work regime', *Journal of Management Studies,* Vol 35:63-94

Legge, K. (2006) 'Human resource management' in S. Ackroyd, R. Batt, P. Thompson & P.S. Tolbert (eds) *Oxford handbook of work and organisation,* Oxford: Oxford University Press:220-241

Liefooghe, A.P.D. & K. Mackenzie Davey (2001) 'Accounts of workplace bullying: The role of the organisation', *European Journal of Work and Organisational Psychology,* Vol 10:375-392

Lewis, D. & C. Rayner (2003) 'Bullying and human resource management: A wolf in sheep's clothing?' in S. Einarsen, H. Hoel, D. Zapf & C. L. Cooper (eds) *Bullying and emotional abuse in the workplace,* London and New York: Taylor & Francis:370-382

McPhail, B. (2002) 'What is on the line in call centre studies?' Accessed on August 10, 2005 from http://www.fis.utoronto.ca/research/iprp/publications/mcphail-cc.pdf

Miles, M.S. & A.M. Huberman (1994) *Qualitative data analysis: A sourcebook of new methods,* California: Sage

Mirchandani, K. (2003) 'Making Americans: Transnational call centre work in India', unpublished paper. Accessed on August 31, 2008 from http://merlin.mngt.waikato.ac.nz/ejrot/cmsconference/2003/proceedings/postcolonial/Mirchandani.pdf.

Mullholland, K. (1999) 'Back to the future: A call centre and new forms of direct control', *paper presented at the 17th Annual International Labour Process Conference,* March 29-31, 1999, School of Management, Royal Holloway: University of London

Mullholland, K. (2002) 'Gender, emotional labour and teamworking in a call centre', *Personnel Review,* Vol 31: 283-303

NASSCOM (2005) *Strategic Review 2005,* New Delhi: NASSCOM

NASSCOM (2006) *Strategic Review 2006,* New Delhi: NASSCOM

NASSCOM (2007) *Strategic Review 2007,* New Delhi: NASSCOM

NASSCOM-McKinsey (2005) *Extending India's leadership of the global IT and BPO industries,* New Delhi: NASSCOM-McKinsey

Noronha, E. & P. D'Cruz (2009) *Employee identity in Indian call centres: The notion of professionalism,* New Delhi: Sage

Patton, M.Q. (1990) *Qualitative evaluation and research methods,* California: Sage

Peetz, D. (2002) 'Decollectivist strategies in Oceania', *Relations Industrielles/Industrial Relations,* Vol 57:252-281

Poster, W. (2007) 'Who's on the line? Indian call centre agents pose as Americans for US outsourced firms', *Industrial Relations,* Vol 46:271-304

Ramesh, B. (2004) 'Cybercoolies in BPOs', *Economic and Political Weekly,* Vol 39:492-497

Rayner, C., M. Sheehan & M. Barker (1999) *Bullying at work (1998 research update conference proceedings),* Stafford: Stafford University

Sturdy, A. & S. Fineman (2001) 'Struggles for the control of affect: Resistance as politics and emotion' in A. Sturdy, A. Gruglis & H. Willmott (eds) *Customer service, empowerment and entrapment,* London: Palgrave

Taylor, P. & P. Bain (1999) 'An assembly line in the head: Work and employment relations in the call centre', *Industrial Relations Journal,* Vol 30:101–117

Taylor, P. & P. Bain (2005) 'India calling to the faraway towns: The call centre labour process and globalisation', *Work, Employment and Society,* Vol 19:261-282

Taylor, P. & P. Bain (2006) *An investigation into the offshoring of financial services business processes,* Glasgow: University of Strathclyde

Tracy, S.J., P. Lutgen-Sandvik & J.K. Alberts (2006) 'Nightmares, demons and slaves: Exploring the painful metaphors of workplace bullying', *Management Communication Quarterly,* Vol 20:148-185

van Manen, M. (1998) *Researching lived experience,* Canada: Althouse

Looking behind the line:
privatisation and the reification of work in a Brazilian telecommunications company

Simone Wolff

Simone Wolff *is a professor in the Social Sciences Department at the State University of Londrina, Brazil.*

ABSTRACT

This paper analyses the results of a case study carried out in the call centre of a public Brazilian telecommunications company. The study focused on the working conditions of operators engaged in telemarketing, an activity that relies on computerised data processing as its main working tool. Information was collected on the perceptions of managers and employees of the informatisation of working procedures and of the new forms of management that were adopted to enable these processes to be handled using the new technologies. The analysis was guided by the hypothesis that the application of Information and Communications Technologies (ICTs) in the context of changed organisational parameters inspired by the so-called 'participative administration' approach, has enabled a new kind of exploitation of living labour to emerge, one that is marked by an expropriation and commodification of workers' knowledge, in its cognitive dimension.

Introduction

This paper presents the results of a case study carried out in the call centre of a telecommunication company[1]. The case study focused primarily on working conditions in telemarketing; a service created and outsourced in response to the new competitiveness in the sector that emerged in the post-privatisation period in Brazil. It was during this period that a customer care function was created within the organisation with the sole purpose of expanding the company's market share. This was a radical departure from the previous situation, where customer support had only the technical function of providing telephone lines and service. It is this crucial role of expanding and preserving the market that gives telemarketing an unprecedented strategic importance, not just for this particular telecommunications company, but for several other contemporary enterprises as well.

Although this was a public company, the competitive scenario stemmed from the break-up of the former state monopoly and followed the same organisational and technological

---

1   The study was carried out as part of the PhD thesis 'The reification spectrum in a telecommunication company: the working process under new management and technological parameters' (O espectro da reificação em uma empresa de telecomunicações: o processo de trabalho sob os novos parâmetros gerenciais e tecnológicos), defended in 2004 at the State University of Campinas (UNICAMP), available on http://libdigi.unicamp.br/document/?code=vtls000331335. The company investigated was a Brazilian telecommunications company owed by a municipality in the southern region of the country.

patterns as those adopted by private companies. In line with the neoliberal policies that had created the break-up, it had to operate on a commercial basis and compete on equal terms with private telecommunications companies. Thus, the provision of a public utility service where profit simply provided the means to invest in improving quality and expansion of the service, which was its original purpose, was replaced by a market view in which profit became the object of the exercise, and the marketing strategies the means to achieve this.

It could therefore be said the services were 'commodified' (Huws, 2003), even though this company was state-owned. The main means for attaining this was the creation of a marketing unit to which the telemarketing department investigated in this study was linked. In this outsourced enterprise, the new market focus resulted in the application of management models aimed at promoting strong standardisation and control of workers' attendance. This was considered to be the key to obtaining 'total quality' in the products and services that were supposed to capture new markets and keep existing customers satisfied. These processes rely strongly on the use of Information and Communications Technologies (ICTs).

The standardisation of tasks that is enabled by informatisation also makes possible a form of flexible automation – promoted by software that makes it possible to optimise productivity by collecting information on all aspects of the working process and providing feedback on it. After this information has been screened and codified, it becomes data which can be crystallised in the company's software and used for improving its products and services.

In the call-centre processes, these data are obtained from the customer-operator relationship whose characteristics it is usually impossible to capture by the normal monitoring to which operators are submitted (and that is also informatised). In other words, the software does not just collect the usual quantitative call-centre metrics concerning duration of calls, speed of response etc. but also analyses the actual content of the calls. In this way, agents' tacit knowledge about imperfections and gaps in the service arising from their direct contact with the customers can be collected. This information is highly valuable to the company. Flexible automation thus requires active involvement and 'collaboration' from operators in the continuous adjustments of attendance and consumption patterns implied by the term 'flexible'. This is indeed the aim of the 'participative management' paradigm which guides the human resources policies of this and other contemporary enterprises. It is thus the case that not only their labour but also their knowledge is taken from the workers in the commodification process, and this occurs through its expropriation and materialisation into the company's data processing system and products.

Contrary to the thesis that argues that work is enriched through the advent of ICTs (Castillo, 2008), the hypothesis guiding our analysis was that such technologies, when applied under the new organisational parameters that form part of current entrepreneurial strategies, make possible a new kind of exploitation of living labour[2] based on the

---

2   Marked by the introduction of machinery to the productive process, the phenomenon of reification of work refers to the transference of complex operations, which come from the worker's empirical experience, to, machines, leading to the primacy of the latter in the shaping of both working procedures and temporality (Marx, 1984). Thereafter, the machine's operations determine the functionality and employability of living labour in production, making the concept of qualification equivalent to its reification.

commodification of workers' knowledge in its cognitive dimension. The more they are involved in the production processes of large companies (as we can regard this customer service function), the more workers' space for creativity is systematically inhibited by a management policy which demands both quality and uniformity, yet, through increasing automation, control, intensification and simplification, leads to low pay, instability, stress and precariousness[3].

This paper focuses on how these developments affect those workers who are included in the process, drawing on the perceptions of the company staff involved in this kind of activity (employees and managers) and an analysis of working procedures, the process of informatisation and the new management forms adopted to implement this process. The research was carried out through direct observations at the workplace, supplemented by semi-directed interviews.

When production relations are simultaneously information relations

In Brazil, it was under the government of Fernando Henrique (1995-1998) that privatisation policies were first implemented, with the privatisation of telecommunications occuring in 1998. This event led many state companies, to restructure themselves to make their acquisition attractive for the large transnational enterprises which were about to invade their exclusive markets. In the case study company, Sercomtel Telecommunications S.A., this productive restructuring started in 1993.

The trajectory of Sercomtel was very unusual compared with other telecommunication companies in Brazil, not only because it belonged to a municipality, while the majority of telecommunications companies were state-owned, but also because it remained, and still remains public. The first step towards enabling the necessary changes was to use a legal subterfuge that, although it was a state company, could allow it to raise investment and access other fund-raising opportunities in the market. In 1993, Sercomtel transformed itself into an 'Anonymous Partnership of Mixed Economy', whose stocks were municipally controlled. As a director at that time said (in an interview), this change could also pave the way for a possible privatisation, an option that has never been completely discarded by the city administrators.

These were the specificities that made it an interesting object of research. First, it raised the question whether privatisation was the only solution that could guarantee the enterprise's competitiveness. Second, the fact that it operated within the tradition of a public company made it more open to investigation, with managers providing almost unrestricted access to its facilities for research. And third, there was a commitment to providing its staff with stability so that, unusually, there was continuity of employment over the change period. These conditions were extremely favourable for collecting data (documents, interviews, observations, etc.) and made it possible to compare the old technologies and organisational structures with those that resulted from the restructuring. Such a comparison was essential for identifying the issues described here.

---

3   It can also be considered for productive chains of transnational corporations which set a new international division of labour in which R&D activities, rfequiring more aggregated knowledge, are typically located in the head company's origin countries while the work which is limited to the transference of knowledge with a lower technological impact is relocated to peripheral countries (Huws, 2003).

Neoliberal policies and discussions about the privatisation process in Brazil did not only lead to a new legal status but also to the modernisation of the organisational structure of the company. Although mostly still funded by public capital, it decided to modernise its new management and technological standards on the same lines as the large private companies.

The first step in the restructuring was the implementation of total quality programmes (TQP). This marked the beginning of the informatisation of the working processes, and also the 'acculturation' of its personnel, (Feldman, 1998), aimed at gaining their consent and commitment to the structural changes which would come. One of its main purposes was to inculcate a marketing perspective among the employees. Little by little, the old conception of providing a public and high-quality services for the community was replaced by the idea of generating profit for the company. Such a perspective was fundamental to achieving the new kind of commodification, both of the work and of the services that would result from the informatisation of the company's processes.

Commodification that results from the introduction of ICTs comes from two apparently paradoxical resources for the productivity of contemporary capitalism (Zuboff, 1989). First, there is a qualitative increase in the trend, already well known in the history of capitalism, of using automation as a means of standardising and simplifying living labour and replacing it by machines. Second, the logic of informatisation requires workers' creativity to contribute to the development and improvement of its software. In order for this to be achieved, it is necessary to ensure that everyone involved in the development process has a 'marketing attitude' (Zuboff, 1994; 1989).

In an attempt to solve this paradox, what might be called 'management by processes' has been developed, in an approach that adopts a type of information management designed to encourage greater interaction between different areas, enabling employees at all levels to develop ideas linked to the interests of the company (Wolff, 2005). This management by processes is embedded in a participative form of administration that aims to develop a 'marketing attitude' among employees, motivate them and direct their communication and cooperation in this direction.

It is for this reason that the company currently uses the term 'collaborators' to describe its staff. Such new management paradigms are usually introduced into companies by means of initiatives such as TQPs. These mark the beginning of the restructuring, mainly because they provide a methodology for the standardisation of working routines that, after being codified as 'work instructions'[4], will eventually be automated. 'Participative management' prescribes techniques (such as brainstorming and team work) that aim to encourage workers to disclose their old working procedures and 'collaborate' by offering suggestions for improving productivity (Wolff, 2005; 2004).

These new management methods are essential for acquiring the information feedback that is required to respond to the highly diverse and competitive consumption market which emerged in the neoliberal context. They are also necessary to adjust this information to the continuous technical-operational alterations that are needed to launch new products and services.

---

4   A common term in the literature on TQPs.

Far from being enriched, work which deals with information thus undergoes a process analogous to those that affect manual activities related to production. According to Huws (2006):

So-called 'knowledge workers' are those who process units of information in the same way that 'manual workers' are those who process units of physical matter. All these workers, whether 'mental' or 'manual', are intricately linked to each other by the logic of capital, through their complementary positions in the division of labour.

Drawing similar conclusions, Castillo (2008:37) asserts that the codification of tacit knowledge and its commercialisation, that is, its transformation into a commodity brings to "knowledge workers" the same effects that manufacturing workers, with low qualifications, suffered in the past. In this author's view, 'standardisation procedures or the introduction of requirements or metrics, such as the ISO regulations' play an important role in this commodification process.

The introduction of management by processes was the purpose of the second step in Sercomtel's modernisation plan, launched in February 1997 with a project entitled: 'Entrepreneurial Transformation'. It was at this stage that the marketing unit was formed, a unit which had not been needed before because the company was the sole supplier in the local market. This unit was given an important strategic role in the company, at the top level of management, where previously only telecommunications technology and engineering units had been represented.

Sercomtel was digitised in 1999 and its range of services expanded from telephony to voice, data and image communication, enabling it to provide so-called 'multiservice' marketing.[5] In this development, information started to act simultaneously both as an input and as the final result of its production process. In such companies it can therefore be said that the relations of production are at the same time relations of information. This makes a company's productive process highly innovative but also makes it even more essential that the information should be commodified.

This is the sort of situation that led Zarafian (2001) to conclude that, despite the indisputable differences between them, the famous distinction between the secondary and tertiary sectors is no longer appropriate for describing the new business model that has emerged from economic liberalisation, since flexible automation is no longer restricted to manufacturing industries but also covers the major service companies. In manufacturing, information that has been completely reified and embodied in a robot, will create a material product, either partially or fully. In services, the process ends during the actual phase of service transmission, since this is its 'final product'.

The emphasis on multiservice and marketing were decisive at Sercomtel in enabling it to take a further step towards the private company model: the outsourcing of its customer service function. In the beginning of 2000, Sercomtel created the 'ASK! – call centre National Company', which is legally constituted as a separate outsourced company, despite being an essential part of its overall corporate model and playing a direct part in its production process. ASK! was conceived as a company that would

---

5   This term refers to services that add new functions to the products and systems involved in communication transmission, such as voice mail, automated call transfer and Internet services.

supply telemarketing and customer support services both to Sercomtel and to other companies across a wide range of sectors in southern Brazil[6].

The outsourcing model adopted was described as 'mixed outsourcing', It was Sercomtel's responsibility to provide the personnel: coordinators, supervisors and operators, whilst ASK! provide the logistics and infrastructure. Sercomtel thus acted simultaneously as the customer and employer of its outsourced company. This was the legal situation at ASK! at the end of the research period, in mid-2004.

ASK! assumed responsibility for the customer service function as well as for a new key function in the marketing profile drawn up by Sercomtel's senior management as a result of its restructuring projects: telemarketing. With this crucial new function established, the outsourced company became the main channel for selling and marketing Sercomtel's services and, therefore, the main tool used to develop its core busines – the development of technological telecommunications solutions, particularly corporate ones. The creation of this function enabled the company to eliminate the costs and time previously spent on training related to new projects and on advertising campaigns, which had become increasingly frequent since it became a multiservice enterprise.

ASK!'s attachment to Sercomtel's marketing unit was determined by its marketing function. Within this unit, it was linked to the Customer Relations function, which was given responsibility for supervising the new company. Specific communication channels were established between the two companies so that this relationship would not be characterised as one involving a direct commitment as an employer. Thus, Sercomtel's contacts with ASK! are mediated by so-called 'contract inspectors,' and at the ASK! side of the relationship, liaison with Sercomtel is managed by 'contract supervisors.'

The work carried out by ASK! for Sercomtel is broken down into separate projects that are regulated through service contracts. These projects are linked to two basic activities: 'receptive' services relating to incoming demands from customers regarding the provision of telephone lines, services, questions, etc., and 'active telemarketing', involving outbound calls from operators who offer new products and services to potential customers. This research study focused on the working processes in the latter group of activities.

When the working process is simultaneously a worker commodification process

Although Sercomtel remained public, it did not escape from the broader trends that have marked the productive restructuring that private telecommunications enterprises have embarked on since privatisation. Of course, the outsourcing of customer services made a major contribution to keeping it competitive after its monopoly was broken up.

Indeed, Sercomtel considers its active telemarketing to be ASK!'s 'golden egg'. It is critical to the company's success because it is both a sales channel for its services and plays an important role in contributing to innovation in marketing. The information collected through contacts in the active telemarketing serves as a thermometer for

---

6   All the technical and administrative data on ASK! presented here were taken from the company's website: http://www.askcallcenter.com.br, complemented by information from an interview with ASK!'s Business Manager who was also acting as a Project Manager at ASK!.

Sercomtel to obtain market trends and deepen its relationship with its customers. It thus has a direct impact on the company's income. All the organisational and technological standards assembled by Sercomtel were transferred to ASK!, which was created according to the parameters inscribed in the TQPs. As one business manager who was around when ASK! was first set up put it, 'the company was born with Total Quality in its blood; it was already in its DNA.'

The telemarketing operators are the personnel responsible for collecting and digitising the data that can be considered as the raw material of this working process. Once analysed by the head company, these data will serve as the ingredients for the development both of new products and services and of marketing strategies.

Using a customer relations management programme, the information, in its unprocessed state, is integrated and standardised in a large database at the head office of the company, becoming the raw material for further developments. As well as automating certain working processes, the software also systematises and links the data related to each customer's purchasing habits, providing a detailed report that makes it possible to predict the potential for the purchase of other products and services, which can also lead to further fine-tuning and improvement of the programme itself and well as better targetting and an increase in sales. Using this software has enabled Sercomtel to achieve another major competitive goal: product diversification through personalisation of services.

As the most important of Sercomtel's projects at ASK!, active telemarketing' service requires the most experienced operators. 'Sercomtel Telemarketing,' the project chosen for this study at ASK! employs only 25 operators, working in six-hour shifts from Monday to Saturday. These reasonably limited working hours are possible because the calls are initiated by the team, unlike the inbound call-centre agents dealing with customer queries, who have to be available round the clock and work 24-work shifts.

As well as carrying the responsibility for being part of this strategic operation for the customer company, these workers have to deal with a working process that is surprisingly complex, because it enters the customer's space and is much more prone to generate unexpected situations. 'Active' work is thus much more difficulty to standardise fully than 'responsive'. work Nevertheless, its temporality is more determined by the machines than is the case for inbound calls because the calls are sent to the operators at a continuous stream, generated by the company in its search for new customers. This is why active telemarketing requires more experienced operators, and only employs agents who have already worked on other Sercomtel projects of Sercomtel. As ASK!'s Business Manager put it:

When you get into the customer's home, you must be prepared to answer all their questions. We can't take the risk of the customer saying: 'How can you call me and you don't know the answer to what I'm asking you? So telemarketing needs a higher qualification than the other projects because the agents must be more aware of the client company's business.

This 'higher qualification' certainly has to do in large part with knowledge of ITCs, which are not just a tool but the very organiser of these operators' working processes. This also demonstrates that the systemic operational perspective, recommended by

TQP is crucial to the company's business processes. The agents sit at workstations, referred to as 'attendance positions' (AP), that are connected to a local network server, which automatically sends them a screen filled with information about each customer whose number will be dialled.

Calls are made using predictive dialing , enabling the system to send a new call as soon as the previous one has finished . Besides monitoring which operators are logged in at any given time, the system also makes it possible to check the average length of conversations, the time adjustment, and the number of calls made and connected to each AP, as well as automatially rebooking missed calls. This flexible automation does not allow the telemarketers any control over the rhythm of their activities.

Informatisation is also used to standardise the *modus operandi* of the working process. This is carried out through programmes that predict the dialogue that will take place between operator and customer in the form of pre-written scripts, that appear on the agents' screens as each new call is sent and provide a pattern of dialogue that directs them in the conversation with the customer, as well as leaving gaps to be filled in with the answers obtained from the customers that will afterwards serve as raw material for new processes and be incorporated into new scripts.

These screens are developed jointly by teams from ASK!'s IT section, and Sercomtel's IT and marketing section. The entire process is carried out within the TQP parameters which in turn fall within the 'management by process' procedure that is incorporated into the latest version of the company's ISO international business standards. The principles guiding script development are success in customer persuasion and customer satisfaction in relation to the relevant multiservice package. In this sense, the script is a flexible tool of automation that accepts data changes and additions in response to variation in the consumer market, and it can also be amended according to suggestions given either by customers or by operators. As the Business Manager explained:

The script is able to get feedback if the (marketing) campaign is already in process. So, if an operator has an interesting idea, we discuss it with Sercomtel, analyse whether the suggestion should be implemented or not, and redirect everything accordingly.

Within the TQP concept, the script works as an 'action plan' for standardising the production flow. It also works as 'labour instruction' because the information collected from customers functions as data which, once inserted into the system, standardises both the temporality of the work process and its *modus operandi*. In the words of the Business Manager:

The script is also an optimising tool because it has some internal controls which assure that what the customer requested will be delivered on time and with the quality laid down by the company. It is the 'control tools' called: 'Service Orders,' 'Implementation Schedule' etc., that show me if what the customer asked is being done as he asked, and at the time and quality that the company wants. These variables are given by our Total Quality Programme.

This is how TQP uses informatics as a tool within ASK!'s processes, a tool that normalises the operational work that defines the new kind of the reification of living labour in this company. This reification can be understood as such because the operators function like information transmission antenna that contribute to the preparation and updating of the scripts that will determine how to carry out their work. The way the Business Manager refers to the operators reflects such reification:

The call centre operation is fundamental to our success. It is the first to feel if things are going well or not. The perception they have, and the cooperation they give will produce the final result, in the telemarketing actions themselves.

Because they serve as antenna of the market, these operators' experiences make it possible to capture demands and consumption trends much more effectively than the marketing department. Their suggestions are vitally important at the moment a new script is being elaborated. This moment denotes the expropriation of their tacit knowledge (the suggestions and ideas that originated from their daily work experience) through informatisation. The same manager describes how this expropriation takes place:

Each operator has an immediate supervisor who makes this happen. In the case of telemarketing, before the operators start using a new script, they are trained to use it. If at that time they notice that any of the questions are likely to interfere in any way with the process of approaching the customer or in the data collection, the operator signals this and a message is sent to Sercomtel. Generally, Sercomtel is with us at this time. We work in a very integrated way when a script is introduced to the centre. Normally, the person who is responsible for the campaign at Sercomtel is with us and the operators make their suggestions. Because they have the experience. So, the suggestions that come up from the operations area are extremely important for the progress of the campaign.

The alliance between informatics and Total Quality also becomes a way of optimising control over the operators. The 'action plans' that establish the workflow, are based on the TQ methodology that defines 'preventive actions' and 'corrective actions' and are supposed to ensure the quality of the final result. Based on these criteria, the operators are exposed to a continuous and double monitoring process. It is continuous because its target is to cover 100% of the operators, generally in real time (because the process is carried out online). It is double because such monitoring is performed both by ASK! and by Sercomtel. The 'contract inspector' from Sercomtel assigned to monitor contracts with ASK! describes this procedure in detail, explaining how this aspect of flexible automation actually functions:

The script is a flexible tool, but only when feeding in data for the company. You can't jump a question; the script must be followed as a whole. That's why an internal monitoring process is needed. All the calls are recorded 100%. Indeed, we do the monitoring online. Once a month we call the agents and show them their assessments individually. We give them a score telling them the positive and negative points. The scoring and the assessment are carried out together by ASK! and Sercomtel. ASK! monitors there and I monitor here. What they don't catch there, I catch here.

The operators live under a continuous pressure in their work once it is made clear that the monitoring is used for assessment purposes. This monitoring also reveals individual 'non-conformities', and consequently can lead to warnings. The new kind of control provided by the informatisation of production became very evident in the interview with the 'inspector,' who had previously been a telephone operator at Sercomtel and was thus in a position to make a comparison with the control system that was in place before the informatisation of customer service work. This interview also made the operators' resistance to this change visible.

> In the past, everything was done on paper. There were paper cards that were modified with a pencil. With the paper, I completely lost the information. In the computer the information is permanently available. I see it as a way of centralising the information. With the paper system, the information was concentrated in just one person's hands. She saw herself with power, with strength. But in the computer, with Sysonline[7], the information is available to everyone. There is the question of 'non-conformity', which is a control tool that, in some areas, operators consider as an aggression. Thus, we say some things are cultural. It is as if the person who generated the 'non-conformity' wanted to sabotage it; they don't see it as a way to correct eventual mistakes at work. The quality system aims at making work easier. (Contract Inspector, Sercomtel-ASK!)

At the same time that the informatisation of production was making work faster and easier compared to that of the telephone operators under the old system, the new marketing tasks that were added to the job descriptions were creating new demands, broadening the range of tasks and requiring new types of behaviour. The requirements needed to exercise the function of 'call-centre operator' in the company were described in the following terms:

> Cordiality, helpfulness, ability to compromise, responsibility, interest, empathy, objectiveness, a knowledge of how to identify the customers' needs, enchanting them, presenting alternatives and solutions, organisation, emotional stability, motivation, oral and written communication, agility in using microcomputers and devices used in the office's basic automation, customer service and persuasion techniques [that is, 'knowing how to listen and propose solutions' to overcome possible objections]. (Source: Internal Document, HR Department, ASK!)

A variety of means are promoted to ensure that operators are sufficiently motivated to fit this profile. These include 'motivational programmes' and meetings called 'word workshops' that are used to measure their 'satisfaction level' with the aim of 'lowering their stress' (Jornal Mural, 09/02/2000). This need to lower the agents' stress levels, recognised by the company itself, clearly shows the difficulties of this kind of work: highly determined, intensified, supervised. These problems are especially severe in the 'active' process of telemarketing, where the contradiction between the extreme standardisation of the tasks conflicts with the unpredictability of the 'work objects' – the customers. Such contradictions are common in a context where the qualification concept is equivalent to the reification of the work; as can be observed from the way the work is perceived by managers, exemplified in this quotation:

---

7   *Sysonline* is the software that links the ASK! and Sercomtel networks and manages the information flow between them. It is lined to the on line monitoring but also integrates and registers customer information. It was this system that replaced the paper-based record-keeping formerly implemented by Sercomtel's telephone operators and technicians.

*Our human material is our working tool, so attitude and voice are two extremely
important things in the call centre. It is important that the professional is well,
good humoured, with a good voice and without abackache, so that he or she can
work well. Operators are people and they are our working tools. As they say, this
is 'who does the hard work'. (Business and Project Manager, ASK!-Sercomtel)*

The perception of the telemarketing workers

In both the managers' statements and the documents the workers are viewed as having
become an information source for the machines since informatisation. Simultaneously
their condition as subjects of the production process has been disadvantaged. Moreover,
although a monitoring system has been established that is both ubiquitous and
continuous, it is hidden and depersonalised by the use of computers. Zuboff (1988)
regards this type of monitoring as what she called 'informatics panoptic power,' which
occurs, especially in operational areas, where the uses of these machines is already
normalised by management methodologies .

Something similar seems to happen with ASK!'s operators. In fact, Sercomtel
adopts a much more authoritarian relationship with its outsourced workers than
with the operators who are under its direct employment. Excessive concern with the
standardisation of attendance in its production 'frontline' at ASK! imposes a degree of
surveillance and control ('100%' and 'online' monitoring). that is never witnessed among
its own employees. This concern was justified by an administrative officer linked to
Sercomtel Business Management Area, as follows:

*Look, when most of the customer contact is made by others, things must be very well
specified, in writing, standardised. Mainly in the call centre which has a high
rotation of staff. To control all this, we must have everything well standardised.
For this reason we have the Total Quality procedures and the company's
information system [Sysonline]. All of this is very important in the call centre
because, when serving a customer, the amount of information is usually too
large [to remember], then the agent must have resources to search for the
information. So, he just needs to take a glance at it and soon he can remember
exactly what to answer and how to operate.*

It is interesting to note that, in the outsourced company, standardisation and control
are, more than ever, understood as a synonym for 'quality' in customer service. This
manager's comments also bring to mind the metaphor used by Rebecchi (1990) who
described the worker who operates in a heavily computerised environment as a 'glass
man', a term that suggests the same sort of vulnerability as that suggested by the term
'panoptic power'. In this view, the worker becomes fully visible, exposed, and, most
importantly, capable of being individually singled out by the company.

Certainly, the 'glass man' metaphor was very apparent in the operators' discourse:

*It is a great pressure upon the operator. I think it doesn't have to be like this, so
constant. You feel policed. The monitoring is like this: you know how you
work, but the good things never appear. When being monitored you never see
a customer praising you, and during six hours of work there is always someone
who praises you [...] During monitoring they only show you your mistakes.*

> *They don't praise you, they don't cheer you up. They call you to the monitoring room, make you listen to the conversation they thought was not within the standard, and they 'recycle' you.*

The 'glass man' condition is exacerbated by the fact that the company's strategic information will never reach the operators. According to one agent:

> *It is unilateral [the monitoring], because only the company has all the knowledge about us. We don't have the total knowledge about the company. What the company does with the data about us we don't know. Of course, we know that this information has a purpose: to access the time card control, monitoring control [...] We know this will reflect on our activity, our security in the company, but we don't have information about the company, or how it will achieve that.*

The 'panoptic power' given by the informatics monitoring often results in very arbitrary and despotic management. This kind of despotism is related to a serious contradiction pointed out by Heloani (1997) in modern forms of management, especially in outsourced companies.

According to this author, the excessive simplification that is so common in informatised outsourced work, enables a company to continuously threaten these workers with unemployment, arguing that their work is 'fully replaceable.' Such threats contradict the attempt to seduce workers to 'wear the company's T-shirt', one of the main goals of TQ management. This dissociation between the company discourse and the management practice results in an ambiguity which causes a highly stressful state of uncertainty. According to Heloani, the remaining discourse is one that emphasises

> *[...]the importance of 'playing in the same team', but, at the same time, they show that what is really valuable is 'save yourself if you can'. [...] The double message is not free: it is part of an inverse and perverse logic – the logic of capital and seduction. When the organisation commands: involve yourself; devote yourself; get closer to me; at the same time it is implicitly signalling the possibility of being fired. [...] Within the entrepreneurial logic this is perfectly normal... In the workers' logic it is pathologic, inhuman. (Heloani, 1997:150 – author's emphasis)*

In fact, the physical, and especially mental, stress caused by the management's excessive pressure and authoritarianism was a common complain in the outsourced operators' testimonies.

> *I feel that I became very sensitive. I can't listen to music at a certain volume any more. Television at a slightly high volume, the telephone, any kind of noise, disturbs me. And I realised it was after I started to work directly with the headphones, because you are in contact with the customer for six hours a day, every day. When you arrive home, you aren't very patient.*

> *I think there should be more breaks[8]. Really, it is not enough. It is hard labour. At the end of the day, we have sore throats because of speaking too much, because we don't have much break time. This, as time goes by, will cause problems in the vocal chords or because of sitting and typing for a long period of time.*

---

8   The Collective Work Agreement stipulates a break of 10 minutes for each hour worked. However, according to some interviewees, those breaks were not followed by the company, which gave the operators only one break of 15 minutes during their six-hour working day.

The illusory nature of participative management in the outsourced company can also be seen when the operators refer to the constraining and coercive manner in which the TQ management is conducted there:

There was some pressure [on the TQPs implementation] because we knew that they were doing an internal audit, so we had to know the most frequent questions of ISO. There was a requirement from the company for the operators to be involved. In a way, we had to get involved, we had no other alternative. It was a forced involvement.

Antunes (1995) describes this kind of pressure as 'co-opted involvement', drawing on an analysis of the management practices of Toyota that inspired the TQP concept, whose aim is the 'subordination of the worker's creativity.' Encouraging the worker's participation in all the production stages, the Toyota style of management fits the current economic environment, making it 'qualitatively different from that existing in the Fordist age'. Consequently, it is much more 'involving' and 'persuasive' than the Taylorist style of management, whose rigidity better matched the model of mass production and consumption (Antunes, 1995:34).

It was also in the outsourced company that we found the most routine and meaningless 'informational work,' involving the inputting of raw data into the company's software (Dantas, 1999a). These data do not require any reflection from the operators. The only thing they know is that they will help the customer-company to launch it new marketing strategy, which will result in more work and, finally in more unemployment since not all the operators can get used to the speed these changes bring to their working process.

I think it is a very fast process. Sometimes we aren't prepared to receive such sudden changes. This causes unemployment. In the company there are several people being fired so they can hire new employees with lower salaries. I think these changes interfere with the training. One day we're having one campaign, and the next day it's a new one. It is very active; it is a very fast and endless process.

We work with many codes and that overloads us. It is a lot of information. There are many numbers, many codes. So, you sometimes really make mistakes.

These effects are exacerbated by the use of scripts, which reduces the space for autonomy within these activities The resulting high standardisation, combined with the computerised monitoring, creates a situation where these 'glass men' feel controlled in their work, just as though an unseen manager is wielding a 'remote control.' They perceive themselves as being like the machines themselves:

For me there has been no professional development. If I leave this company and look for a new job, I'll only get one in another telephone company because I didn't get much knowledge from this one. There are times when you are no longer reading the script, you're speaking without reading. There is too much memorisation. I feel like a robot with it, we are like machines!

Everything is really easy. What you have to say is ready, you only have to say it. They only use your voice - your knowledge is not exposed.

The standard phraseology provided by the scripts deepens this feeling of being a robot:

With the phraseology they want you to acquire you become even more mechanical. Then you keep on trying to talk to the customer in a natural, normal way, trying not to become too mechanical, and this is where you make a lot of mistakes because you use your everyday words. And they [the company] don't like it very much, not really. You have to do what they want you to do.

This extreme simplification, resulting from the excessive standardisation and control of these operators' activities, conflicts with the unpredictability which is so characteristic of 'active' telemarketing. Because the customers' responses do not follow the same kind of standardisation, the operators usually receive answers which do not fit the standard ranges established in the scripts. At these moments, the agents' 'robotisation', collides with the discrepancies in customers' answers making them 'abandon the script.' When this happens, the fear of punishment resulting from this deviation being monitored, makes them deeply stressed. But the alternative of following the script is equally stressful because it often results in even more inconsistency from the customers who, according to the agents we interviewed, usually feel very angry because of the impression that they are 'speaking with robots'.

You sometimes want to talk to the customer. It isn't that they [the supervisors] prevent you from doing that, but Sercomtel demands it… And we sometimes have to talk to a customer … I think that if I talk to a customer in 'active telemarketing' the company will gain much more than if I keep on speaking like a robot. The customer asks me something and I answer a different question because I have to follow the script.

It is already boring for us who have to approach the customer, but, imagine what it is like for them to answer questions over the telephone from a robot!

In order to resolve such contradictions, which are intrinsic to the competing logics of automation and informatisation, these agents adopt some of the same strategies as those found by Zuboff (1988) in her research: dissimulation and hidden 'tricks' that can lead to improved performance scores. Thus, the way that informatics is applied in the outsourced company can endanger precisely the most important purpose of the overall telemarketing project: maximising customer retention.

I made suggestions about the script. Because it becomes very tiring at the end, you spend too much time with the customer on the line when it isn't necessary. There is a place in the script where we have to ask: 'has this bill already been paid'? But, sometimes, as soon as we called ,the person has already said that the bill has arrived and will be paid on a certain day. So if the customer has already given me an answer, we shouldn't need to ask it again. But the script requires that…

Such inconsistencies do not prevent these operators from using tricks hidden from the management, showing that the creativity common to living labour can bloom even in environments where their autonomy is repressed. Often, this is the only moment when their work demands any inventiveness which effectively differrntiates them from machines. Here is what the interviewees answered when asked about autonomy and creativity within their job:

These atypical situations usually occur. We didn't predict that question or answer from the customer and we have to be flexible to overcome that situation, finding the solution for the customer at that moment without going to the supervisor.

It often happens when we have to trick the script. The script is opening and you don't know who you are going to talk to. Then you have to use your experience to open the other screen, faster, in order to see who will get in there to talk to you.

We must be flexible because some unpleasant situations happen, like when the system doesn't make the search and you don't know what is happening to it... Then, you have to try to convince your customer that you have to execute your work, but in such a way that you don't invade your customer's space. The difficulty is here. Indeed, I've already told the supervisor, but they take a little while to solve it...

The problems mentioned by these operators are related to the extreme subordination of their work to digital time, which, when applied to entrepreneurial production, becomes market time. In the case of a company providing telemarketing service, market time is directly linked to the time of the customers who are called. The customers therefore participate directly in the production process. For this type of company, they are not only a potential source of profit, but the very object of work. The fusion between the machine time and the customer's time, because of the technical dependence the former exercises upon the latter, generates what Rebecchi (1990) has described as 'stress of waiting' among the operators.

This kind of stress occurs when the system gets stuck in the middle of a call. In this situation, the operators have to be able to deal with customers flexibly because they have been contacted by the agent and do not know what is happening, a situation that makes them impatient. The 'stress of waiting' that affects the telemarketing operators in their own right becomes more serious because they have to deal with the customer's stress as well as with their own.

Something that makes this scenario even worse is that the monitoring system does not capture those technical failures as a problem of the system, but, instead, records them as mistakes of the agent, so system delays are reflected as the operators' delays. In extremely controlled working conditions this situation causes an evident fear of warnings from the company on the one hand and rudeness from customers (already common, even when there are no technical problems) on the other. As one operator said:

In both the inbound and the outbound areas, the time is determined by the customer, but of course an inbound call never takes more than thirty seconds on average. What happens in the outbound area is that your script isn't open for long between one call and the other. The monitoring is based on this time measured by the computer. Some campaigns have a target call time of three minutes, others five. Then, when you disconnect, you have some time to input the data if you have not been able to do it with the customer online. Then, you have to take a break to finish the input or another call comes. The company frowns on excessive use of breaks, which suggests that something wrong is happening. We have to record this in a notebook, explaining the reasons for the break. It is much more controlled [than for inbound calls].

Ironically, it is in just such cases that the operators' tacit knowledge is most relevant. It is through their information about problems of a qualitative nature that the company canremedy faults in the system or incorporate suggestions for improvement, which confirms how such knowledge may be extremely important for the company's overall productivity:

They [the customers] complain a lot – 'talk to me in the right way'… But the company also provides us the opportunity to say what we think is not OK in the script, to give our suggestions. What can be taken out, what can be inserted…

However, the stressful condition of having work that is deeply standardised and determined by the market often just causes apathy and disinterest in these operators. This somewhat explains the high turnover of staff in the call centre.

In the future, I'm looking for another job for myself; I don't want to stay there, because it's very stressful. There are a lot of complaints, and, in fact, it isn't very rewarding: there is little gain for what you live for. I see myself as the sort of company employee that if I leave tomorrow, I'll make no difference, nothing will change. I'm just a number for the company, only that.

No, I'm not satisfied. Because it isn't something I enjoy doing. Of course, I enjoy working with people, but it isn't in this activity that I feel good. That isn't what I'm looking for in the future. Because the work is stressful, also because of payment, I think we're stuck here. I expect some growth for myself.

We can conclude that the excessive concern with the standardisation and control of the working process produces an effect which is precisely the opposite of the intentions of the recruitment to the service. Instead of 'gentle' and 'helpful' agents, the dominance of 'dead work' in their jobs, created by flexible automation, deepens the reification in their work, producing operators who are apathetic and uninterested, if not actually angry with their working conditions. Moreover, the results aimed for by the major investment in technology, paradoxically, have created situations of failure that are quite undesirable for the contractor company[9].

Final considerations

In more than a decade of constant changes, Sercomtel has managed to keep itself competitive despite being public and operating in a restricted market. This was achieved mainly because of the rapid innovation brought by the introduction of ICTs to its production and working processes. The evidence indicates that the company can only keep this position by conforming precisely to the marketing and technological

---

9   Some more recent data show that these circumstances are not just a peculiarity of the company studied, but are common right across the sector. The computerised systems and cheapened connections enabled by the Internet have made possible an increase of between 20% and 80% in the number of calls made by each operator since the 1980s. Probably, the 20,000 calls and 1,300 hours on the phone enabled by the intensification of these activities is one of the explanations for the high job turnover that call centres face each year, standing at 39% globally, and 26% in Brazil. In contrast, the high rate of complaints about call-centre services has led many governments to introduce protective measures against overly intrusive telemarketing practices, as well as against excessive waiting time and automation of services, which deprive consumers of easy and quick access to the agents. The US Government's Do Not Call Registry has more than 145 million records. In Brazil, in a decree of December 2008, the government introduced a series of changes that provide monitoring of and penalties for such abuse and laid the ground for the implementation of a Do Not Call programme similar to the American one (Garattoni; Magarotto, 2009).

rules that characterise contemporary capitalism post-privatisation and, in particular, to an organisational model that is tuned to this scenario. This model increasingly cuts down on its use of living labour at the same time that it qualitatively deepens the exploitation and commodification of the workforce that is still employed.

This process relies for its success on the expropriation of older forms of technical knowledge through their materialisation in the machines, whose consequence is the simplification of work and tighter forms of control over productive activities.

For those employed in such working conditions, a paradoxical situation is established whereby extreme standardisation is combined with requirements for abilities to communicate and adapt, stemming directly from the new procedures, leading to the intensification of activities, with severe consequences for these workers' physical and mental health, which in turn explains the high labour turnover in call centres.

As a result, new fields of conflict are opened up for digital or informational workers. Not only do they have to fight to reappropriate their knowledge and autonomy; they also have to struggle against the high vulnerability that is generated by the increasing precariousness of their work. A better understanding of the aims of the new business strategies and their effects on the commodification of 'operational-informational' work may be essential ammunition for those workers who are literally 'entangled' in this new battle between capital and labour.

© *Simone Wolff, 2009*

ACKNOWLEDGEMENT

Special thanks to Cristina Mott Fernandez, for her valuable help with the translation.

REFERENCES

Antunes, R. (1999) *Os sentidos do trabalho: ensaio sobre a afirmação e negação do trabalho*, São Paulo: Boitempo

Antunes, R. (1995) *Adeus ao trabalho? ensaio sobre as metamorfoses e a centralidade do mundo do trabalho*, São Paulo: Cortez

Ask! (2009) *Cia Nacional de call centre.* Accessed on fev., 4, 2009 from http://www.askcallcenter.com. br.Bernardo, J. (2004) *Democracia totalitária: teoria e prática da empresa soberana,* São Paulo: Cortez.

Bernardo, J. (2000) *Transnacionalização do capital e fragmentação dos trabalhadores: ainda há lugar para os sindicatos?,* São Paulo: Boitempo

Bolaño, C. R. S. (2003) *Políticas de comunicação e economia política das telecomunicações no Brasil: convergência, regionalização e reforma*, Aracajú: Ed. Da Universidade Federal de Sergipe

Bolaño, C R. S. (2004) 'A reforma do modelo brasileiro de regulação das Comunicações em perspectiva histórica', *Estudos de Sociologia*, Araraquara, No. 17:67-95. Accessed on set., 5, 2004 from http://www.fclar.unesp.br/soc/revista/artigos_pdf_res/17/04bolano.pdf

Bolaño, C R. S. (2004) 'Trabalho intelectual, comunicação e capitalismo: a reconfiguração do fator subjetivo na atual reestruturação produtiva', *Revista Eptic On-Line,* Aracaju, Vol. l, No. 3:67-97, set/dez. Accessed on set., 8, 2004 from http://www.eptic.com.br

Bolaño, C. & Lacerda, R. O. (1999) 'As tecnologias da informação e da comunicação e o desenvolvimento regional', *Revista Eptic On-Line,* Aracaju, Vol. 2, No. 2, jul./dez. Accessed on ago, 3, 2002 from http://www.eptic.he.com.br

Bolaño, C. & Massae, F. (1999) 'O novo panorama das telecomunicações no Brasil', *Revista Eptic On-Line,* Aracaju, Vol. 1, No.1. Accessed on jan, 3, 2003 from http://www.eptic.com.br

Brandão, C. (1996) *Telecomunicações e dinâmica regional no Brasil,* Tese (Doutorado) - Instituto de Economia. Universidade Estadual de Campinas – UNICAMP, Campinas

Castells, M. (1999) *A sociedade em rede*, Rio de Janeiro: Paz e Terra. (A era da informação: economia, sociedade e cultura, v. 1)

Castillo, J. J. (2008) 'Las fábricas de software em España: organización y división del trabajo: el trabajo fluido en la sociedad de la información', *Política & Sociedade: Revista de Sociologia Política*, Florianópolis, Vol. 7, No. 13:35-108

Chesnais, F. (Org.) (2005) *A finança mundializada: raízes sociais e políticas, configuração, conseqüências*, São Paulo : Boitempo

Chesnais, F. (1996) *A mundialização do capital*, São Paulo: Xamã

Coriat, B. (1985) 'O taylorismo e a expropriação do saber operário' in Pimentel, D. & Costa E Silva, F. (Org.) *Sociologia do Trabalho*, Lisboa: A regra do jogo

Coutinho, L., Cassiolato, J. & Silva, A. L. G. (1995) *Telecomunicações, Globalização e Competitividade,* Campinas: Papirus

Dantas, M. (1999[a]) Da produção material à 'virtual': esboço para uma compreensão 'pós-clássica' da teoria do capital. In: Tapia, J. & Rallet, A. *Telecomunicações, desregulamentação e convergência tecnológica: uma análise comparada,* Campinas: UNICAMP/IE. (Coleção Pesquisas, 2)

Dantas, M. (1996) *A lógica do capital informação,* Rio de Janeiro: Contraponto

Dantas, M. (1999b) 'L'Information et le travail: reflexions sur le capital-information', *Revista Eptic On-Line,* Aracaju, Vol. 1, No. 2, jul/dez. Accessed on set, 9, 2002 from http://www.eptic.he.com.br

Especial (2007) 'Dez anos de privatização das telecomunicações no Brasil', *Revista Eptic On-Line,* Aracaju, Vol. 9, No. 2, maio/ ago. Accessed on fev, 4, 2009 from http://www2.eptic.com.br/eptic_pt/ interna.php?c=19&ct=572&o=1

Feldman, E. (1998) *SERCOMTEL: 30 anos de História,* Londrina: Midiograf

Freyssenet, M. (1990) 'Automação e qualificação da força de trabalho' in Soares R. M. S. M. (Org.). *Gestão da empresa: automação e competitividade; novos padrões de organização e de relações de trabalho,* Brasília: IPEA/IPLAN

Freyssenet, M. (1989) 'A divisão capitalista do trabalho', *Tempo Social: Revista de Sociologia da USP*, São Paulo, Vol. 1, No. 2

Garattoni, B. & Maragotto, E. (2009) 'Do outro lado da linha', *Super Interessante*, São Paulo, No. 262:54-57, fev.

Hansen, D. L. (1999) 'Tecnologia e mudança espacial', *Revista Eptic On-Line*, Aracaju-SE, Vol. 2, No. 2, jul/dez. Accessed on ago, 4, 2002 from http://www.eptic.com.br

Heloani, J. R. (1997) 'Organizações qualificantes ou neurotizantes?,' *Pró-posições*, Campinas, Vol. 8, No. 3:147-153, nov.

Huws, U. (2003) *The making of a cybertariat: virtual work in a real world*, New York: Monthly Review Press: London: The Merlin Press

Huws, U. (2006) 'O que mudou foi a divisão do trabalho' [entrevista], *Ihu On-Line*, Unisinos, São Leopoldo, 24 abr. Accessed on fev , 12, 2008 from http://www.unisinos.br/ihuonline/uploads/ edicoes/1158345977.61pdf.pdf.Kumar, K. (1997) *Da sociedade pós-industrial à pós-moderna: novas teorias sobre o mundo contemporâneo*, Rio de Janeiro: Zahar

Leal, S. A. G. (2000) 'Algumas considerações sobre o modelo de regulação do mercado brasileiro de telecomunicações: os mecanismos de controle público presentes na regulamentação do setor e o papel da Agência Nacional de Telecomunicações – Anatel', *Revista Eptic On-Line,* Aracaju, Vol. 2, No. 3, dez. Accessed on jan, 2, 2001 from http://www.eptic.com.br

Leal, S. A. G. (1999) 'O Sistema de Telecomunicações no Brasil: as alterações no modelo de monopólio público de Sarney a Fernando Henrique Cardoso (FHC)', *Revista Eptic On-Line,* Aracaju, Vol. 1, No.1, jan./jun. Accessed on jan, 12, 2001. http://www.eptic.com.br

Sercomtel Telecomunicações S.A. (2009) Accessed on fev, 23, 2009 from http://www.sercomtel.com.br

Leal, S. A. G. (2000) *Informativo de Comunicação Social: Sercomtel as novas fronteiras*, Londrina Accessed on jan, 21, 2001 from www.comunic@sercomtel.com.br

Lojkine, J. (1995) *A revolução informacional*, São Paulo: Cortez

Marx, K. (1984) *O Capital: crítica da economia política*, São Paulo: Abril Cultural. (Os Economistas, v. 1, t. 1/2)

Marx, K. (1985) *Capítulo VI inédito de O Capital*, São Paulo: Moraes

Morris-Suzuki, T. (1997) 'Robots and Capitalism' in Davis, J., Hirschl, T. A. & Stack, M. (eds). *Cutting Edge: technology, information capitalism and Social Revolution*, London: New York: Verso.

Rebecchi, E. (1990) *O sujeito frente à inovação tecnológica*, Petrópolis: Vozes

SERCOMTEL. (1996) *Jornal Informativo da Sercomtel*, Londrina, ago. *(*Edição histórica)

SERCOMTEL.(1997) *Qualidade: vamos vencer mais essa*, Londrina, Nov.

SERCOMTEL.(1997) *O desafio da ISSO*, Londrina, dez

SERCOMTEL.(1998) *Edição especial. O sócio*, Londrina, jul.

SERCOMTEL. (1998) *Relatório Anual'97*, Londrina

SERCOMTEL.(1999) *Relatório Anual'98*, Londrina

SERCOMTEL. (2000) *Relatório Anual'99*, Londrina

SERCOMTEL. (2001) *Relatório Anual'00*, Londrina

SERCOMTEL.(2002) *Relatório Anual'01*, Londrina

SERCOMTEL.(1999/2003) *Jornal Mural*, Londrina

Sicsú, A. B. (1999) Sociedade do conhecimento: integração nacional ou exclusão social?, *Revista Eptic On-Line*, Aracaju, Vol. 2, No. 2, jul./dez. Accessed on ago, 25, 2002 from http://www.eptic.com.br

Vasconcelos, D. S. (1999) 'Privatização das Telecomunicações, neoliberalismo e os rumos do capitalismo no Brasil', *Revista Eptic On-Line*, Aracaju, Vol. 1, No. 1, jan./jun. 1999. Accessed on abr., 25, 2001 from http://www.eptic.he.com.br

Wohlers, M. (1999) 'A reforma do modelo de telecomunicações: o menu internacional e a opção brasileira' in Tapia, J. & Rallet, A. *Telecomunicações, desregulamentação e convergência tecnológica: uma análise comparada*, Campinas: UNICAMP/IE. (Coleção Pesquisas, 2)

Wolff, S. (2005) *Informatização do trabalho e Reificação: uma análise à luz dos Programas de Qualidade Total*, Campinas: Ed.da UNICAMP; Londrina: Eduel

Wolff, S. (2004) *O espectro da reificação em uma empresa de telecomunicações: o processo de trabalho sob os novos parâmetros gerenciais e tecnológicos*, Tese (Doutorado), Instituto de Filosofia e Ciências Humanas – IFCH / UNICAMP, Campinas

Wolff, S. (2004) *O espectro da reificação em uma empresa de telecomunicações: o processo de trabalho sob os novos parâmetros gerenciais e tecnológicos*, Tese (Doutorado) - Instituto de Filosofia e Ciências Humanas – IFCH / UNICAMP, Campinas. Accessed on mar., 21, 2009 from http://libdigi.unicamp.br/document/?code=vtls000331335

Zarafian, P. (2001) 'Mutação dos sistemas produtivos e competências profissionais: a produção industrial de serviço; Valor, organização e competência na produção de serviço – esboço de um modelo de produção de serviço'. in Salerno, M. S. (org). *Relação de serviço: produção e avaliação*, São Paulo: Ed. Senac São Paulo

Zuboff, S. (1994) 'Automatizar/informatizar: duas faces da tecnologia inteligente' *Revista de Administração de Empresas*, São Paulo, Vol. 34, No. 6:80-91, nov/dez

Zuboff, S. (1989) *In the age of the smart machine*, New York: Basic Books

Double workload:

a study of the sexual division of labour among women telemarketing operators in Brazil

Claudia Mazzei Nogueira

Claudia Mazzei Nogueira *is an Assistant Professor in the Department of Social Science at the Federal University of São Carlos, Brazil.*

ABSTRACT

This paper discusses the sexual division of labour both in the workplace, that is, in the space of production, and in the home, which is termed the space of reproduction. The author discusses the close relationships that exist between the division of tasks in domestic labour of women workers and their functions in the world of work. The study draws on in-depth qualitative research in a telemarketing company. The aim of this study of telemarketing operators was to obtain a deeper understanding of how these workers experience the dimensions of their work in terms of the sexual division of labour in both production and reproduction. The term 'productive work is not used in the strict Marxist sense of work that directly creates surplus value but in a more generic sense, to designate the salaried act of working, whether in productive or unproductive work, as it is performed in capitalist society. The expression 'reproductive space' refers to the domestic sphere.

Introduction

In recent decades a noticeable feminisation of the workforce has taken place. Although the participation of men in the world of work has grown very little since the 1970s, the increasing presence of women has been an important demographic feature in Brazil. Nevertheless, this growth has been restricted largely to low-paying jobs, where exploitation is usually more pronounced. This situation is one of the paradoxes, among many others, of the globalisation of capital in the world of labour. The impact of policies for 'flexibilising' labour as part of the restructuring of companies has been accompanied by serious risks for the entire working class, but especially for women.

There is no doubt that although the process of precarisation has affected a great many people in the working class, the disadvantage for women has been more noticeable. As one analyst has concluded, flexibilisation of the number of hours worked by women has 'become possible because there is social legitimation for employing them for shorter periods of time. Such jobs are offered as an opportunity to reconcile family life and professional life, and it is presumed that this reconciliation is the women's exclusive responsibility' (Hirata, 1999: 8).

It is also assumed that women's work and wages play a supplementary role in meeting the needs of families. But today, for some families, this premise no longer holds good because the 'complementary' value of women's wages is often essential for balancing the family budget, especially for families in the working class (Hirata, 1999: 8).

Many women today work for salaries as men do and are taking on new functions in companies (including jobs that, until only recently, had been filled almost exclusively by men), and are sharing the responsibility for supporting their families or sometimes even doing so alone. For this reason, it might be expected that their domestic work is also undergoing substantial transformations in the sexual division of labour.

Before going on to address the question of whether and how this transformation is actually taking place, we will first discuss the space of labour in telemarketing and then, more specifically, analyse the position of these women in their role as workers. For a fuller account of the research on which this paper is based, see Nogueira (2006).

The work of telemarketing operators

In Brazil, telemarketing operators form a sub-category of the broader occupational group defined as telephone operators. This type of work usually consists of providing information to users who call in to a telephone exchange, the only tool used being the operators' voice mediated by computers and headphone (Vilela & Assunção, 2004). The work process poses a range of hazards to the workers' health, thus resulting in an intense pace of work, a constrained physical posture and a lack of rest breaks for their bodies to recover. These are combined with tight control, fatiguing productivity targets, repetitive movements, constant pressure from supervisors, unhealthy working environments and unsuitable furniture and equipment. The effects of the substandard working conditions in call centres place heavy burdens on the physical and psychological health of the labourers. According to Vilela and Assunção *(2004)*:

These workers often go their labour unions with complaints of physical fatigue and mental exhaustion, depression and feelings of powerlessness in the face of the demands of their employers. They are emphatic in their statements and are aware of the association between these problems and their occupation.(Vilela and Assunção 2004:1069):

The rigidity of the companies' management style often generates disruptions in the relationship between the workers and their tasks, thus reducing the full use of their skills. This type of work also tends to 'automatise' thought. The most intense mechanisms of control over work in telemarketing operations involve control over working time, content, behaviour, the amount of work done and the results. Call-centre companies depend on the mental and emotional efforts of their operators to interact with their clients. They aim for client satisfaction but want to solve problems without going beyond the Average Operational Time (AOT), or average contact time, stipulated by their commercial goals; nor do they want to reduce the control exercised over the workers. These conflicting objectives create such a stressful situation for the workers that there is a high likelihood that they will become sick.

The field of telemarketing was chosen for study because it constitutes a salaried occupation comprised mostly of women that is currently in a process of expansion in the Brazilian capitalist system. It is therefore consitutes a favourable field for examining whether a more egalitarian division of labour might be emerging.

The case study company

The company discussed in this paper is Atento-Brasil. It began operating in April 1999, in the city of São Paulo, Brazil, with a little over 1,000 employees. By late 2003 the company had 29,434 employees, 28,960 of whom were involved directly in company operations, having handled 489 million calls in 2003. In October 2008, Atento-Brasil had 65,000 employees, working in 13 contact centres distributed across six of the largest cities in Brazil (São Paulo, Rio de Janeiro, Belo Horizonte, Porto Alegre, Salvador and Brasilia), and had 31,007 work stations. These numbers indicated that it was one of the largest private employers in the country (http://www.ranking.callcenter.inf.br/pesquisa/detalhe/?empId=105).

Telemarketing companies, including Atento-Brasil,[1] provide a range of telephone-based services including answering queries from customers, providing information such as addresses and telephone numbers, telesales and advising customers on how to access or use products or services.

The operators' perspective on their work

Interestingly, the company no longer refers to its workers as 'operators' but has redesignated them as 'consultants'. Gisele[2] explained why.. She said that:

This is why they change the names of our occupation. Like ... We're called consultants instead of operators because, by law, employees classified as operators, or telephone operators, earn a basic wage of R$ 700 to R$ 800 [US$ 250 to US$ 350] per month and they don't want to pay us that much. So we're 'consultants'. They always get around problems like that.

The telemarketing operators are, nevertheless, referred to as 'operators' in this paper.

To carry out their work, the operators remain seated for 85% to 90% of their daily working hours with total attention focused on their individual computer screens, the keyboard and the headset. The former operator Ignez had the following to say about her work:[3]

I worked from 2 p.m. to 8 p.m., which means that I had to stay sitting down for 6 hours straight, with only 15 minutes for a coffee and bathroom break. For all the rest of the time I answered one phone call after another. There was no way of getting up again after the break. Either you went to the bathroom during your break, or you didn't go at all. It was six hours straight on the phone.

---

1   An interview schedule was drawn up for this study. The first part of the semi-structured questionnaire included questions designed to clarify how the respondents' labour relationships operate in the sphere of production. Here the purpose was to grasp some of the elements that are characteristic of women's work, such as their duties, rights, the women's own consciousness (or lack of it) of exploitation in the workplace, the varied forms of control, the health problems involved and, finally, the precarious situation of this group of workers in general. The questions in the second part were geared to investigating how activities carried out in the reproductive space express dimensions that are also strongly affected by the sexual division of labour.

2   Gisele was 23 years old and childless at the time of the interview, in 2005, and unmarried, but she married shortly afterwards. She has an eighth-grade education and until her marriage was living with her parents, a brother and a sister. Before going to work at the company she worked at a shopping mall, which she left because she had to work nights there. At the time of the interview she had been with the company for three and a half years as an operator (or, as she herself ironically described it, as a 'consultant').

3   Ignez was 26 years old, married, without children. She had completed high school and hoped to study more. Having left the company, in 2005 she was working as a receptionist and secretary at a small language school.

In addition, a supervisor is always present, demanding higher productivity and control over the operators' AOT. As a result, a number of employees have contracted occupational diseases. Luiza[4] described the situation in these words:

> You have a target to meet, so when you give someone information you're always paying attention to your AOT, in other words, how long it takes you to give the person the right information. For example, they say you have 29 seconds, but there are people who want more than that to get their information. They want to say something else, so you aren't nice to them. For example, you don't pay enough attention because you know your AOT is going up. So that makes you tense at your work. And then they keep saying that productivity fell and so we don't even get our 5-minute break[5] because they say: 'girls, let's lower the AOT'. But how am I supposed to lower my AOT? People want information, they don't want robots. If they wanted a robot they could just call and hear 'the information is such and such, the information is such and such, the information is such and such'.

The control over work is intense, greatly facilitated by the advanced technology used in this sector. The machines do so much that there is almost no possibility for the existence of interpersonal relations. Fernanda[6] said that:

> It's funny when we come in. We look at each other and, 'Bye!'. There's no time to talk. You have to talk before you come in, because once you're inside there's no way to talk anymore. And when you've finished working, you're so beat that you just take the elevator and say 'One more day is over', and the other person manages to say 'One more day'.

Control over time is extremely rigid. It can be seen as functional control for the survival of the capitalist mode of production, since it consists of a mechanism for extracting extra work, a factor that is essential for the accumulation of capital. All this intensification of working hours involves more time without freedom forced on workers with the specific purpose of accumulating capital. In Marx's words:

> Wherever part of society has a monopoly over the means of production, workers, free or not, must add, to the time of working needed for their own self-conservation, a time of extra work to produce the means of subsistence for the owner of the means of production. (Marx, 1988, p. 181, vol. I)

It is not by chance that time sheets and workflow charts are integrated into the rigid methods for controlling time, productivity and the quality of work. Many telemarketing companies have standardised the operators' scripts and established regulations for behavior that even specify the operators' tone of voice. They have discovered that the response given to the client is often accepted or not depending on

---

4   In 2005 Luiza was aged 41, single, with one son. She had completed senior high school and was living at her parents' home, together with a sister. She had worked at a number of other companies before joining this one, where she had worked as an operator for four years.

5   Personal breaks are the five minutes during which each operator can go to the bathroom during a six-hour work period.

6   In 2005 Fernanda was aged 27, single and without children. She had a senior high-school education and hoped to study pharmacy at a university. She lived at her parents' home, together with a brother and a sister. Before joining he company she had beenunemployed and, in 2005, had been with the company for five years, as an operator.

the tone of an operator's voice. But there can be no doubt that the central objective of this system is to guarantee the company's goals of productivity and thus sustain its accumulation of capital. According to Vilela and Assunção,

> Language is the expression of human acts and, therefore, always carries meanings and tones of affection expressed in words, gestures and simple intonations of the voice. In telemarketing companies, language literally takes on the nature of an instrument of work. The company recommends the expression of affection as a tactic of approximation of the client to the company's services. Affect is controlled and even fashioned in accordance with the requirements of good manners with clients, but without encouraging them to stay on the line any longer than strictly necessary. (Vilela and Assunção, 2004, p. 1077)

The company's way of controlling the operators' emotions shows clearly how this area of labour is closely related to their emotional lives. It highlights the need for self-control by workers because situations of anger, rudeness and even harassment have to be handled and corrected. And this implies the ability to listen and communicate. The experience of the operator Fernanda illustrates this type of situation:

> One lady wanted to talk about the 103 line (repairs and complaints). She had tried to use it but it didn't work right. She said she had tried to dial 103 a number of times and couldn't get through. This irritates clients. It would irritate anybody. Then the woman shouted into the phone and said: 'Listen here, you bunch of bitches'. Then she said, 'You lousy bums! What do you do there, anyway?' Swearing is routine. It happens all the time. And when you hear somebody call you a bitch, it shocks you. And she kept on shouting: 'Just shut up. Now you're going to listen to me'. and all I could think was, 'Oh goodness, what about my time'.

Regardless of the clients' aggression, operators have to maintain the standard of service, both in terms of their tone of voice and in sticking to the predetermined script. Gisele also discussed the need to control her personal reactions:

> When the system crashes you get the worst of it all the same because then you have to talk to each client, one by one and you have to say a long phrase, like: 'We are sorry, but at the moment our system is down. Please call again after thirty minutes or check out the company's Internet site, www.telefonica.com.br'. Then the client bangs the telephone down and you go to the next one and say: 'We are sorry, but at the moment....' and so on. You have to give them a long phrase and the clients don't accept it, they don't understand.

By robotising and routinising their workers the telemarketing companies do not just determine the exact phraseology for each service. They also dictate their tone of voice in order to avoid personal expressions of emotion by the operators. This demonstrates the way in which language has become just a working instrument, and the balancing act created for the operator who has to remain polite but without letting the dialogue go on for too long (Vilela and Assunção, 2004, p. 1074). Control is exercised through a hierarchical structure, which can be represented in the following way: the senior officers pressure the managers (the coordinators), who pressure the supervisors, who pressure the operators, who thus bear the psychological brunt. Deborah[7], a supervisor, explained the dynamics of this process:

My relationship with the operators is what I consider good, but some days it gets complicated. As soon as you come in, there's is pressure from the managers, but I know they're under pressure, too. So I have to pressure my personnel and that's the way it works. It's like a sandwich. Each one keeps squeezing the next guy down and so everybody is under pressure. You're fine when you start off in the morning, but the atmosphere gets you down.

Another indicator of the pressure of work in telemarketing is the control that is exercised over rest periods. When they start working at the company the women are told that they have a 15-minute break for eating or drinking during their six-hour working day (time which is deducted from their daily pay which is based on six hours of work) plus a five-minute individual bathroom break. Luiza described the resulting dehumanisation:

There are very few breaks. They include five minutes to use the restroom, which they call an individual pause, and a coffee break of about 15 minutes. That means if you bring in something to eat, you don't exactly eat it. You have to gulp it down. Otherwise it's impossible. Some people can't use their restroom break. I try to hold it in, but some of the workers can't do that because of urinary problems or because they are taking medicine. So it's hard. It's hard and the company has no respect for you. Some people have to go to the bathroom and they can't. They have to wait, and so you have that problem too.

Monitoring of calls in real time by the supervisors, to ensure that they don't exceed the maximum times (which are often stipulated in contracts with client companies) is another mechanism of control designed to keep costs down. The aim of the monitoring is not only to guarantee that calls are answered within the standard time of ten seconds but also to control the quality of the service. This procedure allows the company to hire as few operators as possible. In the words of Katia,[8] a supervisor:

You have to hear the person, listen to the call, the service, the connection. I'm not monitored. I do the monitoring because I'm a supervisor. But the operators are monitored. We listen in on their conversations to know what the client is saying and what the operator answers.

In 1996 the company distributed a 'Code of Principles for Ethical Conduct in Telemarketing', which was revised in 2003. This code says that 'recording for the purpose of monitoring does not require the awareness of the attendants and should only be used for this purpose'.

But the reality from the worker's point of view is different. When we asked about this aspect of the monitoring, Ignez had this to say:

---

7   Deborah was aged 32 in 2005, separated from her husband and with a son aged nine, with whom she lived. She had a college education and had been working at the company as an operator for 18 months before being promoted to the position of supervisor, which she had held for a further two and a half years.
8   Katia was aged 35 in 2005, divorced,with a daughter who was finishing high school. She lived in a house behind that of her parents (she made it clear that they only shared a common yard). Before joining the company she had worked in a small shop. She had been at the company for four and a half years, having begun as a personnel assistant, but now worked as a supervisor of telemarketing operators.

We're monitored around the clock, even with cameras. We can't tell if they're on or not (...) but we know they monitor the phone lines to find out how we treat the clients. They see if you get nervous, if you lose your temper or if you give them wrong information. If you do, the supervisor comes over in a flash to talk to you.

Another kind of control over the operators' behavior is through their time cards. Supervisors check how many times each operator comes in late and how many days are missed. If there is evidence of lateness or absence, the company mounts campaigns to encourage discipline. Havana[9] described one of these campaigns:

This month they're having a 'campaign'. I can't even remember its real name, but it works like this. If you don't take any days off and are never late, at the end of the month you're included in a raffle for a bicycle, a DVD, a television set or a cellphone. So this is an incentive for you not to come in late, because lots of people get medical slips so they take the day off because they're sick.

Maria[10] explained that, in addition to this campaign, there is strict control over lateness and absence:

..You can't get sick at this company. You always have to be normal. You know, perfect health – you can't miss a day. If you get sick you have to make a doctor's appointment a month in advance. Then they dock the time from the time bank for you to go to the doctor. Sometimes a person misses work and it's for a good reason, like a death in the family, but that time can also be docked from the time bank.

All the women from Atento whom we interviewed mentioned the time bank. No monetary payment is made for overtime, not even when the company itself asks the operators to work longer. And, as Carla[11] made clear, this is not an occasional practice but an everyday part of working life.

There's no overtime here. If you work on a holiday it goes to the time bank and if you agree to work overtime it's the time bank. You can't take time off when you want.

Another important feature of telemarketing work, from the management point of view, are the campaigns to encourage productivity. These campaigns are usually organised by the quality control department, and are known as 'motivational incentives', designed to encourage competitiveness among the employees. Here, the employers' strategy is to increase productivity by increasing the pace of work. Mechanisms that prevent the workers from becoming conscious of this scheme are also used. The supervisor, Joana[12] described how this works:

9   Havana was 23 in 2005, single, and without children. She had a high-school education (and hoped to go to college to study nutrition). She lived with a friend, because her family lived in another state. This was her first job and she had been with the company for three years, working as an operator.
10   Maria, who was aged 21 in 2005, was single and had no children. She had graduated from high school, and hoped to go to college to study advertising or hotel services. She lived with her parents and a brother, and this was her first registered job, although she had had several informal jobs before. She had been with the company as an operator for two years and eight months.
11   Carla was aged 36 in 2005 and married with two daughters, aged five and two. She had a high-school education and intended to study business in college. She had been working at the company as an operator, but could not remember how long she had been there.
12   Joana was 35 in 2005, divorced, with a daughter. She had studied advertising in college but had not finished the course. She lived in a house behind her mother's. She had worked in other areas, including at a factory, and had been at the company for four and a half years. She began as an operator and was later promoted to the position of supervisor.

As a matter of fact, this is how I operate. I always have quality campaigns in the
department to raise people's awareness about the importance of their work for
their personal life and for the company. Really, on the whole, I always try to
raise people's awareness. I call team meetings, lots of group meetings, for them
to understand the importance of all this in their life. The company doesn't pay
so well, so I always try to make my staff aware of how they should value their
work and work with quality, you know. It's always this way, like..., I give them
candy, gum, popcorn, stuff like that. This way I'm always encouraging them so
they value their work. And I give them things. Candy is what they like the most.

But quality campaigns are not only about meeting performance targets for answering
calls. They also include other aspects, such as group meetings of workers set up by the
supervisors to discuss their work and performance in order to improve the company's
productivity. This is one important instrument for capital to appropriate the intellectual
and cognitive know-how of labour (Antunes, 1999, p. 55). Gisele gave us an example of
this:

As for our satisfaction, they ask us about our working environment. They are the kind of surveys that
never come to anything because we always answer the same thing. We say that the snacks
are terrible and it's the same thing every day. They encourage us to write down what we
think and so on, but they don't do anything anyway. Oh, yeah! They even put a suggestion
box in the coffee room. If you have something to write down, you write it and put it in
the box. But you can guess what happens: it's always the same complaints and always the
same answers. In the end you're always guilty for anything that goes wrong, you know. You
don't have enough willpower, you don't want to improve, and so forth. 'Your professional
success depends on you, don't you know that?' So then the coordinator calls a meeting and
gets people together in the snack room and she asks everybody if they need anything, it's
just psychological pressure. And then she says what she has to. She needs her job.

Another aspect of performance that affects the work is related to the
company'saspirations to earn quality certifications, like the ISO, that set up rigid norms
for the different kinds of services supplied. Managers try to impart standardised values
and rules among their employees and encourage merit[13]. They are constantly looking
for productivity improvements and qualitative indicators of excellence by adapting the
information. But from the viewpoint of the workers, the ISO certification has a different
meaning. Luiza commented on certification:

When they want to change the ISO we always have to get in on the act. We have to
study business and information in the book about the company's qualities. I
never know what that means, but it's about quality in the company. So when
they renew the company's ISO they come in and explain. They tell you what
each quality item means, for them to get a higher ISO. They always ask workers

---

13   The International Standards Organisation, better known as ISO, lays down international standards
for work and quality guarantees in companies. It has issued a number of norms since 1987, known as ISO
9000, which set in place a system for managing quality. The ISO 9000, which many believe is the name of the
certificate, in fact only sets down guidelines. Its objectives are to clarify the differences and inter-relationships
between the main concepts of quality, and to provide guidelines for choosing and using the norms. They serve
both for managing internal quality processes within companies (ISO 9004) and guaranteeing quality externally
(ISO 9001, 9002 and 9003) (ABES, 2004).

who have higher status to answer the questions about quality. Then they train
everybody, just to be sure, because they never know who will be chosen to
answer the questions. All the companies do this – to get people to say that the
quality of the company is excellent and so forth. So they train you for a few
days to say 'our company is excellent'.

We can therefore conclude that, as Antunes (1999) has written, this is really 'a process for organising work' that results in the 'intensification of the conditions for exploiting the labour force' (Antunes,1999:53) by greatly reducing, or even eliminating, work that is considered 'idle' or unproductive, especially activities such as maintenance. Re-engineering, lean production, teamwork, elimination of work stations, productivity increases, total quality and certification are all a part of the everyday ideology (and practice) of a 'modern company'.

Another crucial issue, which, to some degree, is related to all the elements mentioned above is the operators' health. To safeguard workers' health in this sector is difficult even in the best of situations. Health hazards are exacerbated by the poor working conditions in telemarketing companies. One obvious challenge in this context is how operators can comply with the companies' productivity goals. There are many different demands to meet, and this is not only psychologically difficult but is made harder by the fact that the physical conditions for carrying out their tasks are inadequate, with operators having to work against background noise, with broken furniture and insufficient space. These physical constraints are described by Luiza:

As for the furniture, such as chairs, some are terrible. Some of them are broken so the
levers don't work and the backs are out of place, and some of the counters and
desks are broken. People come in to take care of the posture of workers, the
labour safety people come in, but you'll never come to an agreement because
the chairs and desks are always broken. Some of the keyboards have keys
missing. How can you work in a situation like that? How can the company be
first rate? Sometimes you sit down at a desk and you're almost sitting on the
floor because you can't raise the chair, and things like that. So it's bad for your
back and it can give you RSI (...). Why? Because of the material. Besides the
pressure you're under there, it all ruins your health.

It is clear that there are a number of different features that could be expected to lead to discomfort or more serious ill health. In addition to the purely physical aspects of poor work design, strict controls over working time and break time, the mental and emotional tensions associated with meeting their productivity goals within the time allotted mean that it is common for the workers to experience health problems.

Deborah, a supervisor who was very reticent in her answers during most of the interview, was most eloquent on this question of health.

I have a 15-minute break, but that's my job. I'm a supervisor. Some days I can't even take
those 15 minutes. Today was one of those days. When I was leaving, I went to
have some juice. No water or even restroom or anything else. And this is certainly
prejudicial to my health. I shouldn't be working so hard. I had to stop and go
home. I've had bladder infections from not being able to go to the bathroom. The
company knows this is wrong. They should have one more supervisor working

with me, but then there is the thing of keeping costs down. (...) And, since
everybody has to work we have to put up with it to keep our jobs.

The physical health of telemarketing workers is undoubtedly affected. At the Atento unit in 2005, at the time of our interviews, out of 1,863 workers (396 men and 1,467 women), approximately 136 were on sick or accident leave, representing about 7.5% of the total workforce. Of the 136 that were off, only six (1.5%) were men. This provides supporting evidence that the work has both physical and psychological effects on health, including exhaustion, stress, fatigue, etc., especially for the women.

According to Vilela and Assunção (2004, p. 1077), such mental wear and tear on individual workers creates favourable conditions for implanting conditioned behavior to benefit production. Emotional problems arise as a by-product of submitting the body to intensive external demands. As Dejours (1994) puts it, 'Making a body docile is no simple thing, because it is usually subordinated to its natural boss, known as the "personality"'.

Many of the interviewees in this study described the effects of their work on their emotional wellbeing, Antonia[14] had this to say:

My emotional state has a lot to do with it. So I keep holding things in and holding them
in.... But the time comes that... you look at me and don't even have to say
anything at all, and I burst into tears. I had to take some pills to take care of
myself... Yes, the work does affect you!

Fernanda also thought that her emotional state was affected by her work:

I don't think my health is very good. I'm under heavy stress! My emotional state isn't
too good! I realise that I'm talking to a person but pretty soon I'll be yelling! I
don't want... to explain more than twice. And this happens at Atento. You have
to explain everything, but if they ask more than twice I start yelling.

It is clear that, whilst the company's overt goal is simply to 'guarantee the quality of services' and ensure its clients the 'satisfaction' they demand, in fact it aims at meeting productivity goals within timeframes and standards imposed in its process of accumulating capital. The company is extremely rigid in the control systems it imposes for attaining these goals. At the same time, it ignores numerous aspects of its workers' wellbeing, producing working conditions that, in the end, are very prejudicial to the workers. In short, it can be regarded as exploiting its workforce

This exploitation of women's work in *productive* space is related to how they are situated in *reproductive* space, with a complex and contradictory interplay of social relationships within and between each of these spaces. For this reason, in the next section we will discuss the sexual division of labour among the operators in their reproductive space.

The sexual division of labour in the reproductive space of telemarketing operators

There was considerable unevenness in the awareness of the workers surveyed with regard to the sexual division of labour. Many exhibited concerns about creating equality in domestic

---

14   Antonia was aged 34 in 2005, had been married for eight years, and had no children (by choice). She had finished college but was unemployed before beginning work at Attento. She had been at the company for five years.

chores but, at other moments, expressed strong sentiments that supported the traditional sexual division of labour. For example, when Carla was asked about the division of domestic chores in her home, she answered, 'I'm responsible for the domestic chores, even though I hold down a job, too. But my husband helps me.' But when probed further, she admitted, 'No. He helps when he wants.' Gisele's answers were not very different:

We don't have any specific chores to do. Each of us does part of the work. Sometimes I wash the dishes; other times I get home and my mother has done them. I wash my own clothes, my sister washes hers and my mother washes her own and my brother's and my father's clothes, too. Only the women do the domestic chores. My father takes care of the yard and my brother doesn't take care of anything. He just sleeps.

These responses suggest that the standard practice is to attribute domestic and family chores to the women, regardless of the specific circumstances of the family, including whether or not the women hold down jobs. We might say that shorter working days (as is the case in telemarketing) are reserved for female workers because culturally (and due to the interests and logic of capital itself) in a patriarchal society, women's work is required in the domestic sphere. This is quite in line with the responsibilities for taking care of children that often also fall more on the women, even though the men seem to feel more comfortable in this sphere of family life than in others. When we asked the operators with children about who was most involved in taking care of them, we heard practically the same thing from all. For instance, Carla answered:

I like to have this responsibility, but my husband does too. He's a good father and we both spend our 'free time' with the girls, even if we are tired.

Men's share in the domestic chores is much less than women's. The amount of time spent in the domestic space by salaried working women (like those in this case study) raise difficulties in the spatial/temporal organisation of work in the reproductive sphere. The time that the women workers spend on their various activities, in comparison with the time of the other members of the households (husband, children, etc.), is marked by fragmentation and overlapping of chores.

In order to confirm this reality, we asked the interviewees how much time they spent on their reproductive functions in comparison with work at their outside job. Fernanda replied:

At the company we only have our work to think about. As soon as you finish the last call, you leave and don't have any work left over for tomorrow. But at home, if you can't to something today, you have to do it tomorrow or eventually. There's no way out.

Havana answered this question in a similar way:

At the job you have to work six hours straight, but at home there's no schedule. When I get home I make my bed and wash the dishes. There's no specific schedule. I just go on doing things until it's all finished.

Here, it is apposite to recall the words of Simone de Beauvoir, who wrote that the inclusion of women in the world of work was not enough to change the sexual division of labour or make it more just. Despite their growing participation in the labour market, many women are still subjugated to men, connected by their homes and by their work, by emotional ties, by economic dependence (on their father or husband).

As de Beauvoir noted, the ties that unite women to their oppressors are not comparable to any others. In the patriarchal family, couples have the perspective of reproducing this institutions's 'logic of being'. The family is a fundamental unit whose halves are indissolubly bonded to one another (de Beauvoir, 1980).

Our study showed that financial dependence and emotional ties are the main factors that keep operators joined to their partners or families. Emotional ties, specifically, are a way of maintaining the relationship of male domination over the women in the family. Antonia went through a difficult experience of violence in her marriage but nonetheless justified the aggressive attitude of her companion, saying that she was emotionally dependent on him:

I've suffered a lot with my husband. There was a time when he was unemployed. He drank and I suffered a lot, but since last month my life, thank God, has taken a turn for the better. We are fine together, while he is employed. He's a very loving person and we talk about everything. He was without a job for a year. He only did odd jobs and that's not the same thing as a real job, especially because I was working and studying and he was at a standstill. I cried so much. I knew that I was going to get home and he would be drunk. A few times, I won't deny it, my friends came to help me. The last time he even hit me. I couldn't even go home the next day. I don't even like to think about it.

But, according to Antonia, after her husband got a regular their relationship improved. She described her relationship of emotional dependence in the following terms:

After he got the job he gradually stopped being violent. But, in spite of everything, I didn't want to live without him. I don't know how to explain it. I think it's because of his way of being so loving with me, it's like I depend on him. For example, I can't go to the supermarket unless he goes with me. It feels like something is missing. And I earn more than he does and so I try not to touch on this point! I know it's a touchy point and if I bring it up it will upset him and we might go back to the same terrible situation again.

This response is related to the 'regulation' of gender relations. In patriarchal families men attempt to regulate women's lives and get a good amount of domestic work out of them. Many women accept this situation because it is an emotional issue. Nothing changes the underlying reality of oppression but superficial changes may make it more complex.

Domestic work (in other words, 'taking care' of the family) is a basic reproductive activity that is not aimed at producing merchandise, but producing goods that are useful for the family's survival. And this is one of the essential differences between salaried labour and domestic work. Whereas one is related to the productive space, the other is related to the production of goods needed for reproducing the members of the family. So, albeit indirectly, capital also appropriates the sphere of reproduction.

This is why talking about sexual division of labour does much more than just draw attention to the specificities of gender. It articulates this description of reality with an analysis of the processes by which society uses the dynamics of difference for the purpose of creating hierarchies of activities, as is illustrated in the responses of these women workers.

Some conclusions

Social relationships of gender, understood as unequal, hierarchical and contradictory, both through the exploitation of relationships between capital and labour and the domination of men over women, express the basic articulation of production and reproduction. The findings of gender exploitation, oppression and domination vindicate our approach to this study, based on the sexual division of productive and reproductive spaces and validates our objective of drawing attention to the importance of studying work in the home as well as in the workplace. In order to do so, it was necessary to take into account both objective and subjective dimensions, as well as the individual and collective aspects of this relationship.

The sexual division of labour is a historical phenomenon that changes in function according to the structure of the society of which it forms a part. In contemporary Brazilian capitalist society, this division still assigns domestic work largely to women, whether or not these women are also present in the productive space.

We can conclude that the sexual division of labour is not at all neutral: women's work and men's work are distinct categories not because of the technical nature of the work they do, but because of the relationships of power and the interests that these imply (Pena, 1981: 81).

The sexual division of labour in both the domestic and the productive spheres thus expresses a hierarchy of gender that strongly influences the downgrading of women's salaried work. It has the effect of devaluing their work in the home and this causes a chain reaction whereby women's work in the labour market is also devalued. We have tried to depict this reality as it is illustrated in women's work in telemarketing in Brazil. This situation is perpetuated because

The reproduction of the capitalist social relationships of production is also the reproduction of the sexual division of labour. Here the relationship of capital to labour as a historical reality can be seen to incorporate a hierarchy of gender, expressed in categories such as qualification, responsibility and control, which are neutral neither in relation to gender nor to social class. (Pena, 1981: 81)

Domestic work includes a large portion of socially-necessary production. The domestic space of the family is necessary for capital to guarantee the reproduction and maintenance of the working class. This allows us to state that a relationship of substantial equality in both the reproductive and the productive spaces is not a concern in society, nor does it fit into the logic of capital. What we can see today is the existence of a relationship of merely formal equality (Meszaros, 2002: 271).

The articulation between the sphere of production and the sphere of reproduction thus takes place on the basis of the logic of the sexual division of labour that exists both in the world of salaried work and in the patriarchal family. The sexual division of labour in the productive and reproductive spaces makes it possible to articulate the two dimensions that define this relationship, namely, labour and reproduction.

In the contemporary world of production, the service sector is one of the fields that most absorbs women's labour. This sector is typical of those that employ female labour in the monotonous, repetitive and stressful character of the tasks and the prevalence of part-time work, all of which are evidenced in telemarketing.

It has been said that 'when someone speaks of part-time work, one thinks of women's work' (Maruani, 2000: 80). A first glance, this might look like an advantage. But our study shows that this reality is contradictory and often negative, since women who work in telemarketing for six hours a day have to perform very intense work, without creativity, in very inadequate working conditions. These women do not even have time to satisfy their basic biological and social needs.

In contrast, women's work in the reproductive space gives them greater flexibility in terms of working hours and allows for emotional involvement and personal interaction, albeit at the price of submission to male authority. It should be noted, however, that it is the capitalist system itself that benefits from this patriarchal model, and is the agent most responsible for these inequalities in class and gender.

Telemarketing provides just one example of a situation where the most substandard jobs are occupied by women. This can lead to the conclusion that labour relationships are also directly related to the relationships of power present in the historical assertion that women's work has less value that men's because of the priority of their 'natural' qualities of mother and wife. Even though this reality is replete with contradictions and antagonisms, it holds true in any situation where the interests of capital impose their logic. As Meszaros has noted, 'it is apparently impossible to integrate the unequal sexual division of labour into the dominant logic' (Meszaros, 2002: 272).

In this study of telemarketing workers, the articulation of the categories of *work* and *reproduction* have made it possible to show the positive and negative factors that exist in these contradictory dynamics. Women's participation in the world of labour is certainly positive in many respects, and represents a step ahead in their emancipation, even though this is partial and limited. Nevertheless, it has not significantly lessened the double burden of their work. On the contrary, the load has become even heavier since domestic work has no monetary value, even though it is fundamental for the reproduction and maintenance of the labour force in general. It continues as a priority for women although it represents their unacceptable exploitation in the world of work, in a clear relationship with male domination over women in the domestic sphere.
© *Claudia Mazzei Nogueira, 2009*

REFERENCES_

Antunes, R.(1999) *Os Sentidos do Trabalho*, São Paulo: Boitempo Editorial
de Beauvoir, S. (1980). *O segundo sexo*, vol. 1 e 2. Rio de Janeiro: Nova Fronteira
Dejours, C. (1994)'Trabalho e saúde mental: da pesquisa à ação'. *In*: Dejours, C.; Abdoucheli, E.; Jayet C. (orgs.), *Psicodinâmica do trabalho: contribuições da Escola Dejouriana à análise da relação prazer, sofrimento e trabalho*. São Paulo: Atlas
Hirata, H. (1999) 'Flexibilidade, Trabalho e Gênero', GEDISST/CNRS, Santiago (Mímeo)
Maruani, M.(2000) *Travail et emploi des femmes*, Paris: Éditions La Découverte
Marx, K. (1988) *Capítulo VI Inédito de O Capital*, São Paulo: Editora Moraes, S/Data
Marx, K. (1988) *O Capital*, Livro I/Volume I/Tomos 1 e 2, São Paulo: Nova Cultural
Mészáros, I. (2002) *Para Além do Capital*, São Paulo: Boitempo Editorial
Nogueira, C. M. (2006) *O Trabalho Duplicado*, São Paulo: Expressão Popular
Pena, M. V. J. (1981) *Mulheres e Trabalhadoras*, Rio de Janeiro: Editora Paz e Terra
Vilela, L. V. de O. & A.A. Assunção (2004) 'Os mecanismos de controle da atividade no setor de teleatendimento e as queixas de cansaço e esgotamento dos trabalhadores', in *Caderno Saúde Pública*, n. 20(4):1069-1078, jul-ago

Resisting Call Centre Work:
The Aliant Strike and Convergent Unionism in Canada

Enda Brophy

Enda Brophy *is a postdoctoral fellow in Atkinson College at York University, Toronto, Canada.*

ABSTRACT
Countering the more placid depictions of call-centre work on offer from academic literature, this paper illuminates the labour antagonisms currently being produced within this growing form of employment. It brings into sharper focus one of the ways in which call centre workers are organising to protect and their interests, by describing their participation in the emerging model of 'convergent' trade unionism of the Communications, Energy, and Paperworkers Union of Canada (CEP) and their 2004 strike against the Canadian telecommunications company Aliant. The five-month strike was provoked by a set of processes that characterised the transformation of the Canadian telecommunications sector in the 1990s, including the privatisation of public telephone companies, corporate convergence, and the restructuring of the labour process at the telecommunications companies that emerged. Drawing on the descriptions offered by a group of call-centre workers who are members of Local 506 of the CEP, the paper focuses on the transformation of the Aliant customer contact labour process from its 'help-desk' functions towards conditions prevailing within non-unionised outsourced call centres across New Brunswick, and recounts the 2004 strike. It concludes by assessing the significance of these events for unionised call-centre workers in the Canadian telecommunications sector and reflecting on how convergent unionism might be extended to include non-unionised workers at outsourced call centres across the region.

introduction

Broadly optimistic discussions of call-centre labour, emerging primarily from business and management perspectives but also within fields such as occupational psychology, have tended to steer clear of discussing industrial conflict in these new workplaces (D'Cruz & Noronha, 2007; Frenkel et al, 1998, 1999; Holman 2004; Srivastava and Theodore, 2006). In so doing, this research has offered a view in which neither exploitation nor resistance is prominent in the apparently placid world of call-centre work. More critical perspectives have, over the last decade, focused their attention on the labour processes within call centres, offering an increasingly textured portrait of the insecurity, routinisation, surveillance, and emotional labour characteristic of one of digital capitalism's fastest-growing professions (Baldry, Bain & Taylor, 1998; Callaghan & Thompson, 2001; Head, 2003; Mulholland, 2002; Taylor & Bain, 1999).

Labour process approaches have helped illuminate the contested power relations between employers and workers in call centres, and have also begun to produce much-needed research into moments of resistance by workers (Bain & Taylor, 2000; Taylor & Bain, 2005; Mulholland, 2004). There remains a great deal of work to do, however, to further academic analysis of the different forms that collective resistance by call-centre workers is taking, to explore the relationship between such resistance and the labour processes that provoke it, and to evaluate the effectiveness of these forms. Such concerns are central to a small but growing academic literature on call-centre work that is the product of research carried out in an explicitly collaborative manner with the collectives, associations, and unions formed by and/or representing call-centre workers (Guard, Steedman & Garcia Orgales, 2007; Rainie and Drummond, 2006; Stevens & Lavin 2007), research that aims both to extend the power of those organisations and to provide a counterbalance to the more antiseptic representations of call-centre work on offer within the academic literature.

Adding itself to such research, this paper describes the 2004 strike against the Canadian telecommunications company Aliant by call-centre employees and other workers who were members of Local 506 of the Communications, Energy, and Paperworkers Union of Canada (CEP). It shows how the five-month strike was provoked by a set of processes that characterised the transformation of the Canadian telecommunications sector in the 1990s, including the privatisation of public telephone companies, corporate convergence[1], and the restructuring of the labour process at the newly privatised telecommunications companies. Soon after its formation out of a merger between four privatised telephone companies in Atlantic Canada,[2] Aliant began to experiment with the adoption of new technology, facility closures, layoffs, the electronic transfer of work, and the repurposing of workers for new portions of the production process. In the process, as is described below by its employees, the company's in-house telephone help desk functions and the clerical labour enabling them were restructured towards the intensified rhythms, tightly-controlled customer interactions, and increased surveillance that characterised outsourced call centres in the region.

Workers at Aliant in Moncton, New Brunswick were familiar with the labour conditions of these emergent digital workplaces however, and were not keen to be subject to them. By one estimate, one out of every twenty of their fellow New Brunswickers in the workforce is employed in a call centre (CBC, 2008) in a province where the communicative labour sustaining corporations such as AOL, UPS, IBM and Air Canada has long been a focus of economic development. Karen Buckley, who provides technical support at Aliant, describes the impact of the industry on those close to her:

---

1   The process of convergence within the media and telecommunications industries has been a key conceptual lens for critical political-economic analyses of the sector (Winseck, 1998; McKercher, 2002; Mosco, 2008). More recently, the concept has been applied to labour organisations as well (Chaison, 1996; Mosco & McKercher, 2006).

2   The companies involved in the merger were NBTel (New Brunswick), Island Telecom Inc (Prince Edward Island), Maritime Telegraph and Telephone Company (Nova Scotia), and NewTel Enterprises Limited (Newfoundland and Labrador). In early 2000 Bell Canada Enterprises increased its controlling interest in the new firm to 42 % (Rideout, 2003: 119), and by 2004 its stake had risen to 53 % (Wong, 2004).

The call-centre industry is getting a bad name because of the stress level that is added to the individual who's working that particular job. The expectation that one person is going to extrapolate that kind of quality from interacting with a person on the telephone… it's unreasonable, it's unbelievable, and it's landed so many people in stress leaves from work that the unemployment office actually has a way to deal with them. You know that there's an issue when you go to unemployment and tell them that you're out on stress leave, and they'll send you back to school to re-educate you to do something else, provided you never ever, ever, ever, go back to call-centre industry. Because my daughter took it. Yeah, they'll pay her [Employment Insurance] for the whole time she's in school provided she never goes back to a call centre. She was working at Client Logic. And she was their top salesman for 2 consecutive months prior to leaving on stress! And they were still hounding her because her calls weren't less than 12 minutes. She was their number one salesperson.(Buckley, Karen, personal interview, April 6, 2006)

This paper brings into sharper focus one of the ways in which call-centre workers are organising to protect their interests by describing their participation in the emerging model of convergent trade unionism (Mosco & McKercher, 2006), the organisational response adopted by North American unions such as the CEP, the Telecommunications Workers Union, and the Communication Workers of America to confront the ongoing turbulence within the telecommunications industry. This unsteady scenario has seen convergence of ownership across previously distinct industry sectors (eg cable and telephony), supported by technological convergence (towards digitisation as a common language), through which production is increasingly coordinated across emergent conglomerates like Sprint, Bell, Telus, and Aliant (Winseck, 1998; McKercher, 2002; Mosco, 2008).[3] In an attempt to harness these processes, trade unions of communication workers have merged with others nationally in order to produce larger and stronger organisations that are capable of confronting labour restructuring and the outsourcing of unionised positions to non-unionised companies. As we shall see, in-house, unionised call-centre workers within the telecommunication industries have played a key role in this process.

In what follows, mindful of the fact that a great deal of research on call centres has offered portraits of these workplaces in which they are abstracted from their political and economic contexts (Ellis & Taylor, 2006: 108), the paper begins by describing the restructuring of New Brunswick's political economy during the 1990s and the processes of convergence that both created Aliant and gave it its union. I then focus on the transformation of the labour processes in the company's functions from those of

---

3   In the United States, examples from the telecommunications sector include Verizon's purchase of MCI in 2005, the $16 Billion USD acquisition of AT&T by regional phone giant SBC Communications Inc. and the $35 billion USD merger of Sprint Corp and Nextel Communications (Noguchi, 2005). The effect on telecommunications workers and their unions has been devastating. According to Jeffrey H. Keefe, a researcher at the Economic Policy Institute (a Washington research institute), from 1998 to 2003 traditional wire-line companies in the United States eliminated 15.5 % of their jobs, which paid 26% more than those in the cable industry, where employment grew by 22.6% (cited in Belson, 2004). Overall, the number of telecommunications workers represented by a union fell 23% between 2000 and 2004 to 273,000 according to the Bureau of Labor Statistics (cited in Belson, 2004).

a 'help desk' towards the conditions prevailing within non-unionised, outsourced call centres across New Brunswick, and then move on to examine the 2004 strike. I conclude by assessing the significance of this restructuring for unionised call-centre workers in the telecommunications sector, and reflecting on how convergent unionism might be extended to include non-unionised workers in outsourced call centres across the region.

The research draws on 14 open-ended interviews conducted with Aliant call-centre workers and CEP members in Moncton, New Brunswick in April 2006. These workers had all been present at the telecommunications company when it was NBTel, and had thus experienced the merger that would turn it into Aliant, their own unionisation through the CEP, the ongoing restructuring at the company, and the 2004 strike. They were therefore able to offer invaluable testimony concerning these events and processes. Their accounts were supplemented by a review of papers from archived issues of daily newspapers from the four Atlantic provinces describing the transformations at the company and the 2004 strike, by CEP and Aliant newsletters, press releases and collective agreements, by various documents and decisions of the Canadian Industrial Relations Board (CIRB), and by business press and other papers dealing with the development of the call-centre industry in the Maritimes, particularly in New Brunswick.

Restructuring of New Brunswick's political economy

The 'New Economic Strategy' enacted in New Brunswick during the 1990s by Frank McKenna's Liberal government rapidly transformed the composition of labour in the province. The rationale supporting this restructuring was simple: if the province's traditional forms of employment were dying, then a wave of new opportunities for profit existed in the form of an emergent call-centre sector, which, with the right incentives, could be lured to the province to replace the jobs lost on the fish-packing line, at the railway yards, and in forestry. Bolstered by its close relationship with the provincial government, telecom provider NBTel invested heavily in fibre optic and digital switching technologies. The result was a state-of-the-art-telecommunications infrastructure that offered potentially seamless integration between the headquarters of major American and Canadian companies and their New Brunswick operations (UNCTAD, 2005: 197). As Tom Good and Joan McFarland (2005:104) have documented in their research on the development of call centres in the province, by 1999, NBTel was offering to cover virtually all of the costs associated with telecommunications hardware and software, as well as its maintenance and regular upgrading, for companies that were considering relocating their call-centre operations to the Province.

If NBTel offered companies the cutting edge technology, the provincial government took care of providing the workforce and financial incentives (Balka, 2002; Buchanan & Koch-Schulte, 2000). The most important features of the New Brunswick 'business climate' promoted by McKenna's government to prospective buyers were one of the lowest unionisation rates and one of the highest unemployment rates in Canada.[4] The entrepreneurial spirit of the Liberals went well beyond the standard advertising of the

---

4   As McKenna promoted his strategy for the province, a full 12% of the active labour force (roughly 40,000 people) was officially unemployed, a figure that did not even include part-time or casual workers seeking full-time work (Good & McFarland, 2005: 99).

region however, manifesting itself in enthusiastic pronouncements in promotional literature regarding the weakness of organised labour in the province. As the New Brunswick Department of Economic Development and Tourism website proclaimed in 1999:

The industry that reflects call-centre activities the most is the communications industry and [in that industry] New Brunswick has the lowest rate of unionisation in Canada… NBTel is the only telephone company in Canada with non-unionised clerical employees … There has never been an industry attempt to unionise [call centres in the province]. (quoted in Good & McFarland, 2005: 111).

There is some irony in the fact that the non-unionised NBTel clerical employees in question would soon become a barometer of the deteriorating labour relations at the company, unionising in 2001 and striking in 2004. In the years before this labour unrest, McKenna's Liberals went about the business of expanding the existing pool of skilled, non-unionised, and chronically unemployed workers with call-centre skills. During the 1990s, educational initiatives were enacted that were designed to ensure the continued reproduction of the call-centre workforce in the decades to come. Computer literacy became mandatory for high school graduates, and both public and private institutions began to offer call-centre training programs in the province (UNCTAD 2005, 197).

In addition to state-of-the-art infrastructure and an obedient workforce, McKenna's government also promised billions in forgivable loans to lure call-centre operations to New Brunswick. Companies were enticed, and by one count at least 35 call centres were established in the province between 1991 and 1996 (Jaimet, 2006). By 2002 in Moncton alone there were 43 call centres employing an estimated 6,000 workers (Warson, 2002).[5]

The labour process at Aliant was deeply affected by the broader transformations occurring outside of it. The 1999 merger produced the third-largest telecommunications company in Canada and the largest in the region, worth $3 billion and employing 9,000 people(Aliant, 1999). Newly convergent companies like Aliant quickly compensated for the revenue lost from their former long-distance monopolies by offering new services like wireless, Internet access, and satellite television. In a move that was enabled by the Canadian Radio-Television and Telecommunications Commission through its loosening of service requirements, corporate re-engineering programmes gutted the workforces of these companies and, in the process, carried out a sustained attack on their unions (Niemeijer, 2004; Shniad, 2005; 2007). Aliant was no exception. After the merger, it closed its operator service operations in Nova Scotia, Newfoundland and Prince Edward Island, centralised significant parts of its other operations, downsized its workforce by several hundred employees and transferred a major part of its Network Surveillance operations and Buildings Real Estate management to its parent company, Bell Canada.

---

5   By 2004, roughly one-quarter of all employment in the Canadian call-centre industry was in Atlantic Canada, most notably in New Brunswick and Nova Scotia (this compared with the region's 7% share of total employment both in the service industries as a whole and in all industries combined (Statistics Canada, 2005). In New Brunswick 22,000 people (Canadian Broadcasting Corporation News, 2008) currently work in an estimated 100 call centres, producing $1 billion yearly for the provincial economy (Kitchener-Waterloo Record, 2006). This has allowed New Brunswick to become part of a 'nearshoring' trend that belies simple models describing the offshoring of communicative labour as flowing solely from developed to developing countries (Austen, 2004; Mosco, 2006).

By 2000, however, Aliant was having to face its own version of the convergent trade unions that were organising workers across the communications, information, and media sectors. The union representing its workers had pursued its own growth strategy since the 1990s, merging with two other unions to create the CEP in the early part of that decade.[6] This union convergence was supported by the Canada Industrial Relations Board (CIRB) which followed the state of labour relations at Aliant closely in the aftermath of the merger. Prior to the amalgamation, the Atlantic companies contained nine bargaining units. The CEP represented craft, clerical and operator units in Newfoundland and Labrador at NewTel (Local 410) and Prince Edward Island at IslandTel (Local 401), but only craft and operator bargaining units in New Brunswick at NBTel (Local 506). In Nova Scotia, the historically more militant Atlantic Communications and Technical Workers Union (ACTWU), that, by all accounts, had the best collective agreement, represented employees in all three occupations. The workers studied in this paper were the only non-unionised clerical/call-centre employees of these four companies prior to the Aliant merger and the subsequent proceedings before the CIRB.[7]

On the heels of the merger, the CEP began its third campaign to organise clerical workers in New Brunswick in March, 2000. After a card-signing meeting with the majority of the workers, the CEP applied to the CIRB for certification in August, 2000. Aliant sought a review of the bargaining unit structure in the same year, requesting the consolidation of the nine bargaining units in an application to the CIRB. The existing bargaining units agreed to the merger, and, by order of the Bureau, in 2001 a single bargaining unit was formed, representing all of Aliant's unionised workers. The bargaining agent for the new unit was to be the Council of Atlantic Telecommunication Unions (CATU), formed through an agreement between the CEP and the ACTWU. The CIRB thus granted Aliant its wish, yet in its decision the Board *also* ordered the inclusion in the newly convergent bargaining unit (now some 4,300 workers strong) of the nearly 800 clerical employees in New Brunswick. Sensing that the newly unionised call-centre workers could send an important signal to other workers on the province's digital assembly lines, Vice-President of the CEP's Atlantic Region, Max Michaud,

---

6   The CEP's 'communications section was born in the early 1970s when the Canadian contingent of the Communications Workers of America opted for secession from its US-based parent (McKercher, 2002).

7   Why these workers were not unionised before the Aliant merger is unclear. The CEP had tried to unionise them at least twice previously in the 1990s, without success. As one worker described it: 'We were presented with it, and we were asked to join the union throughout my career at least twice before we actually did. […] And we voted on it, and voted against it because whatever [the other unionised clerical/call-centre workers in other provinces] had, we also got. Without paying the union dues or anything like that. I mean in terms of money and hours of work […]. As far as protection and stuff like that, we didn't have what they had, but we didn't feel the need to have it, at that point in time'. (Aliant worker 1, personal interview, April 6, 2006) Frequently cited reasons for this lack of unionisation were either that clerical workers at NBTel were suspicious of established trade unions, or that they had a reasonably good relationship with management, or both. Whether the suspicion arose from personal experience or elsewhere, it often included views that trade unions were overly bureaucratic or inclined to focus on petty aspects of the labour-management relationship. Others pointed to what they suggested was New Brunswick's lack of a strong labour history, or to the strong work ethic of its inhabitants. One worker's comments are typical: 'It's lacking compared to the other provinces. Especially in Moncton, because it's more of a service city, not an industry [city]. If you go up north, where the economy runs on paper mills and other wood products, they're all unionised right, so union[s] [are] a lot stronger in the Northern economy' .(Aliant worker 2, personal interview, April 6th, 2006).

marked the decision by suggesting that these were 'among the first-ever call-centre workers to join a union in Canada' and that the CEP hoped their unionisation would 'open the door for others who desperately need the protection of a union' (CEP, 2001). In February of 2002, the arbitrator produced an interim collective agreement until a new agreement could be reached.

The transformation of the customer contact labour process at Aliant

In the literature surrounding the merger, whether in union publications, press releases, CIRB decisions or quotes from representatives of Aliant, the call-centre workers who form the focus of this paper are most often defined as 'clerical' workers. This differentiates them from 'operator' services (who, despite the automation affecting their jobs still carry out a contemporary iteration of the roles they have played since the emergence of telephony) and 'craft' or 'outside' workers, who make repairs, install new services at homes and businesses, etc. At the same time, clerical employees at Aliant are increasingly referred to (including by themselves) as 'call-centre workers', a name that registers the changes in their labour process unleashed by the transformations described above.

Telecommunications companies increasingly need employees who can interact with customers over the phone in both an efficient and affectively productive manner. These workers must tell customers about the packages on offer, bargain with them, or sell them more expensive packages than they already have, but their role does not end with sales. A range of technical difficulties can emerge once the customers are signed up, and these workers must also act as the front line solvers of such problems, helping the customer keep the services running and, if possible, avoiding putting the company to the expense of a physical visit to the location. Clerical/call-centre workers must also coordinate the visits of outside workers to homes or businesses for repairs or to install services if this is necessary.

These tasks require a set of skills that are linguistic, communicative, and affective. In Arlie Hochschild's classic formulation (2004), they are prime examples of the 'emotional' labour increasingly in demand in contemporary economies. This labour is far from unskilled: not only is the generic human faculty of communication put to work at Aliant, but it must also by necessity be paired with the ability to speak two languages in a bilingual province.[8] Specific cultural knowledge is a key part of creating an affective bond when workers speak to customers from their province:

I get a lot of calls from the French communities also, and I know pretty much all the different areas, so I can relate to customers a lot.... sometimes they have different dialects from different areas, and you can recognise what region they're from, and right away you can empathise with them (Philippe Roy, personal interview, April 5ᵗʰ, 2006).

---

8   The province's entrenched bilingualism has made New Brunswick a strong candidate for the outsourcing of call-centre work. A legacy of the Acadians who trickled back into New Brunswick after their 1755 expulsion by the British, 45% of call-centre workers in the province speak both English and French, a factor which makes them attractive employees for Canadian or American companies who need to manage their interaction with bilingual Canadian customers.

This extends, as Sandy Brideau (who has moved from clerical to craft duties at Aliant) suggested, to knowledge of regional dialects composed of a mixture of English and French:

> Some people mix their French and English, and if you're only French or only English you're not able to understand that type of language. You need to be able to switch from French to English rapidly, because a lot of people do that.'
> (Brideau, personal interview, April 6th, 2006)

Aliant clerical/call-centre workers are also highly educated, with the majority having a post-secondary degree.[9] This is described by Philippe Roy who entered the company shortly before the merger:'I saw a lot of faces that I recognised from university. [...They had] different backgrounds, lots of backgrounds: commerce, arts, science, engineering' (Roy, ibid). Not only is communication put to work at the company, but many of the affective abilities gained *outside* Aliant become the raw ingredients of the labour process, whether these derive from the public education system, the service sector at large, or even a simple aptitude for dealing with people. When asked what management expected of their interaction with callers, workers frequently underscored the affective demands of their job: 'They want me to build a relationship with a customer, definitely' said one worker (Aliant worker 2, personal interview, April 6th, 2006). This dimension of the job was stressed to Donovan Richard from the beginning: 'I got to Aliant, [and] they said, 'we can train for computers, but not for customer service' (Donovan Richard, personal interview, April 4th, 2006).

Since the merger, this complex skill set has been pushed closer to its limits by management in an attempt to extract as much labour from these workers as possible. At the same time as they are expected to develop productive relationships with the customer, balancing several responsibilities and finding solutions to their problems, virtually all of the workers interviewed suggested that, since the merger, Aliant has subjected these responsibilities to a different series of logics and rhythms, ones that are much closer to those of outsourced call centres in the rest of the province. Sandy Brideau charted the transformation of their labour process through management discourse, suggesting that prior to 2001 management referred to their labour as 'help desk work'. As he pointed out:

> There is] a big difference between a help desk and a call centre... And then, three years after, they sent an email [and] for the first time it says '...the call-centre working hours.' So we said, 'what happened with [the] help desk?' 'Ahhh [they said]... by the way, no, we're a call centre. (Brideau, personal interview, April 6th, 2006)

Brideau further notes that the term 'call centre' entered the management lexicon 'shortly after we signed our union card' (Brideau, ibid). Indeed Aliant management could not have been unaware, as it began to implement these changes, of the well-entrenched methods of disciplining call-centre labour – and the lack of unionisation – reigning within the typical outsourced call centre in New Brunswick.

The transition from help desk to call centre has been much more than a matter of semantics for the workers, however. Philippe Roy suggests that since the merger

---

9   This is consistent with call-centre workers across the province, 70% of whom are estimated to have a post-secondary education (Good & McFarland, 2005: 106).

his work is 'very structured: call flows, you know, productivity and sales quotas and everything. It is very call-centre structured now, more than it was before' (Roy, ibid). For most of the call-centre positions among the Moncton CEP 506 members, this increasingly involves processes that unite the workers with their non-unionised colleagues across the province in a most unwelcome form of convergence: greater electronic monitoring and discipline based on performance. As Roy suggests, '…if the performance isn't there, they notice fairly quickly' (Roy, ibid). When asked about this increased surveillance at work, the Aliant workers were unanimous in their dislike of it. Keenan Richard described it as like having 'an extra pair of eyes behind you all the time' (Richard, Keenan, personal interview, April 4th, 2006).

The upshot of this shift toward an outsourced call-centre labour process, the workers suggested, has been a decreasing ability for them to affectively connect with and adequately assist the customer, a tension that marks the call-centre industry at large (Taylor & Bain, 2005). Many of the CEP 506 workers immediately connected this problem with the kinds of work rhythms their non-unionised counterparts are facing across New Brunswick. As evidenced by the quotation from Karen Buckley at the beginning of this paper, Aliant workers are very familiar with these, as many have direct experience at other call centres or have friends and relatives who have worked in them.

While there are increasing similarities between their labour processes and those of their non-unionised colleagues, Aliant employees still retain a greater ability to resist such pressures when they impede them from from carrying out their responsibilities as they feel they ought. For several interviewees, personal standards of professionalism supersede management's demands, and, doubtless bolstered by the fact that there is a union behind them, the workers are sometimes able to take matters into their own hands:

>…with the Quality Care they want you to talk on average X amount of minutes on each call, but to me numbers aren't as important. I do very well on certain things where I know, but there are certain things that they're going to ask and I know I won't do as well as they want me to do, but I still take the time anyways. […] I don't think they can fire me for taking the time to help the customer, so I just take the time! (Aliant worker 2, ibid)

Although they resisted such changes to their labour process, the greater Taylorisation in the work of some call-centre workers was still not evident to all the workers or present across the board at Aliant. Within some forms of clerical labour, such as technical support, expertise still resided with workers rather than being embedded in the software. When asked whether she had more knowledge of her job than her supervisors, Buckley (who provides support for IPTV and web hosting) responded:

>Yeah! Far more! They remind me of a group of people playing with toy soldiers. All the little plastic men are lined up, but they don't have a clue what's going on in any of their heads. (Buckley, Karen, ibid)

Donovan Richard experiences this as well:

>…probably because our group is a little bit more experienced, we've been there a long time… the supervisors we have now don't really know what we do. (Richard, Donovan, ibid)

These are some of the key areas in which, amid a transforming labour process, the contest for control between management and call-centre labour at Aliant was played out. The early changes towards an outsourced call-centre model were warnings of the newly converged company's approach to its unionised employees. By 2003, Aliant management was determined to break the convergent union that had been created in the wake of employer convergence and to restructure the labour process as it saw fit.

The 2004 Aliant Strike

If Aliant management had begun to tinker with the labour process of a newly converged corporation, the labour strife to come would be an early example of a convergent strike.[10] The 2004 conflict was a test of the soundness of the CEP's organisational decisions in a rapidly changing economic landscape. In an age of outsourcing, success for it and CATU would primarily mean maintaining the kind of job security for Aliant employees that telecommunication workers had achieved under what Vanda Rideout has called Canada's 'permeable Fordist' telecommunications regime established in the post-World War II period (2003:3-46), as well as defending the traditional Defined Benefit pension system against the plan offered by Aliant. On the other side of the divide, as Niemeijer (2004:6) has suggested, management was focused on 'cutting costs by reducing workforces, eliminating restrictive contract language, and reducing benefits.'

On December 1, 2003, Aliant workers across Atlantic Canada voted by a 92.5% margin to give their negotiating committee the authority to call a strike. Aliant and CATU had been squaring off for three years since the Bargaining Council was formed, and by the time the strike vote was called Aliant workers had not had a contract in almost two years. Despite the strike vote, Aliant was unwilling to offer CATU what it wanted on pensions and outsourcing. Negotiations broke down, and, in March 2004, the CEP negotiators secured a new strike mandate following Aliant's offer.

As the strike approached, Aliant management played up its ability to circumvent strike action by a combination of automation and managers carrying out the jobs of striking workers. 'We've got pretty good systems, a good network,' suggested the company's public affairs manager Brenda Reid, 'we don't expect if there is a work stoppage that it will have any major impact on the network itself' (quoted in Macphee, 2004). The company was training over 1,800 of its managers to fill in for call-centre workers, and a strike would see the company pit its managers and automated telephone networks against the workers' withdrawal of their labour.

For its part, the CEP's strategy became clear: while it would probably not be able to shut down Aliant's networks entirely, it might cause enough of a slowdown to routine maintenance, repair, and support functions to jeopardise the influx of new

---

10   The 2004 strike was part of a cycle of struggles in the telecommunications sector in Canada. As the strife broke out, trade unions and convergent telecommunications companies across the country were paying close attention; indeed the issues on the table in several situations appeared to be remarkably similar. In Ontario and Quebec, 7,500 CEP technicians were locked in contract talks with Bell Canada, with similar issues (outsourcing, pensions and wages) coming up as key. On the west coast, the TWU and Telus were in the middle of a four-year dispute. Thousands of TWU members had been without a contract for years, and eyes were turned to Atlantic Canada to assess what might happen when push came to shove.

customers, diverting them towards competitors and putting a squeeze on Aliant's profits. Considering the size of Aliant's operations and the fact that it was in the midst of restructuring, the strategy was by no means far-fetched. This would put enormous pressure on Aliant's managers, who would have to 'keep the lights on' as CEP President Brian Payne suggested (cited in Canadian Press, 2004), for an estimated two million residential customers and 80,000 businesses across Atlantic Canada.

On April 23rd, pickets went up across four provinces. In Moncton, the newly unionised workers were facing the unknown: '90% of the people [...] going out the door had no idea what a strike was, they'd never gone on strike before' (Brideau, ibid). While the strike was mostly played out within the framework imposed by the Canadian Labour Code, it produced a great deal of friction across the Maritime Provinces. In a tactic that would feature prominently in the Telus strike on the west coast, Aliant employed private security guards to monitor and intimidate the striking workers:

We did get harassed quite a bit by the security guards. Several tactics, fear tactics, were used and stuff like that. So it was kind of rough, you know, they showed us our home address on a piece of paper, just to rub it in that we know where you live. They delivered letters at my home about conduct and stuff, they were saying I was harassing people and all that which, you know, is kind of scary... (Aliant worker 3, personal interview, April 6th, 2006)

Tension was high between strikers and managers, who belonged to the same union but were in different bargaining units, meaning that the latter crossed picket lines to carry out the former's work. Assault charges were laid against picketers in several locations as the hustle and bustle of strike activity soon took on an analogous life in the courts (Bouzane, 2004).[11] Since work was being outsourced to call-centre workers at non-unionised companies and installations and repairs continued across the city of Moncton, CEP strikers also used roaming pickets: 'people got in cars and looked for vans to picket. And then there was the Xwave[12] parking lot, because they were doing our job' Buckley recalls (Buckley, ibid).

An old staple of labour struggles, sabotage, also surfaced during the spring and summer. In May, an Aliant automated systems building in Holyrood, Newfoundland suffered fire and smoke damage to its exterior and an Aliant vehicle had its tyres slashed (Bouzane, 2004). In June, primary and backup cables in the Aliant network were severed, disrupting telephone, cellular and Internet services on the Avalon Peninsula and Corner Brook, Newfoundland. The same tactic was also employed on the east coast of Nova Scotia (Bradbury Bennett, 2004a).

As the strike hit the two-month mark, the parties met in order to resume negotiations, but these exploratory talks ended after two days (Cronk & Macdonald, 2004a). With strike pay offering little more than $200 per week (Bradbury Bennett, 2004b), there was growing pressure both on the strikers and the union coffers.[13] At

---

11   Aliant and CATU ended up in the Newfoundland Supreme Court in July after a riot squad was called to the St. John's Aliant to watch over about 200 striking workers who were holding up managers trying to enter the building (Bouzane, 2004).

12   Xwave is a division of Bell Aliant offering 'business solutions', or, more colloquially, call-centre services.

13   At the end of July, national treasurer Andre Foucault stated that the CEP had spent roughly $3 million on the local union's strike fund (Bradbury Bennett, 2004b).

roughly the same time, the TWU contributed $1 million to the Halifax-based Atlantic Communication and Technical Workers' Union, an early sign that there were financial difficulties at the Nova Scotia organisation.

When Bell Canada technicians in Ontario and Quebec accepted a contract their bargaining committee had advised them to reject in mid-August (one which fell short of CATU's own bargaining objectives), it seemed to be an indication that they did not see things proceeding well in Atlantic Canada. Workers in Ontario and Quebec agreed to a contract that allowed outsourcing and also agreed to Bell Canada's pension plan demands. Their capitulation provoked a special member update from CATU's bargaining team urging strikers at Aliant not to be discouraged by what had happened elsewhere (Cronk & Macdonald 2004b).

By mid-summer, the strike was cutting into Aliant's bottom line. The company's second-quarter financial results at the end of July revealed that the strike had cost it around $21 million, with a drop of $9 million in revenues and a $12 million increase in costs (CBC News, 2004). Considering that it was relieved of the burden of paying its unionised workers, these figures support the idea that Aliant was prepared to pay a hefty price for future control over its labour processes. With the strike approaching its fifth month, in August, provincial Labour Minister, Joe Fontana announced that a federal mediator would try to resolve the dispute. The parties met with Elizabeth MacPherson in Halifax on August 30th, and four days later it was announced that a tentative agreement had been reached.

Not all was peaceful within the CATU alliance, however. As its workers were reviewing the tentative deal, friction was developing between the CEP and the ACTWU. The Nova Scotia ACTWU members were far from happy with the Aliant offer, in particular, it appears, with the outsourcing contract language and how long it would take them to reach wage parity with Aliant workers doing the same work in other provinces. As the ratification of the agreement by union members was pending, the CEP withdrew its support for the 1,800 Nova Scotia workers through its strike fund. 'The CEP has really kicked us while we are down – our union brothers' one ACTWU member lamented, 'in my opinion, they are trying to force a yes vote' (cited in Halifax Chronicle-Herald, 2004). Indeed, with the ACTWU on the rocks financially, Nova Scotia workers were facing the prospect of receiving no strike pay if they rejected the tentative deal and continued striking. While some Nova Scotians may have felt the offer was the best they could get from the company, the sentiment of betrayal appears to have been widespread. 'It was [a] real blow,' said Nova Scotia dispatcher Joan Ross, 'my own personal feeling is I think we should be contacting the Auto Workers and Teamsters, and saying: "we're here, take us" And leave the CEP in the dust' (cited in McLaughlin, 2004). CEP Local 410 president, Tom Retieffe added his voice to the chorus: 'The contracting-out language that we enjoyed for years in Newfoundland has been completely left out of the collective agreement and all we have now is basically a no-layoff clause…' (quoted in Bradbury Bennett, 2004c). Indeed while unionised workers at Aliant are protected by a series of measures against layoffs, or 'workforce reduction' as it is referred to in the collective agreement (Aliant and CATU, 2004), they may still be shifted to other positions so long as they are unionised ones. In addition, once a unionised worker leaves or retires, the position does not have to be replaced with another unionised worker.

The five-month strike came to an end when workers at Aliant accepted the contract offer with a 76% 'yes' vote. The last act of the strike was the disappearance of the ACTWU, which in January of the following year opted to merge with the CEP because of its financial difficulties. The strike that began with corporate convergence thus ended with an intensification of trade union convergence.

With employees back at work across the four provinces, Aliant immediately resumed its restructuring, albeit within the boundaries of the new collective agreement. That September, the company announced the closure of a walk-in phone centre in St. John's (Vaccaro, 2004). In November 2005 it announced that it would outsource 129 permanent call-centre jobs (including technical support for dial-up Internet, high-speed Internet, telephone repair and mobility repair) to a non-unionised company and drop around 100 temporary employees from the payroll (Tutton, 2005). The positions were shifted from call centres in St. John's, Halifax and Moncton to the non-unionised ICT Group, whose two call centres in Miramichi already provided the help-desk service for a portion of Aliant's dial-up Internet customers.

The company's strategy since then appears to be one of moving to outsource its call-centre support work and keeping its call-centre sales work in-house. For many of the clerical/call-centre workers in Moncton, this has meant regular upheaval as portions of the labour process are spun off to other companies:

I was doing the technical support at first for the dialup portion of it; then they got me into high-speed, and then the company decided to move their dial-up to a contractor. So we lost the dial-up part that we were doing, and we were doing high-speed up until now and now they've outsourced the high-speed as well. So all of the technical side has been outsourced. And they're keeping the unionised force for service. (Worker 2, ibid)

For the call-centre workers at Aliant, the ongoing experimentation means that they face permanent uncertainty at work: '[Management's] always telling us, "you know, you guys can always be moved around to other trouble resolution groups"', says Donovan Richard (Richard, ibid). Ferdinand Leblanc sums up the indeterminacy of their labour conditions: 'you have a job, but not necessarily the job that you want to have' (Leblanc, Ferdinand, personal interview, April 3rd, 2006). For those who remain in technical support, like Richard, work has been further intensified: 'same workload, just less people' as he says (ibid).

After the strike, Aliant employed about 8,400 people, and its 2004 revenues were more than $2 billion with profits of $137 million (CEP, 2005). In March of 2006 the company announced further restructuring in the formation of Bell Aliant. This entailed Bell Canada Enterprises (BCE) taking over Atlantic Canada's wireless operations, with Bell Aliant now being responsible for the traditional wireline operations in Ontario and Quebec, a move that boosted employment numbers to 10,000. According to current CEP Atlantic Region Vice-President Ervan Cronk, Bell was 'hiving off the growth part of the company' and leaving the more imperilled parts to Bell Aliant, and therefore to its unionised employees (cited in Tutton, 2006). This restructuring seems likely to continue the trend of outsourcing and job losses at Aliant. As one telecommunications analyst suggested: 'they're going to fracture the company and move employees around. Clearly some of the unionised employees will change unions, seniority is going to be affected and over time there will be attrition' (cited in Tutton, 2006). Bell's move could mean further union convergence as well. Bell Aliant will take over the management of 750 unionised employees in rural Ontario and Quebec, represented by three separate unions, including the CEP, the Canadian Telephone Employees Association and the Teamsters.

Overall, Bell Aliant's strategy towards its union appears clear. While for the moment it must keep on unionised positions, over the long term it will be able to reduce the union's presence steadily through attrition as people retire or leave their jobs. Donovan Richard neatly captures the feeling this outsourcing strategy evokes: 'so you see, our department got smaller, and they don't replace people, they just let it go smaller and go smaller until at one point there won't be anybody left' (Richard, Donovan, ibid).

One of the last questions asked to the interviewees was how secure they felt their positions to be. While responses were not completely unanimous, most employees felt like Aliant Worker 6 who replied 'not secure at all'. Despite their collective agreement, she says, 'anybody can fall' (Aliant Worker 6, personal interview, April 6, 2006).[14]

Convergent Unionism and the Aliant Strike: Lessons and Prospects for Labour

Call centre work presents some diversity globally in terms of its labour conditions (Holman, Batt & Holtgrewe, 2007), ranging from unionised and well-remunerated positions in some public services to the precarious, low paying, highly routinised, and stressful work commonly found in the outsourced call-centre sector. Customer contact labour that sustains the telecommunications sector across developed countries has tended to see a slide across the spectrum from the former to the latter over the last twenty years, as incumbent telecommunications monopolies have been privatised, outsourced their production processes to non-unionised companies, or spun off the call-centre portion of their operations into entirely new ventures. As these companies have seen their need to interact with the customer increase due to the nature and range of products they offer, they have also acted to decrease their dependence on the well-remunerated, unionised portion of their workforces.

This paper has explored the way in which the labour processes of 'clerical' workers at Aliant have, since the 1999 merger, steadily been restructured towards those that are dominant within the outsourced, non-unionised call centres dotting New Brunswick. The latter offer a model of structuring customer contact work favoured by management, in which communicative and emotional labour is extracted from workers predictably, efficiently, and with the aim of keeping the possibility of collective resistance to a minimum. The significance of this transformation at Aliant goes beyond the more immediate forms of control it imposes in the workplace, however. Once management had restructured the labour process towards that of an outsourced call centre, it wasted little time transferring work to some of those very same call centres in the region. The

---

14   The collective agreement was extended in 2007 amid the general uncertainty of the drawn-out ownership bid (the largest takeover bid in Canadian history) for Aliant's parent company BCE on the part of a consortium of investors led by the Ontario Teachers' Pension Plan. The bid fell through in late 2008.

re-engineering of the labour process is used as a comprehensive disciplinary tool against unionised call-centre workers, ensuring greater flexibility in the labour process and creating an omnipresent threat of job loss. As a result, call-centre workers working for the new North American continental oligopolies like Sprint, Telus, and Aliant face serious challenges in the years to come.

The call-centre workers at Aliant actively resisted the transformation of their labour processes. This paper has explored the manner in which their resistance took shape, through their unionisation with the CEP and participation in the 2004 strike. While the CEP's strategy of convergent unionism is relatively new, some of the features it presents are familiar. Aliant workers across the Maritimes are heirs to the kind of company-level collective bargaining process that was typical of Canada's post-World War II Fordist telecommunications regime and dismantled as a part of the restructuring examined above. The case of the 2004 Aliant strike is therefore one where the emergent jobs of digital capitalism and the institutionally enshrined forms of collective action forged within Fordism are united. While this has meant that unionised call-centre workers currently have some degree of protection in the face of restructuring and outsourcing, this paper ends by considering how convergent unionism might be extended onto the terrain of the outsourced call-centre sector.

In the Aliant strike, having a bigger union confront a bigger employer produced some advantages for the workers, including a larger strike fund and a more coherent bargaining position. In addition, contract language was achieved limiting the outsourcing of work, meaning that unionised Aliant workers could maintain some labour security. On pensions, too, losses were limited, as Aliant workers retained access to the Defined Benefit plan. But Aliant call-centre employees could not resist the steady erosion of their positions and continual upheaval in their jobs. Given that Aliant management has had ample time to experiment with restructuring the customer contact labour process and transferring portions of it, and that this process is now quite advanced, the CEP has a weakened bargaining position because of its low presence in the regional call-centre industry as a whole, one which offers a large pool of bilingual labour for (electronically transferred) replacement work. While their particular linguistic and cultural skill-set gives them an advantage in that their work is less transferable to other regions, the same potential for the transfer of work that is allowing companies like Aliant and Telus to get through strike action relatively unscathed means that as long as call-centre workers in the rest of the province are not organised, the 'clerical' workers at Aliant will remain especially vulnerable to outsourcing. It follows that established telecommunications unions must pay close attention to the outsourced call-centre sector.

The problem the Aliant strike raises, therefore, is not one of union convergence in itself as an organisational form, but rather the way in which it is being applied.[15] The CEP, despite its harnessing of the processes that have been unleashed within the telecommunications industry,

---

15   Indeed when we consider convergent trade unionism as a mode of organisation there are a range of varieties existing between the 'One Big Union' idea championed by the Industrial Workers of the World a century ago, premised as it was on a revolutionary solidarity across all capitalist industries, and the kind of convergent trade unionism practiced by the CEP. As documented by Mosco and McKercher (2006) convergent unionism was successful in its application by the Canadian Media Guild during the 2005 CBC strike.

remains strongly premised on the firm-level, Fordist form of collective bargaining whose material basis is eroding due to restructuring (Cobble, 1996; Cranford, Das Gupta, Ladd & Vosko 2006). The combination of the potential for rapid outsourcing and the low union density characterising the Canadian call-centre sector means that the firm-by-firm organising that characterised Fordism is increasingly vulnerable in a regional economy that is open to global forces. As has been suggested by many attempting to critique, fashion, invent and refine forms of labour organisation, unions must begin to experiment with strategies to organise geographically, by industry, by occupation, and across intermittent periods of employment if they are to strike back at employers in the process of flexibly restructuring their labour (Cranford, Gellatly, Ladd & Vosko, 2006; Fine, 2006a; 2006b).

If companies like Aliant have re-engineered their labour processes, convergent unions like the CEP might stand to gain from putting more of their resources into organisational experiments of their own. One of these could involve the adoption of forms of 'social movement' unionism (Moody, 1997) operating on the basis of a particular constituency (call-centre workers) or location (Moncton) as opposed to a particular company. One example of how this is occurring is the growing phenomenon of worker centres, a promising strategy that is being deployed by workers across North America (Fine, 2006a; Tait, 2005). Worker centres are established in low-income communities and act as resources, spaces for organising, and skills-sharing centres for workers in that community. In a city like Moncton it is not difficult to see how establishing a worker centre aimed specifically at call-centre workers and the issues they face might be the first step on the long road of addressing both the union's vulnerabilities and the opportunity to organise the outsourced call-centre workforce.[16]

To speak of this as an opportunity for the CEP and its members is not to suggest that this goal is an easy one. By all accounts, and considering the composition of call-centre labour in New Brunswick, there is little or no experience of labour struggle and collective organisation lying dormant within its ranks. As one Aliant worker suggests:

[Most of] the people going into call centres are people finishing college, university or high school... so the only people who would probably have a background with union people would have to be people that have parents that work in the mill, or at the mine, or something like that. (Richard, Donovan, ibid)

The CEP and its members thus face the challenge of organising a generation of Atlantic Canadian call-centre workers in a completely new industry with little or no memory of struggle to draw upon. One of the unionised Aliant workers describes the mindset of her less fortunate colleagues in Moncton:

I find that people aren't aware, and most of the people never worked for a union before, as was the case for me, I was 19 coming out of college, don't know much about the world... you know. So it's kind of taking advantage of people not knowing what there is out there, and the same things are going through with Xwave and Clientlogic right now, which are little branches of our own companies, just down the street (Aliant worker 3, ibid).

---

16   Efforts such as these are commonly described as 'community unionism,' or forms of collective organisation among workers in low-wage jobs occupying a space between community activism and established trade unionism (Cranford, Das Gupta, Ladd & Vosko 2006; Cranford, Gellatly, Ladd & Vosko, 2006)

The challenges that outsourced call centres present for the labour movement are therefore considerable, but organising the sector is not impossible. Faced with a similar problem, organisers from the Communication Workers Union in Ireland have begun to hand out leaflets regularly outside outsourced call centres and to commit more resources to organising this major source of employment in the country (CWU organiser Ian McArdle, personal interview, February 13, 2009). In Italy, the *Collettivo PrecariAtesia*, a collective of precariously-employed workers at Europe's largest outsourced call centre, Atesia, organised ten strikes against the employer between 2004 and 2007 and eventually achieved permanent contracts for most of its over 4,000 employees, but only after members of the rank and file union Cobas distributed leaflets outside the call centre for almost a decade (Brophy, 2007). The current financial crisis will take its toll on the call-centre sector, but it may also make workers in regions characterised by high rates of outsourced call-centre employment and the associated high rates of turnover more willing to hold on to their jobs and consider collective solutions to their problems rather than simply quitting and finding a job elsewhere. Meanwhile, the engagement with emerging examples of collective organisation by call-centre workers is a pressing task for their allies in academia as they shift their attention, in labour sociologist Michael Burawoy's words (2008), from 'labour process' to 'labour movement.'

© *Enda Brophy, 2009*

ACKNOWLEDGEMENTS

The author would like to thank the Aliant call-centre workers in Moncton, New Brunswick who generously participated in the research, and the Communications, Energy and Paperworkers Union of Canada for greatly facilitating the interviews and the gathering of other material. Thanks are also due to this journal's anonymous reviewers, who provided very helpful advice on a previous draft of this paper, and to the Social Sciences and Humanities Research Council of Canada, which supported this research.

REFERENCES

Aliant (1999) 'Atlantic business combination complete: Aliant launched; enters TSE as $3B growth company', May 31, *Canada NewsWire*. (Available through Factiva database. Url: http://www.factiva.com/)

Aliant & Council of Atlantic Telecommunications Unions (2004) *Collective agreement.*

Austen, I. (2004) 'Canada has U.S. number: A growing number of American companies are finding a cost-effective and reliable destination for the outsourcing of software development and call centres just across their country's northern border', *National Post*, December 1:FP10

Baldry, C., P. Bain & P. Taylor (1998) '"Bright, satanic offices": Intensification, control and team Taylorism', in P. Thompson & C. Warhurst (eds), *Workplaces of the future*, London: Macmillan:163–183.

Bain, P., & P. Taylor (2000) "Entrapped by the 'electronic panopticon'? Worker resistance in the call centre," *New Technology, Work, and Employment*, Vol. 15, No. 1:2-18.

Balka, E. (2002) 'The invisibility of the everyday: New technology and women's work' in E. Riordan & E. Meehan (eds), *Sex and money: Feminism and the political economy in the media*, Minneapolis: University of Minnesota Press:60-74

Belson, K. (2005) 'At traditional phone companies, jobs may not last a lifetime', *New York Times*, December 5. Accessed on March 14, 2007 from: http://www.nytimes.com/2005/12/05/technology/05telecom.html?pagewanted=all

Bouzane, B. (2004) 'Union brings it home: Pickets set up at manager's houses', *St. John's Telegram*, July 30:A4

Bradbury Bennett, T. (2004a) 'Police seek list from Aliant: Want to know who has knowledge to bring service down', *St. John's Telegram*, June 11:B7.

Bradbury Bennett, T.(2004b) 'Strikes draining food bank', *St. John's Telegram*, July 21:A1.

Bradbury Bennett, T. (2004c) 'Aliant workers back to work Monday' in *St. John's Telegram*, September 17:A3.

Brophy, E. (2007) 'Organizing in the affect factory: Lessons for labour from the Atesia call centre workers in Rome', paper presented at the *Union for Democratic Communication Conference*, Vancouver, Canada, October 27th.

Buchanan, R., & S. Koch-Schulte (2000) *Gender on the line: Technology, restructuring and the reorganization of work in the call centre industry*. Accessed on February 25, 2009 at: dsp-psd. pwgsc.gc.ca/Collection/SW21-44-2000E.pdf

Burawoy, M. (2008), 'The public turn: From labor process to labor movement', *Work and Occupations*, Vol. 35, No. 4:371-387

Callaghan, G., & P. Thompson (2001) 'Edwards Revisited: Technical control and call centres', *Economic and Industrial Democracy* No. 22:13-37

Canadian Press (2004) 'Union leader predicts Aliant managers will tire as strike drags on' May 4. (Available through *Factiva* database. Url: http://www.factiva.com/)

Canadian Broadcasting Corporation News (2008) 'Call centre industry needs to change, say economists', accessed February 25, 2009 at: http://www.cbc.ca/canada/new-brunswick/story/2008/03/03/nb-callcentre.html

Canadian Broadcasting Corporation News (2004) 'Strike has cost $21M: Aliant' July 30. Accessed February 17, 2007 at: http://www.cbc.ca/money/story/2004/07/30/aliant_040730.html

Cobble, D.S. (1996) 'The prospects for unionism in a service society' in C. Macdonald & C. Sirianni (eds), *Working in the service society*, Philadelphia: Temple University Press:333-358

Cranford, C., T. Das Gupta, D. Ladd & L. Vosko (2006) 'Thinking through community unionism' in L. Vosko (ed), *Precarious employment: Understanding labour market insecurity in Canada*, Kingston: McGill-Queen's University Press:353-378

Cranford C., M. Gellatly, D. Ladd, & L. Vosko (2006) 'Community unionism and labour movement renewal: Organizing for fair employment' in P. Kumar & C. Schenk (eds), *Paths to union renewal: Canadian experiences*, Peterborough: Broadview Press:237-250

Communications, Energy and Paperworkers Union (2005) 'Phone customers should be rebated for poor service – CEP Canada' in *NewsWire*, September 27. (Available through Factiva database. URL: http://www.factiva.com/)

Communications, Energy and Paperworkers Union(2001) 'Aliant Inc: Call-centre workers among 800 newly-unionized phone workers' in *Market News Publishing*, September 27 (Available through Factiva database. URL: http://www.factiva.com/)

Cronk, E & D. MacDonald (2004) 'Report on exploratory talks' July 16. Accessed February 17, 2007 at: http://www.cep.ca/reg_atlantic/files/aliant/040716_e.html

Cronk, E & D. MacDonald (2004b) 'Council of Atlantic Telecommunication Unions info update: Bell contract offer & CIRB hearing' August 11. Accessed February 22, 2007 at: http://www.cep.ca/reg_atlantic/files/aliant/aliant_040816_e.html

D'Cruz, P. & E. Noronha (2007) 'Technical call centres: Beyond "electronic sweatshops" and "assembly lines in the head"', *Global Business Review*, Vol. 8, No. 1:53-67

Fine, J. (2006a) 'Worker centers and immigrant women' in D. Cobble (ed), *The sex of class: Women transforming North American labor*, Ithaca: Cornell University Press:211-230

Fine, J. (2006b) *Worker centers: Organizing communities at the edge of the dream*, Ithaca, NY: Cornell University Press

Frenkel, S., M. Korczynski, K. Shire & M. Tam (1999) *On the front line: Organization of work in the information economy*. USA: Cornell University Press

Frenkel, S., M. Tam, M. Korczynski & K. Shire (1998) 'Beyond bureaucracy? Work organisation in call centres', International Journal of Human Resource Management, Vol. 9, No. 6:957-79

Good, T., & J. McFarland (2005) 'Call centres: A new solution to an old problem?' in J. Sacouman & H. Veltmeyer (eds) *From the net to the Net: Atlantic Canada in the global economy*, Aurora, Ontario: Garamond Press:99-114

Guard, J., M. Steedman, & J. Garcia-Orgales (2007) "Organizing the electronic sweatshop: Rank-and-file participation in Canada's steel union," *Labor: Studies in Working-Class History of the Americas*, Vol. 4, No. 3:9-31

Halifax Chronicle-Herald (2004) 'Many striking Aliant workers to lose some strike pay, employee says', September 9. Accessed March 1, 2007 at: http://proquest.umi.com/pqdweb?did=699934201&Fmt=3&clientId=14119&RQT=309&VName=PQD

Holman, D., R. Batt & U. Holtgrewe (2007) *The global call centre report: International perspectives on management and employment (UK format)*. Accessed on February 25, 2009 from: http://www.ilr.cornell.edu/globalcallcenter/upload/GCC-Intl-Rept-UK-Version.pdf

Head, S. (2003) *The new ruthless economy: Work & power in the digital age*, Oxford: Oxford University Press

Holman, D. (2004) 'Employee well-being in call centres', in S. Deery & N. Kinnie (Eds) *Call Centres and Human Resource Management*, Basingstoke: Palgrave:223–244

Hochschild, AR 2004. *The managed heart: Commercialization of human feeling,* Berkeley: University of California Press [Orig. pub. 1983].

Jaimet, K. (2006) 'The plot to enslave New Brunswick: Did the former premier make a secret pact or was the Bilderberg just a place 'to meet interesting people'?' *Ottawa Citizen*, June 9:A4

Kitchener-Waterloo Record (2006) 'Canadian call centres at risk; N.B. and other provinces losing ground to lower-cost overseas rivals, analysts say', July 4:C8

Macphee, N. (2004) 'Aliant workers could strike by Friday', *St. John's Telegram*, April 13:D1 / Front

McKercher, C. (2002) *Newsworkers unite: Labor, convergence, and North American newspapers*, Lanham, MA: Rowman and Littlefield

McLaughlin, P. (2004) 'Aliant workers vote on deal' *Halifax Daily News*, September 11:11

Moody, K. (1997) *Workers in a lean world: Unions in the international economy*, New York: Verso

Mulholland, K. (2004) 'Workplace resistance in an Irish call centre: "Slammin', scammin' smoking an' leavin'", *Work, Employment & Society*, Vol. 18, No. 4: 709-724

Mulholland, K. (2002) 'Gender, emotional labour and teamworking in a call centre', *Personnel Review*, Vol. 31, No. 3:283-303

Mosco, V. (2008) 'The labouring of the public service principle: union convergence and worker movements in the North American communication industries', *Info*, Vol 9, No 2/3:57-68

Mosco, V. (2006) 'Knowledge and media workers in the global economy: Antinomies of outsourcing', *Social Identities*, Vol 12, No 2:771-790

Mosco, V. & C. McKercher. 2006. 'Convergence bites back: Labour struggles in the Canadian telecommunications industry', *Canadian Journal of Communication*, Vol. 31, No 3:733-751.

Niemeijer, M (2004) 'Unions slow to develop new strategies: Canadian telecom industry rocked by deregulation, competition, mergers, technology', *Labor Notes*, No *305*, August:6

Noguchi, Y. (2005) 'Telecom is getting another behemoth: Verizon-MCI union is industry's latest', *Washington Post*, February 15:A1.

Rainie, A. & G. Drummond (2006) 'Community unionism in a regional call centre: The organizer's perspective', in J. Burgess & J. Connell (eds) *Developments in the call centre industry: Analysis, changes and challenges*, New York: Routledge:136-151.

Rideout, V. (2003) *Continentalizing Canadian telecommunications: The politics of regulatory reform*, Kingston: McGill-Queen's University Press

Shniad, S. (2007) 'Neo-liberalism and its impact in the telecommunications industry: One trade unionist's perspective', in C. McKercher & V. Mosco (eds) *Knowledge workers in the information society*, Lanham, MD: Lexington Books:299-310

Shniad, S.2005. 'Lessons from the TWU-Telus dispute', *Labor Notes*. Accessed March 4, 2007 at: http://labornotes.org/node/26

Srivastava, S. & N. Theodore (2006) 'Offshoring call centres: The view from Wall Street', in J. Burgess & J. Connell (eds) *Developments in the call centre industry: Analysis, changes and challenges*, New York: Routledge:19-35

Statistics Canada (2005) *Who's calling at dinner time? 1987 to 2004* May 25. Accessed March 14, 2007 at: http://www.statcan.ca/Daily/English/050525/d050525c.htm

Stevens, A. & D. O. Lavin (2007) "Stealing time: The temporal regulation of labor in neoliberal and post-fordist work regimes", *Democratic Communique*, Vol. 22, No. 2:40-61.

Stewart, D. (2004) 'Unions at Aliant predict quick end to work stoppage: P.E.I. union member says public has been supportive as they plan to get back on local picket lines today' in *Charlottetown Guardian*, April 26:A1.

Tait, V. (2005) *Poor workers' unions: Rebuilding labor from below*, Cambridge MA: South End Press

Taylor, P. & P. Bain (2005) '"India calling to the far away towns": The call centre labour process and globalization', *Work, Employment & Society*, Vol. 19, No. 2:261-282

Taylor, P. & P. Bain (1999) '"An assembly line in the head": Work and employee relations in the call centre.' *Industrial Relations Journal*, Vol. 30, No. 2:101-117.

Tutton, M. (2006) 'Shakeup won't mean job cuts, CEO says' *St. John's Telegram*, March 8: D1

Tutton, M. (2005) 'Aliant outsources 129 jobs, slashes 100 temp positions' *Halifax Daily News* November 16:13

United Nations Conference on Trade and Development (2004) *World investment report: The shift towards services*, Switzerland: United Nations

Vosko, L. (ed) (2006) *Precarious employment: Understanding labour market insecurity in Canada*, Kingston: McGill-Queen's University Press

Warson, A. (2002) 'Moncton's core gets urban facelift: City's fortunes have been reversed by new businesses, prompting building', *Globe and Mail*, July 30:B9

Winseck, D. (1998) *Reconvergence: A political economy of telecommunications in Canada*. Cresskill, NJ: Hampton Press

Wong, T. (2004) 'Strike could hit Bell this week: Technicians give union mandate to set up picket lines' in *Toronto Star*, July 13: D01.

INTERVIEWS

Aliant Worker 1. Personal interview. Moncton, April 6, 2006

Aliant Worker 2. Personal interview. Moncton, April 6, 2006

Aliant Worker 3. Personal interview. Moncton, April 3, 2006

Aliant Worker 4. Personal interview. Moncton, April 3, 2006

Aliant Worker 5. Personal interview. Moncton, April 5, 2006

Aliant Worker 6. Personal Interview. Moncton, April 6, 2006

Brideau, Sandy. Personal interview. Moncton. April 6, 2006

Buckley, Karen. Personal interview. Moncton, April 6, 2006

Chaloux, Jim-Bob. Personal interview. Moncton, April 6, 2006

Leblanc, Ferdinand. Personal interview. Moncton, April 3, 2006

Richard, Donovan. Personal interview. Moncton, April 4, 2006

Richard, Keenan. Personal interview. Moncton, April, 4 2006

Roy, Philippe. Personal interview. Moncton, April 5, 2006

Thibodeau, Joseè. Personal interview. Moncton. April 4, 2006

Standardising public service:

the experiences of call-centre workers in the Canadian federal government

Norene Pupo and Andrea Noack

Norene Pupo *is Director of the Centre for Work and Society and an Associate Professor in the Department of Sociology at York University in Toronto, Canada.*
Andrea Noack *is an assistant professor in the Department of Sociology at Ryerson University in Toronto, Canada.*

ABSTRACT

This paper explores the impact of the adoption of neoliberal economic policies and practices on public sector jobs within the Canadian Federal government. In recent years, employment in the public sector has been increasingly shifted to a call-centre format, thereby transforming the working conditions of public servants as well as access to services enjoyed by Canadians. By adopting work practices, technologies and managerial techniques usually found within the private sector, we argue that the call-centre format fundamentally transforms the notion of public 'service' from secure employment and a dynamic career to that of a routine, Taylorised job. In this process, standardised interactions redefine the notion of public service and the role of the public servant.

Introduction

Over the past decade Canadians have witnessed substantial shifts in the structure of the federal public service, impacting both public sector workers and the services they administer. Challenged by the processes of globalisation and relentless pressures to maintain economic competitiveness, the Canadian state has joined with its counterparts in Western economies to abandon its earlier commitment to a Keynesian economic approach, replacing it with policies and practices of neoliberalism. Under a neoliberal regime, the state seeks to strengthen and promote a free market agenda while reinforcing the primacy of private property and capitalist social relations. It does so through privatisation, deregulation, outsourcing, flexibilisation, free trade, financialisation, and de-unionisation. Neoliberal economic policy and its powerful ideological underpinnings represent the social form of rule under globalisation and advanced capitalism (Albo, forthcoming; Shalla, 2007; Broad & Antony, 2006). As a result, public policies and processes have been reorganised, broadly affecting the public sector, including the provision of social services and social welfare and the restructuring of work within the public realm.

To remain competitive within the global sphere, the State has undertaken numerous measures to trim its spending. These measures, including private-sector management practices promoting efficiency and lean operation, have ultimately shaken Canadians' long-held notion of the public sector as an oasis of secure lifelong employment. Instead, new work arrangements adopted within the public domain mirror those usually identified with the private sector. On the one hand, these new forms of work, including flexibility standards, promise to empower workers while promoting organisational efficiency. On the other hand, public sector workers have faced a variety of restructuring exercises, new management practices, and technological changes that are causing them concern about their working conditions as well as their ability to meet the public's expectations in relation to service delivery. Compared to the private sector, jobs in the public sector have typically been regarded as having more 'good job' characteristics, including lower rates of unemployment, higher rates of unionisation, higher wages, better benefits, and overall, greater job security (Stinson, forthcoming; Duffy, Glenday & Pupo, 1997). As a result of recent restructuring initiatives, what Canadians traditionally regarded as the stable pillar of employment - the federal public service - now shares a number of work practices and features with the less predictable private sector. These new trends and practices consequently affect public service workers and their families as well as the quality of service provision.

In this article, we focus on the case of the Canadian Federal government, where there has been a substantial move towards the use of call centres to provide the public with access to services that were previously available through face-to-face contact in regionally located government offices. This shift to tele-service delivery has brought with it many features of private sector call centres, such as standardisation and the imposition of performance targets. The result is a fundamentally changed working environment for some members of the Canadian civil service; what were once respected, high-skilled jobs have become increasingly technical and high-surveillance positions. Workers argue that their ability to provide effective service to the Canadian public has been circumscribed by the changing organisation of their work and workplace. For them, the idea of what it means to be part of the civil service has radically shifted as a result of the implementation of neoliberal practices of standardisation, monitoring, and time management in this sector.

The Canadian public sector in context

In the face of intensifying economic pressures to maintain a Canadian presence in the global economy, the Canadian State has undertaken steps to restructure the administration of its services by adopting new management structures and workplace practices. The purpose of these initiatives is to lower the cost of maintaining the public sector labour force by incorporating technological innovations and adopting new management structures and flexibility initiatives. These changes have raised many questions for public sector workers and their unions regarding working conditions, deskilling, and growing precariousness as well as the risks and benefits to the general public (Pupo, 2007; Pupo & Noack, forthcoming).

Over the past thirty years, governments at all levels have adopted the ideology and practices of neoliberalism in an attempt to remake the Canadian state as a 'lean' operation, trimming redundancies in its workforces and shrinking its reach by cutting programmes and budgets (Broad & Antony, 2006, McBride 2001, Evans & Shields, 1998). The transformation of the public service has meant moving work from the public domain to the private sphere of the household in areas such as education and health care (Sears, 2003; Pupo & Duffy, 2007) and from the public domain to private enterprise, thereby corporatising many aspects of service delivery. Analysts who have studied such transformation have raised questions regarding the impact on the meaning of social citizenship (Siltanen, 2007) as well as on the erosion of trade union rights and freedoms (Panitch & Swartz, 2003). As a means of addressing unrelenting economic pressures and fiscal crises, both the state and governments have imported management practices from the corporate world, including the operation of call centres, into the public domain.

Recent literature on work restructuring primarily considers the changing conditions and structures of work within the private sector. Few studies have considered the state as an employer and the particular pressures to downsize and reorganise within the public sphere. In the light of fiscal crises and the call to implement measures of greater restraint, the state has aimed to exemplify the 'do more with less' approach by streamlining and standardising its operations wherever possible. This approach has had myriad effects on public policies, accessibility of services, and governments' responsiveness. For example, practices of restraint have left unemployed Canadians to wrestle with an Employment Insurance policy that is woefully inadequate, with dozens of regional differences across the country in the preconditions needed to meet the qualifications for benefits.

As an employer, the state has been concerned with the rising costs of its services, especially sustaining the cost of its workforce. In 2007 the overall unionisation rate in Canada was just under 30%, while rates for the public and private sectors stood at 71% and 16.3% respectively (Akyeampong, 2008: 1). Within both private and public sectors, the union advantage is clear: unionised workers have higher wages and better benefit coverage and generally enjoy greater employment security. However, within the highly unionised public sector, the union advantage extends to non-union members of the public service who also enjoy pension plan and health and dental insurance coverage, thereby reaping the benefit of the collective agreements of their colleagues (Akyeampong, 2002).

In its practice of fiscal restraint, the Canadian state has turned to the private sector for means by which to trim the cost as well as the size of the public sector labour force. The state has engaged in a variety of cost-cutting practices to promote efficiency, including a growing reliance on telemediated work arrangements, turning public servants from workers who engage in more time consuming face-to-face or over-the-counter interactions with citizens into call-centre workers with little or no face-to-face contact with the public. Removing public interaction and transforming it into indirect intervention through the 'back office' allows for greater time efficiencies, managerial control and standardisation. As a result of the adoption of a call-centre format for delivering a variety of public programmes, the state is able to amass multiple services, creating the notion of a 'one-stop' government service, while eliminating a number of smaller, regionally-located offices, formerly public contact centres. More importantly, and beyond savings gleaned from operating through fewer centres, the new service format allows for close monitoring of employees who are increasingly subjected to intensified working conditions.

While the call-centre format generally simplifies the labour process and enhances the efficiency and capacity for managing vast amounts of data, the central impact of this use of information and communication technologies (ICTs) is the elimination of spontaneity in interactions, resulting in deskilling and dehumanising working conditions (Huws, 2003). Moreover, the increased possibility of the relocation of work escalates workers' insecurities and thereby makes the search for meaningful work even more elusive (Huws, 2003; Buchanan, 2006). With workplace restructuring, the main concern is that there has been a measurable decline in the social condition of work and insecure, poorly compensated and non-standard work at the expense of quality work. Even unionised public sector workers, who were once envied by their non-unionised private sector counterparts for the security and status they enjoyed as public servants, have faced changing parameters within their workplaces, forcing some to rethink their aspirations to remain within the public sphere. Key processes of public sector restructuring, including privatisation, contracting out, commercialisation, the use of temporary workers, and the reformulation of work to fit a call-centre format are raising new issues for public sector unions attempting to mitigate the new insecurities through collective bargaining processes as well as through legislative change. Public sector unions are currently arguing that the new work arrangements contravene existing collective agreements by removing guarantees of workin rights, security, and in some cases, seniority. It is within the context of these transformations, particularly the standardisation, deskilling and intensification of work within the public services, that we examine work arrangements and conditions within federal public service call centres in Canada.

Compared to the extensive research on call centres in the UK, the largest and most established call-centre market in Europe, there is comparatively little research available about call-centre work in North America, despite its growing prominence. In Canada, employment in contact centres (or call centres) increased five-fold between 1987 and 2004 (Statistics Canada 2005). Generally, there are two competing characterisations of call-centre work that recur in the academic literature: call centres as high-tech, high-skilled work environments in an information economy and call centres as sites of highly regulated, de-skilled jobs in a service economy (Belt et al., 2000). While we certainly acknowledge a range of differences in conditions and experiences of work within various types of call centres, including those located in the public sector, descriptions of call-centre work as involving difficult and intense working conditions, physical relocations, repetition and scripted and highly-monitored client interchanges tip the balance toward negative characterisations in conceptualising call-centre work.

Methodology

This research was a joint project between the Centre for Research on Work and Society at York University and the Public Service Alliance of Canada (PSAC), which is one of Canada's largest trade unions, representing over 150,000 workers in more than 230 bargaining units (PSAC 2006). In the spring of 2006, survey questionnaires were mailed to PSAC members working in federal Contact Centres. Potential respondents were identified by the PSAC officers who represent them. The four-page questionnaire was divided into six sections (Demographics, Work Status, Work Organisation, Job Satisfaction, Working Conditions, and Satisfaction with Union Representation) and was sent to respondents in both English and French, along with a postage-paid return envelope. Two weeks after the initial mailing, a reminder card was sent to all members. The overall survey response rate was 30%. It is not possible to determine how the perceptions and experiences of members who did not return the questionnaire differ from the perceptions and experiences of those who did. It is possible that members who participated in this research are less satisfied with their work environments than members who did not. Questionnaire data was entered into SPSS for further analysis.

Respondents were quite forthcoming in the open-ended questions to the surveys, and in response to the final question asking for additional comments, many wrote extensively, sometimes attaching additional pieces of paper. The final question asked respondents whether they would be willing to participate in a follow-up in-depth interview and 40% volunteered to do so. Among those who volunteered, a representative sub-sample was randomly selected and contacted for an interview in either French or English in the summer or autumn of 2006.

These results reflect the responses of 369 PSAC members who spend more than half their time doing call-centre work[1] and who are employed at Service Canada, the Canada Revenue Agency and Canada Post.[2] Service Canada was launched in 2005 as a 'one-stop service delivery' network for the federal government and now provides services from Human Resources and Social Development Canada (such as employment insurance and pensions), Citizenship and Immigration Canada and Veteran's Affairs (Service Canada, 2006). All of these workers provide services to members of the general public and to business owners who phone the Canadian government's toll-free telephone contact numbers.

Public sector call-centre workers in context

The characteristics of public call-centre workers are slightly different from those of the larger Canadian labour force, workers in Canadian contact centres (both public and private) and the public sector more generally (see Table 1). Most strikingly, this is a feminised workforce compared to both the larger Canadian labour force and the public sector workforce as a whole. Almost three quarters of respondents (73%) were women. Women tend to be over-represented among call-centre employees because they are able to provide the impression of being 'smiling' and helpful service providers, with an even-toned voice and manner (Glucksmann, 2004; Belt et al., 2000; Hochschild, 1983). The proportion of visible minorities (15%) is comparable to that in the Canadian labour force overall, although visible minority men are over-represented among federal call-centre workers. Among men, 21% were visible minorities, compared with only 12% of women.

---

1   Seventy percent of respondents spend 100% of their time doing call-centre work.
2   In conjunction with this project, PSAC members at Statistics Canada were also surveyed, but since these employees spend the majority of their time making outgoing calls (instead of receiving incoming calls) their concerns are somewhat different and thus they are excluded from this analysis.

Like public sector workers more generally, however, public sector call-centre workers tend to be slightly older, especially in comparison with workers in other Canadian contact centres. Many Canadian contact centres rely on college or university students as a portion of their labour force. Van Jaarsveld, Frost and Walker (2007) estimate that 9-13% of the contact-centre workforce are students. Though we did not specifically ask about student status, the age distribution and educational status of respondents suggests that public sector call centres tend to rely less on student labour. In fact, in comparison to Canadian contact centres overall and to the larger Canadian labour force, public sector contact workers tend to be highly educated. Seven out of ten respondents (71%) reported having some post-secondary education; and about a third of respondents (32%) had a university degree.

Table 1: Characteristics of federal government call-centre workers compared with other labour-force groups

Characteristic	PSAC Call Centre Respondents	Canadian Contact Centres	Public Sector Workforce[2]	Canadian Labour Force[3]
Age (average)	42 yrs	32 yrs	45 yrs	n/a
Women	73%	69%	53%	47%
Visible minorities	15%	n/a	7%	15%
Some post-secondary education	71%	54%	n/a	59%
Employed full-time	57%	64.5%	n/a	82%

Sources: data on Canadian Contact Centre workers, from Van Jaarsveld, Frost and Walker (2007); on the public sector workforce, from Treasury Board of Canada (2005); on the Canadian labour force, from the 2006 Census of Canada summary tables.

Call centres jobs are most often characterised as sharing the features of the proverbial 'McJobs', frequently providing only short-term, part-time employment and precarious employment (Huws 2003, Belt, Richardson & Webster 2002, Buchanan 2002, Mulvale 2006). Although government call centres have a slightly smaller proportion of full-time workers (57%) than most Canadian contact centres, more than two-thirds of survey respondents (68%) were permanent employees.[3] The average job tenure of respondents was 5.2 years. Although there were a few long-time employees, about half of respondents had been employed for five years or fewer, and 90% of the sample had been employed for 10 years or fewer in 2006. This reflects the relatively recent shift

---

3   Tellingly, in the Canadian public sector, these workers are labeled as having 'indeterminate' status, discursively rejecting the idea that employment could be permanent and reinforcing the idea that a termination date has simply not yet been determined.

by the Canadian government towards providing services by telephone. Although these call-centre positions appear to be relatively new within the context of the Canadian civil service, these results suggest that they have become a permanent part of service delivery in the public sector.

Under the state's neoliberal cost-cutting agenda and its programme of work intensification in the public sector, call-centre work may seem to be an entry point into employment in the civil service. Sixty-three percent (63%) of respondents worked outside of the federal government before starting in a federal call centre and the vast majority (64%) of respondents had never worked in a call centre before starting this job. Of those who had previously worked in a call centre, most worked in non-government contact centres (31% of all respondents). However, many workers do not anticipate advancing in their jobs. Seven out of ten respondents were not satisfied with their opportunities for advancement. In contrast, in the public service more generally, about five out of ten workers (52%) agreed that there were opportunities for promotion within their department (PSES, 2005). About 40% of these call-centre respondents anticipate that they will still be working in the same job in three years time. Notably, however, only 7% of respondents anticipate working outside of the government in three years time, whereas most others anticipate moving into a different (presumably better) job in the same department (29%) or in another federal department or agency (19%). This is a slightly lower proportion than among the public service more generally, where about a third of workers (30%) anticipate leaving, though most declined to provide information about the timeline of their departure (PSES 2005).

Overall, the majority of federal call-centre workers (62%) are satisfied with their jobs, though in the public service overall, 87% of workers agree that they are satisfied with their current work arrangements (PSES, 2005). Many call-centre workers express pride in being a member of the public service and pleasure in being able to help the public. Respondents made comments like: 'I enjoy the opportunity to help people whenever it is possible to do so', or 'I can make a difference in a stranger's life' or 'What I really like about my job is the fact that I'm helping people in need'. Unfortunately this enthusiasm for helping the public was almost universally paired with concerns about the difficulties of providing effective public service within the context of the high-speed, standardised call-centre environment.

The Stress of High-Speed Service provision

Time pressures and intensification have become benchmarks of work in the new economy. A substantial body of literature addressing the speeding up of work in contemporary work environments points to the use of ICTs and the supervisory and management practices employed in knowledge industries as exacerbating stressful conditions within work environments (see, for example, Huws, 2003; Boisard et al., 2003; Menzies, 1996, 2005; Buchanan, 2002). This has also been reflected in the Canadian public service. For instance, nearly a third of public service workers (31%) report that they 'always' or 'often' have unreasonable deadlines and 15% of workers report that they can 'never' complete their assigned workload (PSES, 2005). The call-centre environment seems to intensify these time pressures and the stress that can be associated with them. In this survey, 69% of call-centre respondents 'strongly agree' that they work in a stressful environment. The key stressor for many of these employees seems to be the pace of work that is required when they are on the phones. Approximately seven out of ten (69%) say that the pace of their work is not manageable. Relatively few respondents (18%) say that they have some control over the pace of their work, suggesting that these employees' working days are structured by the technologies that they work with. Not surprisingly, respondents who reported having some control over the pace of their work were far more likely to say that the pace of their work was manageable (85% of those with some control over their pace of work said it was manageable, compared to only 33% of those who said they have no control over their pace of work).

One issue that was routinely raised by interviewees was their inability to pause between calls. Only 13% of survey respondents indicated that they were able to take downtime between calls. One interviewee commented that 'two seconds between calls is not reasonable. [It's] not possible to take a breath between each call'. Another reported that, 'the calls come in three seconds apart. [There's] not enough time to have a drink of water in between calls.' One worker explicitly compared her conditions in the call centre to the dehumanising conditions found in the informal economy, saying: 'I like my work a lot, however employees are treated like machines and not humans for those stats. Three seconds between each call is like a "sweat shop"'.

Only 45% of respondents said that they were able to take time to respond sufficiently to each call. For many employees, this high-paced environment conflicts with their idea of public service. As one respondent noted, there is more of a focus on 'quantity not quality. Increasingly, over the years, numbers seem to matter more than the people we serve.' Another notes that 'it is called client services but it's more about their "numbers"'. Several respondents reported feeling conflicted that they were not actually able to help people in the time allotted. Others reported situations where they were told to deliberately misrepresent information to the public in order to meet their hourly or daily quotas, and how this left them feeling ineffective in serving clients and in respecting the tradition surrounding their role of trust as public servants. Yet, nine out of ten respondents (90%) agreed that they were able to take regular breaks, as specified in their collective agreement, suggesting that the issue is not one of overwork per se, but rather the structure of their jobs and the intensified conditions that characterise these jobs.

While they are on the phone, workers are continually aware of each call's time score and the way in which this may affect their overall numbers. One worker described the balancing and time management the work involves:

Statistically they ask us not to take more than 300 seconds per call. That's five minutes, 300 seconds... that's an average for the week. Not for a day, but for the week. If you have an average of 300 seconds or less, that's a good score.

The issue of time pressures and keeping scores, as if the work were a basketball game, conflicts with the human service capacity of the job at hand. A worker presents the dilemma of taking a 'long' call:

Sometimes, when we have two or three situations that surface during the call, well the call will end up being 45 minutes. And a 45-minute call massacres your stats. And

because I am part time, it's even worse. One 45-minute call in a week, given that I
work only 3 days ... it will massacre my stats even if I would work five days.

In the context of performance monitoring, it is statistically more advantageous for a single caller to phone in several times with short queries, than to make a single, 20-30 minute call where all of their questions can be answered. For the call-centre employee, a series of short calls increases their performance statistics by increasing the number of calls they complete and decreasing their average call length. Especially in the case of Service Canada, this system seems to contradict the explicit mission to provide 'knowledgeable, one-stop, personalised service to Canadians' (Service Canada 2006: 8). Instead, it is in the workers' interests to answer a caller's questions as superficially as possible and encourage them to call back at another time. In this context, it seems clear that the application of standardised performance monitoring creates a situation in which technological control structures the pace of the work environment without attention to the quality of the services provided.

The Challenges of Standardised Service Delivery

While the pace of work at the phones is heavily monitored and expectations regarding employees' efficiencies are high, there is little time provided for workers to update themselves on new departmental procedures, legislative changes affecting service delivery, or other matters. Only about a quarter of respondents (24%) felt that they had adequate preparation time each day. Workers reported that they are allotted 15 minutes a day 'to read up on our information bank, which is national, to update ourselves in our emails, and to read a whole bunch of readings related to work...'. Respondents routinely referred to the complexity of their work and the difficulty of providing a good service to the public. Because the work is 'too complex and there is too much to read,' many interviewees reported that they used personal time to review material so that they could be confident that they were providing accurate information to callers.

Taken together, this information on the speed-up in the pace of work illustrates the results of imposing performance monitoring in public sector call centres. It is telling that workers who had previously worked in a private sector call centre were less likely to agree that they worked in a stressful environment. The practices that are routinely used to monitor performance in private sector call centres may not translate effectively to delivering services in the public sector.

Private sector contact centres are often oriented towards selling a product, or gathering information about consumers. By contrast, public sector call centres are the nexus through which citizens (or potential citizens) are able to contact their government and access government services. Call centre workers understand that in their capacity as 'information specialists', they perform a valuable service for Canadians, often providing information and services that make a considerable difference in people's lives. In many cases, these interactions are complicated and require a detailed exchange of information. Especially in the case of agencies like Veterans Affairs and Citizenship and Immigration, callers may have complex case histories that need to be understood in order for services to be delivered effectively. In these cases, the conflict between quotas and the time allotted per call, and quality and efficiency is a constant source of tension:

Time around calls can get pretty tense. It sometimes feels like you have no breathing room ... There's something like [a] 300 seconds goal to finish calls; but that's not the reality. It just doesn't always work like that. We have some people with real issues and sometimes they need to vent frustrations, ask a lot of questions, or they need a lot of information explained because they're just not familiar with the procedures.

The disconnection between workers' understandings of and commitment to the notion of 'public service' and their experience of time pressures and heavy monitoring is reflected in the expectations that the Canadian public has of government telephone services. In focus group research asking Canadians about their expectations for telephone-based government services, the Institute for Citizen-Centred Research found that 'participants expected agents to be polite, friendly and resourceful, demonstrating empathy for the callers.' They wanted to know that the person at the other end of the telephone was doing everything he or she could do to help them and not simply trying to 'get rid of us' (Institute for Citizen-Centred Research, 2006:14). Focus group participants also identified the need for telephone agents to demonstrate 'the patience to listen, particularly with regard to a situation that is difficult to articulate, or allow the caller to finish before being transferred somewhere else' (ibid:24). While most call-centre workers surveyed expressed a desire to meet these expectations, they reported increasingly feeling pressured by the need to meet externally determined performance criteria.

Unlike their counterparts in the private sector, fewer than a third of respondents (30%) report that they work from pre-established scripts. Based on interviewees' reports, this appears to be the case because the interactions are too complex to be easily scripted. Instead, these public services must negotiate complex interactions accurately, without a script, but within a designated time period. The result is that this job requires a high level of skill, but workers still lack the flexibility, the resources and the autonomy that would allow them to feel that they are helping the public effectively. Subjecting the work of public service call-centre employees to time monitoring and intensification not only devalues the service these workers provide, but may also erode the public's confidence in their government services.

The emphasis on speed of service seems to be particular stressful for employees who work in French only (16%), the majority of whom also speak French at home and are likely native Francophones. Those who work in French, are substantially less likely to agree that the pace of their work is manageable, that they can take regular breaks, or that they have some control over the pace of their work. They are also less likely than Anglophone workers to report working from pre-established scripts. One Service Canada employee explains why working in French simply takes longer:

The information is there, you just need more time to look for it and integrate it. Because our French clients they have French documentation, but we are a lot faster in English because we are used to it and the English documentation is easier to access. In French or in English, things are termed this or that way.

Another bilingual worker located outside of Québec explains that:

> …we are trained in English. We are not trained in French. The terminology kills us, really. Completely. Because, it's not… [the same]… see I am Acadian, not 'Québequoise'. Our French is not the same … [as] the one in Québec. The terms we use are not the same. So if I have a client that calls from Québec, on line, who has the proper terms, the right terminology, I am completely lost.

As Budach et al. (2003) argue, being bilingual in a standardised environment like a call centre is effectively 'being unilingual twice over, with each [language] being used in a standard, normative form' (Budach et al, 2003:619). Multilingual agents in call centres often draw upon a complex set of skills to interact in one language and interface with a computer programme in another language (Belt et al., 2000), and they do so under intense time pressures and heavy monitoring. In New Delhi, India, for example, call-centre workers are trained to adapt their speech patterns and accents to blend with those of their North American clients, masking both their geographical location and more significantly, their own identities (Mirchandani, 2004). As required by their jobs, these workers undertake mandatory cultural training, learning to adopt accents and diction appropriate to the clientele they are serving. Moreover, this adoption of new occupational identities affect the workers' core relationship to the labour and production process, raising questions regarding their class location, class consciousness and commitment to workplace change (Huws & Dahlmann, forthcoming). These workers straddle the line between the skilled and the deskilled as they often find themselves having to think 'on their feet' and respond quickly, thereby drawing on their knowledge and skills, while carefully balancing their need to remain 'on script'. They are further constrained by the regular evaluation of their heavily-monitored performance and the need for a courteous and respectful response to the client. The same effect is found in Canadian public sector call centres, where, in addition to the numerous tasks workers juggle simultaneously, Francophone workers must negotiate training and instructional materials developed in English, and translate and interpret across a variety of regional dialects.

According to many of the call-centre workers interviewed, the techniques of supervision and micro-management are primary sources of stress on the job, leaving workers looking over their shoulders and fearful of drawing on their own experience and intelligence in responding to calls. Sixty-three percent of respondents report that they are routinely monitored—a practice that is common in large call centres. A number of workers commented on the heavy-handed intensity of the monitoring, suggesting that the techniques went well beyond what they would expect for quality control and assessing performance. For example, workers referred to 'The "Big Brother" aspect of the call centre', the feeling of 'being under a microscope', and the 'zero tolerance' for minor infractions such as being late by a minute. For many, these conditions were more stressful than the work itself. One respondent described being 'timed and required to explain every moment of the day outside of breaks to the point … [of harassment].' Another worker expressed the view that the management system is not simply stressful, but is 'overwhelming' in every way and another referred to the supervisory and management system as 'a dynamic of surveillance.' One worker described it in these words:

...it's the police. And the police is very serious... It's really like the police; it's
surveillance. It's like at school. But there is a lot of policing, in the sense that
they impose things on us, norms toward people, certain sentences we have to
say. Extremely ridiculous. Like, ... robotised. ... but if we didn't say it, we lost
points. And it was a big thing.

Overall, the result of a pace controlled via technology and high levels of time-accountability is a high-stress work environment.

Compounding the surveillance by management, the spaces of work have become increasingly compressed, with workers seated back to back in crowded cubicles. Workers complain that their workstations are in 'open cubicles', or 'not closed off enough', and that their 'neighbours are too close.' Only about a third of workers (36%) indicated that they are satisfied with the level of privacy in their workplace. With four agents to each cubicle, one worker described the workspace as resembling 'veal pens more than work stations.' As one respondent commented, 'the environment we work in could be likened to a "sweat shop". The work itself is manageable, it's the environment ... that's hard to work with or in.'

Under these conditions and 'shackled to a phone', workers say that their work is made to feel 'like a production line' rather than a government service. The working conditions are reminiscent of a Fordist assembly line, as one worker suggests:

I call it a 'factory of voices.' That's all it is. Instead of assembling parts for cars, you're
just processing people or processing calls - 'a factory of voices'. Everybody is
sitting there in their little stalls talking and producing customer service.

By comparing their work settings to factory-like conditions and by characterising their work as 'repetitive, stressful and tiring', these workers' sentiments resonate with the findings of Belt et al. (2000). Their characterisation of call-centre work as similar to that of an assembly line contrasts sharply with the popular conception of work in the public service as reasonably autonomous, high-skilled, white-collar administrative work, and further obfuscates the skills and qualifications of workers in call centres.

Conclusion

The implementation of a call-centre delivery model has substantially transformed the working conditions and experiences of Canadian public service workers. This workplace transformation has taken place as part of the transition toward a globalised economy and the adoption of neoliberal government structures. In the past, the importance of meeting the public face-to-face to attend to diverse and complex needs related to various forms of legislation was the force behind public servants' careers. Canadians had easy access to public service as rights of citizenship. Today, however, new work structures and managerial techniques condition the civil service, transforming the growing number of workers in public service call centres from members of a 'helping' profession to simple bureaucrats paced by advanced technologies and monitored by a super-bureaucratic management. Regardless of the complexity of the questions and problems brought forward by members of the public, call-centre workers must respond to them while remaining mindful of the efficiency measures utilised by their superiors to assess their performance. As a result, the structure under which they operate forces them to offer pat answers and draw upon a formulaic inventory of responses or risk admonishment by their superiors.

In the context of the public sector, the promotion of call-centre jobs replaces the notion of the civil service position as allowing for a degree of autonomy and a modicum of decision-making, based on the educational credentials and career orientation of the civil servant. Within the structure and format of the call centre, the 'civil servant' has become a bureaucratised, standardised employee. Call centre employment destabilises the notion of 'serving' the public and replaces what were formerly secure and well respected positions with precarious, primarily lower level, bureaucratic jobs. Under these conditions, the notion of public 'service' is linked to the idea of interchangeable employees offering standardised interactions with the public. In this process, these standardised interactions then 'stand in' for public service.

© Norene Pupo and Andrea Noack, 2009

ACKNOWLEDGEMENTS

This research was supported by the Social Sciences and Humanities Research Council through the Initiatives on the New Economy Program, Research Alliance, *Restructuring Work and Labour in the New Economy*. This project would not have been possible without the support of Howie West, Public Service Alliance Canada. Research assistants at the CRWS, including Severine Minot and Jonathan Norris also contributed to the completion of this project.

REFERENCES

Akyeampong, E. (2008) 'Unionization', *Perspectives on Labour and Income* , Statistics Canada, Catalogue Number 75-001-XIE, August:5-9

Akyeampong, E. (2002) 'Unionization and Fringe Benefits', *Perspectives on Labour and Income*, Statistics Canada, Catalogue Number 75-001-XIE, August:1-10

Belt, V., R. Richardson & J. Webster (2000) 'Women's Work in the Information Economy: The case of telephone call centres', *Information, Communication & Society* 3(3): 366B385

Belt, V., R. Richardson & J. Webster (2002) 'Women, Social Skill and Interactive Service Work in Telephone Call Centers', *New Technology Work and Employment*, 171, March: 20-34

Broad, D. & W. Antony (eds) (2007) *Capitalism Rebooted? Work, Welfare and the New Economy*, Halifax: Fernwood Publishing

Buchanan, R. (2002) 'Lives on the Line: Low-Wage Work in the Teleservice Economy' in F. Munger (ed) *Labouring Below the Line: The New Ethnography of Poverty, Low-Wage Work, and Survival in the Global Economy*, New York: Russell Sage:45-72

Buchanan, R. (2006) '1-800 New Brunswick: Economic Development Strategies, Firm Restructuring, and the Local Production of "Global" Services' in V. Shalla (ed) *Working in a Global Era: Canadian Perspectives*, Toronto: Canadian Scholars' Press:177-197

Budach, G., S. Roy & M. Heller (2003) 'Community and Commodity in French Ontario', *Language in Society* 32: 603B627

Evans, B. & J. Shields (1998) *Shrinking the State: Globalization and Public Administration Reform*, Halifax: Fernwood Books

Glucksmann, M. (2004) 'Call configurations: varieties of call centre and divisions of labour,' *Work, employment and society* 18(4): 795B811

Hoschchild, A. (1983) *The managed heart: Commercialization of human feeling*, University of California Press: Berkeley

Huws, U. (2003) *The Making of a Cybertariat: Virtual Work in a Real World*, New York: Monthly Review Press

Huws, U. & S. Dahlmann (Forthcoming) 'Global Restructuring of Value Chains and Class Issues', in N. Pupo & M.Thomas, eds, *Interrogating the New Economy: Restructuring Work in the 21st Century,* Toronto: UTP HigherEducation

Institute for Citizen-Centred Research (2006) 'Results of Focus Group Research on 'Answering the Call: Improving the Telephone Channel for Canadians', Fleishman-Hillard Canada. Accessed on March 27, 2009 from http://www.contactcentrecanada.ca/media/77604/telephonyexecutivesnetworkgroupreport.pdf

McBride, S. (2001) *Paradigm Shift: Globalization and the Canadian State*, Halifax: Fernwood Publishing Company

Mirchandani, K. (2004) 'Practices of Global Capital: Gaps, Cracks and Ironies in Transnational Call Centres in India', *Global Networks* 4 (4), 355-373

Mulvale, J. (2006) 'Solidarity Forever' in Cyberspace? Responses of the Labour Movement to Information and Communication Technologies', in D. Broad & W. Antony eds, *Capitalism Rebooted? Work, Welfare and the New Economy.* Halifax: Fernwood Publishing

Panitch, L. & D. Swartz (2003) *From Consent to Coercion: The Assault on Trade Union Freedoms.* 3rd Edition. Toronto: Garamond Press:128-144

Public Service Alliance Canada (PSAC) (2006) Accessed on January 12, 2008 from: http://www.psac.com/bargaining/index-e.shtml

Pupo, N. (2007) 'Behind the Screens: Telemediated Work in the Canadian Public Service', *Work Organisation, Labour and Globalisation,* 1:2, Summer:155-167

Pupo, N. & A. Duffy (2007) 'Blurring the Distinction between Public and Private Spheres: The Commodification of Household Work—Gender, Class, Community, and Global Dimensions', in V. Shalla &W. Clement, eds, *Work in Tumultuous Times: Critical Perspectives,* Montreal and Kingston: McGill-Queen's University Press:89-325

Pupo, N. & A. Noack (Forthcoming) 'Dialing for Service: Transforming the Public Sector Workplace in Canada', In N. Pupo & M. Thomas, eds, *Interrogating the New Economy: Restructuring Work in the 21st Century,* Toronto: UTP HigherEducation

Sears, A. (2003) *Retooling the Mind Factory: Education in a Lean State,* Toronto: UTP HigherEducation

Service Canada (2006) *Service Canada Annual Report 2005-2006*, Government of Canada: Ottawa, ON. Accessed on March 27, 2009 from http://www.servicecanada.gc.ca/eng/about/reports/ar_0506/pdf/ar_0506.pdf

Siltanen, J. (2007) 'Social Citizenship and the Transformation of Paid Work: Reflections on Possibilities for Progressive Change', in V. Shalla &W. Clement, eds, *Work in Tumultuous Times: Critical Perspectives,* Montreal and Kingston: McGill-Queen's University Press: 349-379

Statistics Canada (2006) *Census 2006: Summary Tables.* Accessed on March 27, 2009 from http://www12.statcan.ca/census-recensement/index-eng.cfm

Statistics Canada (2005) 'Study: Who's calling at dinner time?' *The Daily,* Statistics Canada Ottawa, ON. Accessed on March 27, 2009 from http://www.statcan.gc.ca/daily-quotidien/050525/dq050525c-eng.htm

Treasury Board of Canada (2005) *The Human Resources Environmental Scan for the Public Service of Canada: Identifying Current and Future Human Resources Needs,* Ottawa, ON: Government of Canada. Accessed on March 27, 2008 from http://www.tbs-sct.gc.ca/res/esae-eng.asp

Van Jaarsveld, D., A. Frost & D. Walker (2007) 'The Canadian Contact Centre Industry: Strategy, Work Organisation and Human Resource Management', *The Global Call Centre Project.* Accessed on March 27, 2009 from www.gccproject-canada.com

In spite of everything:
Professionalism as mass customised bureaucratic production in a Danish government call centre

Pia Bramming, Ole H. Sørensen and Peter Hasle

Pia Bramming, Ole H. Sørensen *and* **Peter Hasle** *are all senior researchers at the National Research Centre for the Working Environment in Copenhagen, Denmark.*

ABSTRACT
This paper presents a study of the consequences of the transformation of part of the Danish Tax and Customs Administration (TAX) from a traditional white-collar public administration into a call centre. TAX participated in the study using 'Amica' testing methods aimed at improving the psychosocial working environment in call centres. The results showed a surprising and rapid development from a situation where employees reported a stressful and unsatisfying work environment to one where the organisation had taken a giant stride towards improving the work environment, involving a major shift in leadership and employee identity. The paper discusses this change from a traditional white-collar model to a 'mass customised bureaucratic' production one in a New Public Management setting that focuses on cost reduction, customer orientation, performance monitoring and documentation.

Introduction

Call centres have acted as a pivotal point in the international economic development of the last decade, forming part of a trend towards increasing globalisation and embodying the digital revolution that has contributed to a transformation in worldwide economic conditions (Rainnie et al., 2008). Technological innovation has reframed the terms of doing business by increasingly making geographical distance something negotiable. (Ellis & Taylor, 2006; Rainnie, Barrett, Burgess, & Connell, 2008). Globally speaking, the supply of labour keeps increasing while the costs of labour keeps decreasing (Bristow, Munday, & Griapos, 2009; Glucksmann, 2004; Taylor & Bain, 2007) and the call centre aims to utilise the existing supply of diversely skilled labour to maximum advantage. These changes are creating new conditions and forms for work, organisation and productivity (Ellis & Taylor, 2006; Rainnie, Barrett, Burgess, & Connell, 2008; Taylor & Bain, 2007), where the organisation has to deliver the highest possible output at minimum costs whilst also coping with change, ambivalence and immateriality in the pursuit of innovation. The concept of New Public Management (NPM) adapts commercial management techniques found in the private sector for use in the public sector. NPM reforms the public sector by using the market as a dynamic, governing principle. It gives prominence to market-based forms of organisation: privatisation, customer relations, outsourcing, downsizing and industrial production techniques such as lean production.

In order to obtain a grasp of how the customer is constituted in public services, Frenkel et al (1998) introduced the concept of 'mass customised bureaucracy' to denote a hybrid form of organisation while pinpointing the specific problems of call centres. A 'mass customised bureaucracy' balances 'standardisation of processes and products', aimed at lowering unit costs through scale and transaction economies, and 'customisation', aimed at generating revenue by focusing on individual customer requirements' (Frenkel et al., 1998:958). Frenkel et al consider mass customised bureaucracy as a form of work organisation that is both bureaucratic and organised along the lines of a knowledge-intensive organisation. The distinguishing feature of mass bureaucracy is that the combined effects of cost and customer orientation impact all job relations, creating a job function that is essentially based on the ability of each employee to connect with the customer and a dependency on micro-management through coaching, aimed at perfecting productivity in this individualised mass-production model. The 'core' of the mass bureaucratic organisation is the customer relationship. In contrast, the 'core' of a traditional bureaucracy is the rule.

When the customer and the customer relationship are placed at the core of the work arrangement, this has consequences for work organisation and changes skill demands. Research shows that the implementation and use of call centres in customer services often affects job quality negatively (Bain et al., 2002; Batt, Hunter, & Wilk, 2002; Holman, 2003; Sprigg & Jackson, 2006). Typical consequences are deskilling and increased control and monitoring. However, the trend is not unambiguous (Ellis & Taylor, 2006; Schönauer, 2008). Some ambiguities are pinpointed by Schönauer in a recent study of restructured public sector call centres. Fragmentation of employment and more heterogeneous employment conditions (status, contracts, wages, intensity, work time flexibility and job security) are the most distinct results of restructuring. Even though working conditions have worsened generally, public sector units have had more stable working hours and secure job tenure, compared with those in private, outsourced call centres (Schönauer, 2008:141). On the down side, compliance with quality standards and demands for 'commercial' and personal communications have necessitated the development of new skills (Schönauer:143).

A modern sociological interpretation of Schönauer's results is that the professional identity of the employees is a merging of economic and human developmental processes in the life project of the individual (Andersen & Born, 2001; Bason, Agi Csonka, & Nicolaj Ejler, 2003; Florida, 2005; Miller & Rose, 1997; Rose, 1999; Sennett, 2006). Work in modern life is a central element on the road to subjective self-fulfilment (Rose, 1999) and constitutes the locus where personal and professional identity is created in a mutual, internal, indefinable relation between the individual and the organisation (Florida, 2005; Lazzarato, 1996; Lazzarato, 2004; Raastrup Kristensen, 2007). A restructuring process from white-collar work to call-centre work changes the organisation of work and the demand for skills, thus actualising and changing the experiences, knowledge and emotion of the employee (Bauman, 1999; Lazzarato, 1996;

Lazzarato, 2004; Miller & Rose, 1997; Sennett, 1999; Sennett, 2006; Sundbo, 2007). Therefore, we would expect that a transition from white-collar work to call-centre work that involves restructuring of the work organisation and changes the demand for skills will transform the professional identity of the agents.

This paper presents a case-study-based account of the transformation of part of the Danish Tax and Customs Administration (TAX) from white-collar casework into mass customised bureaucratic production as a call centre (TAX-CC). Some of the most important constituents of call-centre work we identified are: the customer-citizen construct, leadership and management systems, and the professional identity of the employees.

The 'AMICA' study

The case study presented in this formed part of a Danish research and development project: 'Improving working conditions in call centres through benchmarking and networking' (in Danish abbreviated as 'AMICA')[1]. The aim of the project was to explore the possibilities for improving the psychological working environment for employees in call centres through the use of benchmarking activities in networks. The project is a three-year intervention project (2007-2010) financed by the Danish Working Environment Research Foundation. The project was implemented in cooperation with DTU (Technical University of Denmark), NRCWE (National Research Centre for the Working Environment) and TeamArbejdsliv (Team Work Life).

The AMICA project involved eight different call centres, representing different sectors: five in-house and three outsourced, seven inbound and one outbound, covering between 40 and 300 employees. The overall intention of the research project was to improve the working environment and job quality in call centres through benchmarking and networking activities. The working environment benchmarks draw on a psychosocial working environment questionnaire developed by The National Research Centre for the Working Environment in Denmark[2], supplemented by a number of questions developed specifically for call centres. These questions had beendeveloped by the research team in a previous research project (Mathiesen et al, 2006; Mathiesen & Wiegman, 2004).

The intervention approach emphasises the learning dimension rather than the control dimension of benchmarking methodology (Christensen & Bukh, 2007). In addition to benchmarks, the networking activities offered the call centres a context in which to discuss their work practices and benchmarking results. The intention was that through these network activities they could be inspired by other call centres. The network was conceived as an incitement and motivation for the participating call centres to implement specific changes by mimicking or learning from practices in other call centres with better benchmarking results. The establishment of the network as a specific 'agent of change' should be considered in light of the fact that many organisations regard their in-house call centres as a marginal appendix to the core of the organisation. Physically, call centres are often situated in remote locations, and organisationally and culturally there is

---

1   The project was funded by a grant from the Danish Working Environment Research Foundation.
2   The 'Copenhagen Psychosocial Questionnaire' can be downloaded from: http://www.
arbejdsmiljoforskning.dk/upload/english_copsoq_2_ed_2003-pdf.pdf

a tendency to consider their services and employees as secondary (Batt, Hunter, & Wilk, 2003; Richardson & Gillespie, 2003). This research project offered support to the call centres to develop internal change projects to improve working conditions.

Methodology

The planned activities of the project fell into several phases. A preliminary survey of all employees produced results which were discussed first in a series of workshops internal to each organisation and then in a benchmarking seminar where representatives from the different centres were brought together to share experiences and discuss solutions. These solutions were further developed in internal workshops at each call centres prior to the implementation of projects at each call centre. A second survey made it possible to assess progress, and these results too were discussed both in internal workshops and in benchmarking seminars involving all the call centres. Finally, follow-up assessments were carried out to evaluate the impact of the changes.

The participating call centres were chosen based on their expressed interests in improving their working environments. Eight call centres were selected (from a total of 14 that expressed an interst) based on 'maximum variation' criteria in terms of tasks, ownership, size, and geographic location (Flyvbjerg, 2001).

In the light of the results of the preliminary questionnaire, the company project group, consisting of both employees and leaders, were instructed to point out at least three areas where they considered that they were successful and could have something to offer other companies. They were also asked to identify three areas in which they believed they could learn from other companies. The researchers did not focus on comparisons between companies, but on how to further a learning process in each company by trying to find areas of possible inspiration. Call centres could take part only if they allowed both employees and leaders to participate in the internal project groups, because involvement was thought to be a very important part of the psychosocial working environment (Holman, Chissick, & Totterdill, 2002).

The qualitative case study material for the case of TAX-CC consisted of five personal interviews, of the key informant style (Andersen, 1995; Spradley, 1979), five focus group interviews with managers and employees (Halkier, 2002). Different kinds of focus groups were used - two groups consisting only of employees, one group consisting only of leaders and two mixed groups. This design took into account possible issues of bias and power. The focus group interviews were conducted after a period during which the employees had been asked to take pictures that captured their perceptions of their working environment and 'blog' about the pictures – a method we dubbed 'snap-logs' (Warren, 2002). In addition, a researcher visited TAX-CC on several occasions, observing work practices and conducting six informal 'walk-and-talk' interviews. This researcher was in continuous contact with the project group in TAX-CC, and had access to internal group communications such as notes taken by the project group while visiting other call centres in the network. The researcher also participated in three workshops and two benchmark seminars, where the group of call centres exchanged experiences and formed networks. An extensive body of data was collected to enable the research team to contextualise and follow the transformations as they were occuring. The drive towards an improved work environment in TAX-CC is seen as a processual translation (Callon, 1986) between the intervention and the existing practice. It was assumed from the beginning that the selected interventions would not necessarily have the desired effect, but would inevitably be modified through a process of translation (Callon, 1986; Mol & Law, 1994)

TAX-CC: from white-collar work to individualised mass production

...and then she said "Thank you, darling", and you know that kind of gratitude from a citizen makes you happy. I mean... you can actually help, by doing such a little thing. (Contextual interview, employee, 2007)

Vibeke works at the switchboard in TAX-CC in the small town of Ribe in Western Jutland. In Danish, the tax authority is called 'SKAT', which also means 'treasure' and is a generally used term of endearment meaning 'dear' or 'darling'. And, as Vibeke relates, citizens calling TAX-CC sometimes in gratitude or sometimes for the fun of it address her as 'darling'.

TAX-CC is the result of a large-scale public centralisation process. In spring, 2005, the Danish Parliament passed a law to reform the municipal system. A single body called TAX was created, uniting what were formerly a large number of separate tax and customs authorities. The former organisation consisted of several hundred formal authorities but the new tax authority system was organised as a so-called 'one stop shop', where citizens could approach the authorities over the phone, by mail or by digital self-service. The intended outcomes of the restructuring process were: economies of scale, more flexible resource utilisation, standardised and equal rulings, enhanced productivity and a more efficient work flow.[3] The TAX authority was divided into 30 local tax centres, a 'payment' centre in Ringkøbing and four customer centres at different geographical locations: Hjørring, Odense, Ribe and Roskilde.

Today, TAX-CC handles all inbound calls and emails from citizens, companies and advisers. The majority of its work consists of answering tax-related enquiries. On a yearly basis TAX-CC answers 3.9 million calls in person (83%). A further 1.4 million calls are either handled through automated telephone responses (with recorded answers) or are abandoned (17%). The initial target was to answer 70 % of the incoming calls. TAX also receives 350,000 emails per annum.

The workload in TAX-CC is estimated to require 400 full time employees per year. But only the equivalent of 321 full time employees were employed at the time of our research. During peak periods, the excess workload is handled by drawing in support from the 30 TAX centres. Around two-thirds of the employees of today's TAX-CC were formerly employees of municipal tax authorities, with around a third drawn from national tax authorities. We attempted to estimate the seniority of the staff based on an approximation between the known seniority of the formerly national employees and the unknown, but probable[4], seniority of the formerly municipal employees and concluded that 13% were between 40 and 50; 31% between 30 and 40; and 15% between, 20 and 30 years of age. We also concluded that 10% had between 10 and 20 years experience in the

---

3   http://www.skm.dk/publikationer/skat/skatau-januar2006/fusionen/. Speech by Minister of Taxation Ole Kjær January 6th, 2006.

4   This approximation is based on the HR-consultants practical knowledge of the case.

same employment, 15% between five and 10 years experience and that 13% were taken on in 2007. A non-replacement policy has been operating in the intervening periods so there were no employees with between two and four years experience. The average seniority among employees was thus high, with more than 60% of the employees aged 40 years or older and 30% 60 years or more. The great majority had few formal qualifications. They were trained as clerks in the municipal or national systems with supplementary tax courses. A small group had been trained as tax accountants and one was a tax lawyer. The employees as a whole represented a huge mass of experience, with some having had their basic training as clerks whilst others had a background in various services. The leaders were a diverse group as well. For some the job in TAX-CC was their first leadership experience, whereas others had also been team leaders under the old system.

When the merger was announced, each employee was offered the chance to express a 'wish' for the new placement that he or she would prefer. However, to retain their job, many had to accept whatever position they were offered. This in effect created two categories of workers: those who 'volunteered' and those who were 'transferred'. The trade unions negotiated the right for transferred workers to return to their former place of work (though not necessarily the same job) after one year. Volunteers, on the other hand, were contracted to their new positions for two years, after which they had the right to seek another post in the parent organisation if they were dissatisfied. The inconstancies in the treatment of these two categories of workers became the subject of a great deal of interest in the national media, and this anomaly kept the trade unions of the TAX employees busy and resulted in a great deal of resentment and frustration. Danish union density is high, at about 80% on average (Due & Madsen, 2008). We believe that the level of unionisation in TAX-CC reflects the degree of perceived trouble related to the restructuring and the rather heavy-handed relocation procedures. However the union aspect will not be discussed further in this paper.

Change in work organisation and work constitution

...But we still have all these people, who were forced to be here...And we know, that by the end of this year, they have 'served their sentence' and they will be gone.(Group interview, leaders/employees, 2007)

This quotation from one of out interviews captures the feelings of dissatisfaction which were prevalent when the study commenced, in 2007. In that year, the the greatest dissatisfaction expressed by the employees was an intense feeling of lack of influence over their job conditions and a feeling that the rigid control system was leading to poorer service for the citizens. They said that they felt they were being treated disrespectfully and that their opportunities for acting professionally in customer interactions had decreased. There was also widespread disrespect for the quality of leadership and management systems.

In 2008, the negative development seemed to turn around. The responses to the questionnaire showed improvements in the employees' perception both of working conditions and of their leaders. The yoke of control seemed to have lifted considerably. Social support from leaders had had its impact and the role and status of the call centre within the TAX organisation had become more clear and positive.

To gain an insight into the background of this positive development in TAX-CC we discuss below three themes: change in the constitution of the customer-citizen construct, change in the leadership and management system, and change in professional identity.

Change in the customer-citizen construct

Well, I have been happy to be here from the beginning. I have to admit. But again, I sought the job voluntarily, and you cannot compare the situation of those who are here by free choice with those who are here by force ... I like [the fact that] that your job does not pile up in big stacks of cases you should have done [any more]. When you are off, you are free. You cannot bring your phone home, so you do not have to speculate before Monday morning ... After 100-500 calls I sometimes have difficulties concentrating, but I like to talk to all these people. And I think there are a lot of nice people calling and you have a lot of nice conversations. I like to have this contact with people on the phone. And I am very satisfied when I am able to help the person calling. They are so thankful 'Oh, could you really help me like that'. It is nice that they are thankful and that you could help them without passing on the call – that you completed it yourself. (Group interview, leaders/employees, 2007)

TAX-CC illustrates how new customer strategies gain a foothold in the public sector through changes in work organisation and management. In the traditional tax organisation, the focal point was the taxation of citizens in general and not the individual citizen. In TAX-CC, servicing individual citizens is the major precept. Consequently, perceptions of the citizen and citizen relations are central to how the working environment is perceived. Earlier, the citizen was an abstraction rarely met in person. Today, the employees and leaders use the terms 'customer' and 'citizen' interchangeably. Because of this, we do not stick to a single term either, but in this paper use the term 'customer-citizen' when writing in 'the researcher's voice' but in interview excerpts we remain faithful to the original term used.

...how are you handling the customers? That is an important part of our work. That they should be treated differently, right? We know the difference between the upset and mad one, who blames us for his own mess, and the one who just wants to talk and tell you the story of his life, right? (Group interview, leaders/employees, 2007)

Employees now seem to 'invest' themselves in their relationship with the customer-citizen. The changes in the job constitution have created a demand for an emotionally-involved employee. This gives employees a feeling of job satisfaction, but also, because the interactions are continuously evaluated, personal interaction with the customer-citizen also contributes to goal-directed service. Employees have to handle the customer-citizen as a person met in conversation as opposed to an abstract number on a case. When TAX-CC was newly established in, 2007, the employees were in the process of figuring out how to invest their emotional and personal life in the job. This process was ambiguous because it both involved a more impersonal attachment to the job and a closer and more personal relation. In the next section, we will expand on this defining characteristic of the job, which is part of the problematic of individualised mass production in a bureaucracy; the employees must deliver a tailored service every time whilst also meeting requirements for a high degree of standardisation and efficiency.

Change in leadership and management system constitution

It is difficult to get into contact with the employee ... [they] are on the phone all the time. When there is something I would like to discuss with an agent, it can be difficult to find the time. And it works the other way around, for that matter. If an employee wishes to speak to the head of department, it is not always possible. I believe that the days where you feel you have have "contact" are the good days – the days with 'interaction' ... We get a lot of stuff from above [the management] but I believe that the conditions are negotiable. We live in a politically-managed system where we cannot always decide for ourselves ... It makes me angry and irritated sometimes, but that will not help me. I cannot change it. (Group interview, leaders/Employees, 2007)

The situation described in this quotation made established forms of leadership practices difficult. In the transformation, the leaders were as much 'under reconstruction' as the employees and had to reinvent themselves as leaders. This was not only because the employees in their teams were on the phone all day, but also because the new minute-by-minute management and monitoring systems were setting new conditions for the leaders.

I believe our heads of department are having a hard time because they are given a lot of work from headquarters. I feel they have difficulties in finishing what they started and – well, excuse me for saying so – are under a lot of stress. (Group interview, leaders/employees, 2007)

The changes in work organisation and the primacy of the customer-citizen left the leaders in a tight spot in 2007. The leadership tools they had used in the old organisation (mainly day-to-day discussions of decisions and yearly employee performance and development interviews) were of no help in the new system, where employees answered hundreds of calls every day.

The new work system made employees responsible for the way they used their individual personalities and the personality was identified as a potential source of efficiency and productivity (Callaghan & Thompson, 2002; Frese, Garst, & Fay, 2007). Under these conditions, the leadership relation became much more complex and channelled into short time bursts while the monitoring system became the most visible way in which the employees experienced management. The professional and social interaction, where norms for decisions had been enacted previously, were contested and almost gone. In 2007, the employees were especially dissatisfied with the lack of common breaks with co-workers that had emerged under the new system. Lunch was planned in such a way that an individual's lunch break could start at 11.30 one day and at 13.30 the next. Consequently, employees were unable to form 'lunch-groups' with their favourite co-workers. In, 2007, the 'common' daily coffee break was also contested after it was officially forbidden 'from above'.

A social atmosphere existed in the beginning – we had a 15-minute break every
morning. That was the only time we had any social activity in our department.
It is a shameful how they treat us – like children instead of grown-ups. (Group
interview, employees, 2007)

And if we gather more than five at a time, we are told we cannot have a common
coffee break (laughter). It is like World War 2. 'We will not tolerate gatherings
on the street corners' (laughter). Well it is actually terrible … (Group interview,
employees, 2007)

In, 2008, the coffee break issue was resolved. What seemed to be an insurmountable problem had been solved by shifting the opening hours by half an hour, thereby allowing for common social activities. In addition, 'daily morning gymnastics' were arranged from 8.15 to 8.30 every morning. The morning gymnastics and the morning meetings created frameworks for social and professional networking. The leaders gained a 'moment' every day in which they could pass on information and get in touch with the employees.

By rescheduling our opening hours – or more correctly the hours where the citizens
can reach us by phone – we have acquired the possibility for professional
meetings. It is so unbelievably important to stay updated, right? (Group
interview, leaders/employees, 2008)

However, the rescheduled opening hours reduced the possibility for social and professional meetings later in the day, because the changed opening hours meant that 'blue hours' (administrative time) later in the day had to be reduced. This resulted in an intensification of the phone work in the afternoon, even though the 'blue hours' weren't meant for socialising but for catching up on administration

By 2008, there was an improvement in the employees' general conception of their leaders, who had been relatively insecure and inexperienced the previous year, when the situation was as new for them as it was for everyone else. Employees showed respect for a leader who they thought was good at 'tampering with stuff' enabling them to feel less restricted by the rules and regulations. The leaders had had to learn how to manage the very stiff monitoring system and the digitally generated rosters and to adjust to a situation where the employees had to be very personal and empathetic in their interaction with citizens, and hence could be sensitive to impersonal and un-empathetic leaders and systems.

It has to do with mistrust – they believe we do not want to put in an effort. They may
even think we are just sitting there picking our noses, when we are busy on
the phones. It is so frustrating. And why? Because it shows a lack of trust from
above. (Group Interview, Employees, 2007)

In, 2007, we identified a tendency of low trust in the leadership system (understood as a combination of the rules, the planning system and the quality of decisions) mixed with a relatively high degree of trust in the leaders as individual people. In, 2008, this had changed into a situation where the employees had higher trust in the planning systems and their leaders' capability of handling the system. The organisation had gained experience and the leaders had demonstrated that they wanted to improve working conditions and support the employees. The leaders seemed to have succeeded in developing a more personal and direct relationship with their employees. In 2008, the leaders re-introduced 'listening in' on employees when they answered calls – a technique that, in 2007, had led to a lot of resentment. We can observe that the perception of the practice of listening in had changed over the intervening period from one of resentment to one that saw it as providing opportunities for learning. It seems that this change has come about as a direct result of enhanced trust in the leaders and their motives for using the techniques. This supports the conclusions of Holman et al (2002) who argue that the perception of control (e.g. listening in) is more positive when employees believe that its purpose is to improve learning.

....you have to see it [listening in] is as an opportunity to develop yourself, right? I like the fact that you can have a dialogue [with the leader] afterwards. It gives you a chance to talk about the concerns and contents of the specific call. 'This one you did well, but you could have gone a bit further by entering these systems...' It is just learning ... and I have had calls, where I said to him [the leader 'It was too bad you were not listening in here, because it was just like this'... (Group interview, leaders/employees, 2008)

The relation between leaders, systems and employees had softened and become more flexible, suggesting that the otherwise alienating control systems and the lack of 'trust signals' in the system had been re-interpreted. Employees interpreted their leaders' behaviour in more positive ways, and the leaders were more willing to subordinate the systems to the employees' needs and not the other way around. It seems that the leaders had implemented mass customised bureaucratic production by linking into the employees' sense of enhancing their actual work performance and by delegating control.

Change in professional identity

I think it is interesting, and the reason why it was so difficult in the beginning could be that we had colleagues, who just did not fit the tasks we [have to] solve. It is important that we get the right people for the job. You cannot have the kind of people engaged here, who like to become deeply absorbed in something. That kind of person does not fit a call-centre job. We have to have people who like action, and quick response – who are able to zoom in on the key problem more or less instantly, ask the right questions and give correct answers. I think a lot about that. When we have employees saying: 'this is me' then we have the right mix. And of course we do not have that yet, because we started the way we did. (Group interview, leaders/employees, 2007)

The changes in work and job constitution have had a serious impact on workers' identities and the relationship between the job and the person. The managers see it as a matter of the right 'fit' – it seems to them to be a question of identifying the person who believes the work 'is' me (Callaghan & Thompson, 2002). As previously noted, the new job relationships and forms of work organisation are defined by the way the agent engages with the customer-citizen, mediated by the organisation of work and the technological monitoring and performance systems. The restructuring of work has resulted in an emotionally-charged process in TAX-CC. Before the restructuring, the professional identity of the white-collar bureaucratic case worker was tied to a professionalism defined by correctness and deep knowledge of the subject matter. The organisational restructuring and the new 'customer based' strategy have created completely different conditions for developing a professional identity.

After the restructuring, new types of employees were recruited with no prior knowledge of the tax field. The 'old', experienced employees had to spend a great deal of time training these new colleagues. Peer training was perceived as a positive element both by old and new employees. However, in, 2007, the old employees were concerned about the professional quality of the work and the possibilities for sustaining their existing competences.

I have not read a single resolution since I came here and new resolutions (court judgements) are coming up all the time. You just feel that you sort of just sit there and tell people something, on a matter of high importance to their personal finances, without really having the newest resolutions from the courts and without having time to read up on the rules – just once in a while. You are using knowledge that is one and a half years old. (Group interview, employees, 2007)

The new form of organisation made peer conversations difficult in, 2007, with no common breaks and only scant possibilities for meeting and discussions. The experienced employees prided themselves on knowing their stuff by heart and giving correct answers to customers. In the new call-centre organisation, employees, on the one hand, have to answer an enormous number of routine questions which do not demand any deep knowledge but, on the other hand, must always be prepared to answer the occasional difficult question. The employees complained that the monitoring system measured only the length of the call without taking complexity into account. Management met these complaints with understanding but emphasised that the employees also needed to understand the service goals of the call centres – that customer-citizens expect a 'suitable service', which means that they should not feel dissatisfied if they are passed on to a more knowledgeable co-worker or even to an employee in one of the tax centres. The employees, however, felt that was unsatisfactory, professionally speaking, not to be able to answer the question themselves. Actually, they saw avoiding the need for a transfer as an extra service to the customer.

It is unsatisfying having to transfer a call. Especially if you have been talking for a while and feel sure that you would be able to finish it. Then another aspect turns up and you are left with no choice but to say: either call back or try someone who really knows what this is about. And that is really annoying both for you and the customer. You can choose to call back, and I do that once in a while, but sometimes you have too many post-it notes [to deal with] and then you have to pass it on, right?' (Group interview, employees, 2008)

The new employees felt that their possibilities for development had become frozen, to some degree. They had an exponential learning curve during the first period of employment and had to learn a lot of different things in a relatively short time. Subsequently, the challenge was to get 'to the next level' and they felt that the balance between learning and using what they had learned was unsatisfactory. The experienced employees felt that they used a more narrow scope of knowledge, but since they already had the basic knowledge - also about the non-routine 'stuff' - their frustrations differed from those of the new employees. However, both groups felt that there were dangers of monotony.

All the employees were challenged, professionally speaking, not because they did not want to talk to the customer-citizens, but because they did not feel they were properly equipped professionally, which made them afraid of not being able to continue delivering a quality service. 'It is difficult to sustain deep competences when there is also concurrent pressure towards keeping up the daily operations' (Employee AB, 2007).

The policies of TAX-CC dictate that difficult questions should be passed on to an employee in one of the tax centres. When an employee either answers or passes on the call the call is 'closed', so having long conversations turns up a smaller number of closed calls. This was perceived as unsatisfactory by anxious employees who felt they had the capability to solve a problem.

The question is whether I want to sit here in ten years time if it is like this. If I am constantly told that it is quantity rather than quality that matters, if I cannot finish my cases and take them all the way and if I am not given the time to do that - because it has to do with time as well - then I do not want to be here. Then I will use my 'job-return-right', because I have been in TAX for 30 years and I am not going to sit around acting as a switchboard. I really am not. (Group interview, employees, 2007)

The problem described was a perceived lack of control over essential features of the job, a feeling that the employees' knowledge and abilities were depreciated, and a fear that this was not a momentary but a permanent condition.

The situation has clearly changed since then. Judging from the reactions of the employees in 2007, we expected a high degree of turnover and disillusioned employees. But, instead, a shift in both relationship management and in the conception of what a professional call-centre employee had taken place.

Interviewer: 'Last year you were quite anxious that you might lose your deep competences?'

Employee 1: 'Something has been done about that. That has been taken care of and now we can attend courses.'

Employee 2: 'Yes, well, it is never going to be a call centre where the telephone service gives you time to go deeply into many things. You have to get used to that, which is the way in which we work. But we are allowed to attend good courses even if we want to learn something in a different area. That is extremely positive – it is just super, that you are allowed ... it is not difficult at all.' (Group interview, leaders/employees, 2008)

A new professional call-centre identity seems to have emerged. The adjusted ICT system has played an important part in achieving a better balance. It was debugged (or 'deloused', in the term used at TAX-CC). The telephone system was adjusted to provide a better fit, and the employees' demand for more flexibility was partially met. After the merger, all known symbols of competence, trust and case work were torn apart. The social system was left in a situation where the management system kept sending ambiguous signals that were often interpreted as expressions of distrust and degradation. But communications between the central and decentralised parts of the organisation now seemed smoother and marked by a higher degree of trust:

Today we experience that the planning department or other central departments say: 'let us try it, and not make a fuss about it. Let us just try it out and see if it works. If heads of department and employees believe it could make things easier, by all means let us try it!'(Group interview, leaders/employees, 2008)

The organisation seems to have been able to handle a substantial shift in professional orientation. The management systems have found a softer and more flexible form. The employees have obviously come to terms with the fact that a professional in a call centre must perform in terms of 'good figures'. They also need to balance the need for knowledge with speed and deliver a service which, on the one hand, is custom-tailored to the specific customer-citizen and, on the other hand, makes it a virtue to get each call closed in the shortest possible time. The employee has to assess the balance of routine calls and when to get involved in the difficult (and hence interesting) calls: 'to deliver the right service against the amount of calls.' In conclusion, we can say that the meaning of 'good figures' has been (re)negotiated, and monitoring and feedback now reflect this new compromise.

Concluding discussion

You could say that we are all in the same boat. We are working under equal conditions. That was different before. Maybe it is different depending on where you originally came from ... I am from the old municipal part of TAX, and some places you could say that people doing tax returns and people doing 'back-office' stuff were perceived differently. There was some kind of hierarchical difference. You do not get that feeling here, and that is great. (Group interview, leaders/employees, 2008)

From a change management point of view, one could claim that this is a conventional story about a management-initiated change process that was met with employee resistance. After a while, when the most resistant employees had been pruned, the changes and the new organisational structure were accepted. This may be true, but to us the interesting aspect of the story is how the work, the employees' professional identity, leadership and the citizen construct became constituted in new ways during and after the transition from traditional bureaucracy to mass individualised bureaucracy. A new constitution allowed employees to construct new meanings in work and to experience job satisfaction again – yet, in new ways whereby professional pride had been shifted from bureaucratic values to encompass the ability to solve citizens' problems as they arise and achieve 'good figures'. This new professionalism demanded that the employees gain knowledge of the 'anatomy of a call' and improve their perception how to handle people directly. Having gone through such a transformative process, the employees have had to cope with crisis and frustration, which some would say were a prerequisite for learning. But as frustration is easily accomplished without leading to learning it should not be a learning goal in itself (Cope, 2003; Deleuze, 2002). Without a clear goal, transformation could become frustration and nothing else. In the case of TAX-CC the goal was obviously the work in itself.

From a call-centre researchers' point of view, the case is interesting because it challenges the notion that the introduction of the call-centre model inevitably creates a detrimental working environment characterised by high levels of monitoring and low job discretion, as described in the introduction. Previous research has documented that it is possible to create work organisation in call centres characterised by high involvement and high job quality (Batt, 2000). The present study provides insight into how a call centre can embark on such a positive trajectory. The intervention project, AMICA, seemed to offer possibilities for learning that TAX-CC was able to use to remedy some of the problems originally created through the change process. The original organisational changes were perceived as unfair and disrespectful by the employees. In particular, they disliked the ways that the physical location was moved, discretion was severely reduced, monitoring was increased and the perceived possibility to perform professionally was considerably reduced.

During the intervention, the leaders became able to *balance* the hard data against a very personal leader-employee relationship that became centred on the concept of the citizen as a customer-citizen. This involved a major change in opening hours. It is rather unusual for call centres to reduce their valuable opening hours to create more time for co-worker interaction and direct management. This, and the reduced focus on monitoring, seemed to be perceived as important signals of trust and respect by the employees. In this process, the employees also changed their perception of professionalismand found a new source of job satisfaction in working with the customer-citizen relationship. Professionalism had come to encompass form as well as content.

Some contextual factors might help to explain why it was possible to deviate from (some) of the negative patterns normally found in call-centre research. One of the explanations is that the TAX-CC is a public administration without competition. Reports from TAX-CC conclude that citizens did not complain when opening hours were reduced. Another explanation is the general Danish industrial relations context. Tension between employees and employers is low in Denmark (Eurofound, 2003), and Danish employees are generally able to use their influence at work (Andersen, 2004). The tradition is to seek cooperation to find mutually-beneficial solutions to issues such as training, HRM and work design (Bicknell & Knudsen, 2006). In TAX-CC, the new leaders regarded the employees' critique as legitimate and acted to remedy some of the problems.

However, there is also a critical edge to this seemingly successful story. Even though the employees regained feelings of respect and trust, the assessment and monitoring systems still exist. The major part of the day is spent talking on the phone in a situation where discretion is low. The traditional pride in bureaucratic values is almost gone and it is possible that the employees who opted out could not live with this loss of professional identity. The remaining employees valued the fact that they had gained the possibility to detach themselves from work. Even though mass individualised bureaucracy focuses on the citizen relationship and customer satisfaction, this relationship only lasts until the conversation is over. So it is possible to value good interactions, dispatch the occasional bad ones and then move on, and there are no piles of unfinished work remaining at the end of the day. In the old case-based bureaucratic organisation, involvement was greater, for better or for worse.

One year might not be enough to determine whether substantial deskilling will occur. The new professional identity is still under construction. In the first year, most employees experienced a steep learning curve related to social and interactional skills. However, the experienced employees feel that more case work is needed to retain and develop their topic-specific knowledge. New employees cannot see how they can acquire the skills of their co-workers who have, 20-40 years of experience given the high workload and the large number of routine calls that have to be dealt with. If the dilemma between the need to produce 'good figures' and to learn by solving complex problems and participating in other learning activities is not solved, in a worst case scenario the new professional identity could simply be reduced only to that of a simple service worker. In that case, substantial deskilling and work segregation would be the result in the long run.

Consequently, it is hard to judge whether the AMICA intervention project was successful or not. Judged by the measurements of job satisfaction and other measurements of the psychosocial working environment, improvements were clear. But because both the fundamental constitution of work and the professional identity of the workers changed during the intervention, it is questionable whether the figures are comparable even though the measuring instrument was the same. Seen from the outside, it can be hard to understand how the employees shifted from a deep resentment over their lack of influence to a high appreciation of one hour off-time with colleagues, when the rest of their working day is still so tightly controlled.

Postscript: the story goes on

In March, 2009 a new organisational change was announced for the Danish Tax and Customs Administration. The call centre will now be subjected to substantial organisational restructuring. The four existing locations handling both business and citizen calls will be transformed into three centres, one of which, in Hjørring in the north of Denmark , will handle only business calls while the other two, in Ribe and Odense, will handle only calls from individual citizens. The location in Roskilde will be closed. This means that employees with citizen competences and business competencies will either be relocated or will have to develop new competences, respectively.
© Pia Bramming, Ole Sørensen and Peter Hasle, 2009

REFERENCES
Andersen, I. (1995) *On the Art of Doing Field Studies - An Experience Based Research Methodology,* København: Handelshøjskolens Forlag
Andersen, J.G. (2004) *Et Ganske Levende Demokrati,* Århus: Aahus Universitetsforlag
Andersen, N.Å. & A.W. Born (2001) *Kærlighed og Omstilling,* København: Nyt fra Samfundsvidenskaberne
Bain, P., A. Watson, G. Mulvey, P. Taylor & G. Gall (2002) 'Taylorism, Targets and the Pursuit of Quantity and Quality by Call Centre Management', *New Technology Work and Employment,* Vol 17, No 3:170-185
Bason, C., A. Csonka, & N. Ejler (2003) *Arbejdets Nye Ansigter - Ledelse af Fremtidens Medarbejder,* København: Børsens Forlag
Batt, R. (2000) 'Strategic Segmentation and Frontline Services: Matching Customers, Employees, and Human Resource Systems', *International Journal of Human Resource Management,* Vol 11, No 3:540-561

Batt, R., L.W. Hunter & S. Wilk (2002) 'How and When Does Management Matter? Job Quality and Career Opportunities for Call Center Workers', in E. Appelbaum, A. Bernhardt & R. J. Murnane (eds) *Low-Wage America. How Employers Are Reshaping Opportunity in the Workplace*, New York: Russell Sage Foundation:270-313

Bauman, Z. (1999) *Globalisering,* København: Hans Reitzels Forlag A/S

Bicknell, H. & H. Knudsen (2006) 'Comparing German and Danish Employee Representatives on European Works Councils: Do Differences in National Background Matter?', *Journal of Industrial Relations*, Vol 48, No 4:435-451

Bristow, G., M. Munday, & P. Griapos (2009) 'Call Centre Growth and Location: Corporate Strategy and the Spatial Division of Labour', *Environment and Planning*, Vol A, No 32:519-538

Callaghan, G. & P. Thompson (2002) '"We Recruit Attitude": the Selection and Shaping of Routine Call Centre Labour', *The Journal of Management Studies*, Vol 39, No 2:233

Callon, M. (1986) 'Some Elements of a Sociology of Translation: Domestication of the Scallops and the Fishermen of Saint Brieuc Bay', in J. Law (ed) *Power, Action and Belief: A New Sociology of Knowledge? Sociological Review Monograph*, London: Routledge and Kegan Paul:196-233

Due, J. & J.S Madsen (2008) 'The Danish Model of Industrial Relations: Erosion or Renewal?', *Journal of Industrial Relations*, Vol 50, No 3:513-529

Ellis, V. & P. Taylor (2006) '"You Don't Know What You've Got Till it's Gone": Re-Conceptualising the Origins, Development and Impact of the Call Centre', *New Technology, Work and Employment*, Vol 21, No 2:107-122

Eurofound (2003) 'EuroLIFE interactive database'. Accessed on June 10, 2009 from http://www. eurofound.europa.eu/areas/qualityoflife/eurlife/index.php.

Florida, R. (2005) *Den Kreative Klasse - og Hvordan den Forandrer Arbejde, Fritid, Samfund og Hverdagsliv,* Randers: Klim

Flyvbjerg, B. (2001) *Making Social Science Matter: Why Social Inquiry Fails and How it Can Succeed Again,* Cambridge: Cambridge University Press

Frenkel, S.J., M. Tam, M. Korczynski & K. Shire (1998) 'Beyond Bureaucracy? Work Organization in Call Centres', *The International Journal of Human Resource Management*, Vol 9, No 6:957-979

Frese, M., H. Garst & D. Fay (2007) 'Making Things Happen: Reciprocal Relationships between Work Characteristics and Personal Initiative in a Four-Wave Longitudinal Structural Equation Model', *Journal of Applied Psychology*, Vol 92, No 4:1084-1102

Glucksmann, M. (2004) 'Call Configurations', *Work, Employment and Society*, Vol 18, No 4:795-811

Halkier, B. (2002) *Fokusgrupper,* Frederiksberg C: Samfundslitteratur & Roskilde Universitetsforlag,

Holman, D. (2003) 'Phoning in Sick? An Overview of Employee Stress in Call Centres', *Leadership & Organization Development Journal*, Vol 24, No 3:123-130

Holman, D., C. Chissick & P. Totterdell (2002) 'The Effects of Performance Monitoring on Emotional Labour and Well-Being in Call Centres', *Motivation and Emotion*, Vol 26, No 1:57-81

Lazzarato, M. (1996) 'Immaterial Labour', in Virno, Pa MH (ed) *Radical Thought in Italy*, Minneapolis: University of Minnesota Press

Lazzarato, M. (2004) 'From Capital-Labour to Capital-Life', *Ephemera - Theory & Politics in Organization*, Vol 4, No 3:187-208

Miller, P. & N. Rose (1997) 'Mobilizing the Consumer - Assembling the Subject of Consumption', *Theory, Culture & Society*, Vol 14, No 1:1-36

Mol, A. & J. Law (1994) 'Regions, Networks and Fluids: Anaemia and Social Topology', *Social Studies of Science*, Vol 24:641-671

Raastrup Kristensen, A. (2007) 'Reconsidering Flexibility - How Employees Constitute Themselves as Individuals between Home and Work Life', Conference: Work, Employment and Society (WES) Aberdeen, United Kingdom, September 12-14, 2007

Rainnie, A., R. Barrett, J. Burgess & J. Connell (2008) 'Introduction: Call Centres, the Networked Economy and the Value Chain', *Journal of Industrial Relations*, Vol 50, No 2:195-208

Richardson, R. & A. Gillespie (2003) 'The Call of the Wild: Call Centres and Economic Development in Rural Areas', *Growth and Change*, Vol 34, No 1:87-108

Rose, N. (1999) *Governing the Soul - the Shaping of the Private Self,* London/New York: Free Association Books

Schönauer, A. (2008) 'Reorganising the Front Line: the Case of Public Call Centre Services', *Work Organisation, Labour & Globalisation*, Vol 2, No 2:131-147

Sennett, R. (1999) *Det Fleksible Menneske - Eller Arbejdets Forvandling og Personlighedens Nedsmeltning,* Beder: Forlaget Hovedland

Sennett, R. (2006) *The Culture of the New Capitalism,* Yale: Yale University

Spradley, J.P. (1979) *The Ethnographic Interview,* Orlando: Holt, Rinehart and Winston, Inc.

Sprigg, C.A. & P.R. Jackson (2006) 'Call Centres as Lean Service Environments: Job-Related Strain and the Mediating Role of Work Design', *Journal of Occupational Health Psychology*, Vol 11, No 2:197-212

Sundbo, J. (2007) *Oplevelsesøkonomi,* København: Samfundslitteratur

Taylor, P. & P. Bain (2007) 'Reflections on the Call Centre', *Work, Employment and Society*, Vol 21, No 2: 349-362

Warren, S. (2002) '"Show Me How it Feels to Work Here": Using Photography to Research Organizational Aesthetics', *Ephemera-Critical Dialogues on Organization*, Vol 2, No 3:224-245

Attracting customers through practising gender in call-centre work

Päivi Korvajärvi

Päivi Korvajärvi *is Professor of Women's Studies at the University of Tampere, Finland.*

ABSTRACT

The aim of this paper is to demonstrate and analyse various ways in which gender is used as a resource when call-centre firms and their employees create customer relationships. Drawing on interviews in a case study call centre it argues that men and women are understood to work differently from the point of view of attracting customers. Men are found important as individuals and through technology-related services, whereas women are conceived as resources through their association with certain products, not as individuals. Thus female gender as a resource is embedded in the commodified products.

Introduction

*It is with the customer that we have to build the contact so that you are able to
    sell something, or to serve them with the product. (Paula, customer service
    representative in a call centre, March 2005.)*
*Since market forces make their way into everything, we have to try to make a profit
    and we have to try to do it by hook or by crook.'(Linda, manager in the same
    call centre, March 2005.)*

These two short descriptions demonstrate the pressures that permeate everyday work in call centres. Every contact that includes a business act or providing advice to a customer forms a piece of the economic growth of the call-centre company. The contact the customer service representative Paula is talking about in the above quotatation is a view from the shop-floor. She implies that a certain kind of interactive relationship is necessary in order to promote a sale to the customer or to serve her or him. Linda, who has a managerial position, expresses the goal of profit-making very straightforwardly. Nonetheless, the aims of the shop-floor employee and the manager are close to each other.

My aim is to show and analyse the various ways in which gender works as a resource when call centres and their employees create relationships appropriately between the customers and the call-centre firm. The core issue addressed here is how employees in different levels of the organisation aim to attract and persuade customers and how they use gender in the fulfilment of this aim. This paper does not examine whether the activities of the call-centre staff are perceived favourably by customers or whether they are successful in terms of the numbers of business deals they conclude.

My argument is that the ways in which customers are assumed to be attracted are closely connected to cultural ways of understanding gender and to ways of using the voice in customer contact in call-centre work. I suggest that in call centres 'practising gender' is a crucial feature in the processes of creating competitive relations through speaking and using the voice in encounters with customers.

The usual view is that call-centre work carries a female label because the jobs in call centres are female-dominated numerically. In addition, interactive service work culturally carries a female label irrespective of whether the jobs are occupied by women or men. Furthermore, the structural features of the jobs refer to female arenas. In most developed countries, jobs in call centres are low paid and do not offer high prospects for career advancement. Thus call-centre work is in many ways feminised (McDowell 1997; Gray 2003).

However, there are also features that oppose the female label of call-centre work. The whole concept of call centres is imbued with the applications and advanced integration of information and communication technology which culturally have a male label (Webster, 2005; Mulholland, 2002). In contrast, it has been demonstrated that women employees in call centres also enjoy the use of technology since they have found that technology can offer positive future prospects in terms of job creation and thus promote the welfare of society in the longer term (Korvajärvi, 2004) . Call centres as working environments thus bear ambiguous and competing gender labels.

In the following, I first present the interactional contexts of the analysis, which includes an insight into the core features of call-centre work, the characteristics of interaction in the case study call centre, the frame of the analysis based on the conceptualisation of Barbara Misztal (2000; 2005) on different interactional realms, and a short description of the fieldwork. Second, I analyse the interviews and look for the ways in which gender is done in the customer service relations and where this takes place. Third and finally, in the frame of the different social spaces of call-centre work, I discuss the various ways in which the aims of attracting and convincing customers and practising gender intertwine. Crucial issues in this interaction are the significance of ways of using voice, the importance of the superiority of men and masculinities in call-centre work and the gendering of the product or service.

The interactional contexts of call-centre work

Speaking on the phone is the space where customer service representatives and customers meet each other. Through speaking and communicating, the customer service representatives need to create a state of mind in the customers such that they start to listen to and reply according to the aims set by the business targets. It is precisely the complexity of the constant fluidity of the communication, including the distance from the customers, which makes call centres an interesting case in the context of exploring the role of practising gender in interaction.

Customer service representatives and managers necessarily have to discover a variety of ways in which a call centre can attract customers. Even more, they have to identify the means that will capture the interest of potential customers. Thus employee skills are not only based on knowledge of the service or product that they are selling, marketing or providing advice about. Instead, skills and knowledge about how to convince the customers have become the central concern in call-centre work. Customer service representatives work at the interface between the firm and its customers.

Thus they have a front-line position which is – as suggested – the most important position for promoting the aims of the capitalist market economy (Frenkel, Korczynski, Shire & Tam, 1999).

Previous studies of call-centre work have focused mainly on the technologically-assisted ways in which work in call centres is organised. Consequently, research on call centres has been dominated by an examination of the managerial mechanisms in place in them. The strict control and monitoring of work has created the impression that call-centre workers are manipulated robots. However, earlier research has simultaneously also shown that employees exert resistance in call centres. Further, it has been shown that employees in call centres support managerial rules by modifying them in order to fulfil the aims set by management (eg Taylor, Mulvey, Hyman & Bain, 2002; Winiecki & Wigman, 2007), as the quotations from Paula and Linda at the beginning of this paper imply.

In spite of the huge number of studies of call centres, customer service representatives as agents have remained in the shadow in the research, and the interactive character of call-centre work as 'a *human relationship*' (Bolton & Houlihan, 2005 – italics in original) is under-researched. Indeed, only a few exceptional studies on call-centre work (Bolton & Houlihan, 2005; Frenkel, Korczynski, Shire & Tam. 1999; Winiecki, 2007) have brought up any more complex and variable aspects. Moreover, call-centre managers have mostly been treated as a group of people who unambiguously carry out their surveillance, control and monitoring of the work and operate as though their interests are directly opposed to those of the call-centre employees. In contrast to this, it has been suggested that managers in call centres do diverse tasks and may aim to 'soften' the strict rules of the call-centre system (Houlihan. 2001). Thus the research on call centres can be divided into those that follow a cost-efficiency logic and those that follow a customer-oriented logic (Taylor & Bain 2005).

In call centres, the core of the work content is characterised by high communication intensity. As has been said, 'communication is not just part of the job description, in essence it *is* the job description' in call centres (Cameron 2000:91 – italics in the original). Customer service representatives' daily activities consist of giving advice, clearing up uncertainties, selling, marketing and convincing, but also of chatting with the customers, listening to them and flattering them on the phone. Thus, apart from its high intensity, the critical characteristic of the communication is also its constant variability and fluidity.

Speaking with the customers is not, however, the only interactive component of the job in call centres. As in every job, there is also the social community of work where employees work together, and learn, support and chat with each other. Furthermore, within the social community of work, interaction is not only horizontal but also vertical. Managers communicate both with their employees and with each other. In these discussions, the ways of speaking and convincing customers are monitored. Thus the social spaces of the work organisation in call centres comprise both the social community of work and the communication with customers outside the organisation. However, the aspect of the social community of work in the sense of what happens among the employees is a matter which mostly goes beyond the questions discussed in this paper.

In call centres, the social space of interaction with the customers is usually twofold, as customer service representatives normally deal with both inbound and outbound calls. An inbound call usually implies a situation where the customer has questions or enquiries concerning a service or a product that she or he has purchased from a firm or an organisation which has outsourced the questions and enquiries to the call centre. In outbound calls, the customer service representative is usually selling or marketing a service or a product to people or giving an overview of marketing opportunities to a client organisation. These tasks may also be outsourced from other firms or organisations to the call centre. The interactive relationships between the customer service representatives and the customers are based on auditory perception through the telephone, supported by information and communication technology.

It is possible to clarify this complex interactive situation by reference to a conceptual approach that differentiates between the realms and styles of interaction.[1] Barbara Misztal (2000; 2005) differentiates between three realms of interaction: encounters, exchange and pure relationships. According to Misztal, these realms of interaction are dominated by corresponding interaction styles: politeness, sociability and intimacy.

In Misztal's model (2000:71) 'encounters' take place between people who do not know each other, as in call-centre work. According to her, the style of these encounters is based on politeness and civility and the content of the interaction is based on respectability. People keep their distance from each other and avoid emotional commitments during encounters. In addition, they use conventional and predictable rules when communicating with each other. Thus the encounters may take place anywhere and accidentally, but still everyone usually knows how to behave in these situations. As Paula's and Linda's accounts imply, however, interaction in call-centre work does not necessarily follow the implicit rules that everyone knows and follows. In particular, selling and marketing also demand emotional involvement instead of keeping a distance.

Furthermore, according to Misztal, although 'exchanges' take place between people who do not necessarily know each other, all participants know the roles that they represent. The style of exchanges is sociability and the content of the interaction is based on reciprocity. When interacting within the realm of exchange, people have certain aims and desires that they try to promote in mutual interaction. Even if they have to follow specific rules and norms, they are free to use the different rules that are available (Misztal, 2000:71). I view call centres as workplaces, and organisations in general, as spaces which typically are realms of exchange between people through sociability. However, interaction in call centres, and doing it 'by hook or by crook', as Linda said, also goes beyond reciprocity and the predictable roles of the participants.

In contrast with 'encounters' or 'exchanges', according to Misztal, 'pure relationships' take place between friends. The style of pure relationships is intimacy and their content is based on responsibility. People develop their own rules when interacting with their friends in the realm of pure relationships. Thus pure relationships belong to the area of life that is often called private life as opposed to life that is regulated outside individual

---

1   This approach was developed in the context of a discussion of trust. Its core idea is to comprehend the reconstruction of the social in society at large and particularly in relation to the possible developments of democracy in society. Nevertheless, I find it as a useful starting point in rethinking interactional processes in work.

aims. (Misztal, 2000) However, call centres are also arenas for creating emotional commitments not only between employees and customers but also between people and products or services.

Within each interactional realm, according to Misztal (ibid), people aim to maintain a balance with the corresponding style of interaction. This ensures that things proceed smoothly without disturbing breaks or conflicts. Furthermore, it means that people are able to anticipate what will come next, which helps assure the continuity and predictability of their activities. When a certain style is used during an interaction, people tie together an appropriate number of formal rules, scripts and legal guidelines with the informal and individual autonomy that they use to regulate their interactional environment.

Gender also takes place in interaction and gender is done in interaction (West & Zimmerman, 1987). Both gender dynamics and gender stability are based on collective and, at the same time, unreflective ways of practising gender (Martin Yancey, 2006). Symbols and images are also intertwined with practising gender (Gherardi & Poggio, 2007). Furthermore, gender dynamics are based in an unreflective cultural work which dissolves concrete ways of practising gender (Adkins, 2005).

Some studies suggest that in the case of creating proper relations in interactive service work in call centres, the unreflective images and normal daily procedures practised as a matter of course have a cumulative weight. However, the images and taken-for-granted facts are closely linked to, and intertwined with the assumed values of customers and client organisations. The assumed and explicit expectations of these customers and client organisations have an impact on the practices at work. Furthermore, the views of these customers and client organisations, as well as those of employees in different positions, are imbued with the images and the discursively produced facts that are pervasive in the society at large (Korvajärvi, 2004; Koivunen; 2006). Thus the concrete practices of doing gender and the gender discourses available in society are tightly bound together, as Martin (2006) has suggested.

The fieldwork and research site

The research material used here comes from a call centre to which other firms, mainly from the private sector, outsource their activities. In these conditions, the spectrum of competences required of the customer service representatives is wide. The inbound calls relate to help desks dealing with different topics such as Internet connection breakdowns in homes, the quality of particular products, such as mobile phones, and enquiries about the invoicing of various services or products. The outbound calls are concerned with selling and marketing different products and services such as Internet connections to individual citizens, advertisements in phone books for firms and candy for the retail trade, among other things. During the history of the call centre, the importance of inbound and outbound activities as the main business has varied. The trend during the data collection period, in 2005, was to slowly attach more weight to the inbound calls and this meant that more customer service representatives were replying to incoming calls and fewer were making calls to customers than in the past.

The call-centre employees in the case study organisation presented themselves to customers as representing either the client organisation or the call-centre firm, depending on the decision of the client organisation. Even though the call-centre employees' employer is formally the call centre, at the same time, however, the client organisations often define in great detail what the customer service representatives need to say and how they must say it. Thus the boundaries of the work organisation are fluid, because the content of the employees' activities is defined by actors outside the firm. From this point of view, the customer service representatives need to 'speak' in the voices of many different bosses and managerial strategies when they talk to customers. Furthermore, the rules of these exchanges and the definitions of the styles of interaction have to be based on the aims of the call centre and understandings of how its business is best promoted.

In this paper the amount of the data used is seemingly small. The empirical analysis is based on three interviews conducted in one call centre in March 2005. The interviewees represent different hierarchical levels: the CEO of the firm, a manager and a customer service representative. They are all women: Laura the CEO, Linda the manager and Paula the customer service representative. There were about 150 employees in the call centre at the time of the fieldwork, which, in the Finnish national context, is a big call centre. Roughly one third of the employees are men, including among the customer service representatives.

The selection of the three interviewees and the analysis was processed in relation to information that I have gathered and analysed in a larger number of call centres over a longer time period. I conducted fieldwork, including observations, but mainly interviews and discussions, in several different kinds of call centre between 1996 and 2005. In this particular call centre, the interviews took place in several phases between 2000 and 2005. During the first phase, in 2000-2001, I conducted 24 interviews. In 2003, I carried out a further six interviews with a research assistant. Later, in 2005, a younger colleague interviewed 17 employees. On each occasion, the interviewees were from different levels of the company: managers, supervisors and customer service representatives. The largest numbers of interviews were conducted with customer service representatives. All in all, there were 47 interviews from this call centre, of which 18 were with men and 29 with women. The interviews usually took place in a separate meeting room during working hours. Each interview lasted for about one hour.

The turnover in the call centre was high, particularly in managerial positions. This is why the interviews with managers and supervisors were mostly carried out with different people in each interview period. Only three employees were interviewed twice in the call centre between 2001 and 2005. Linda, the manager, is one of them. No employees were interviewed three times. We also made field notes, although it was not possible to do actual non-participant observations in this call centre. Thus we were not able to listen to phone calls with the customers or observe personnel meetings in the call centre, for example.

The three interviews used here were conducted in the most recent phase of the research. They were selected for several reasons. In earlier phases of the analysis it appeared that the expectations of the managers and the experiences of the customer service representatives of the demands of interaction were close to each other (as the quotations at the beginning of this paper indicate). Even though the managers and customer service representatives had opposite opinions on salaries, for example, they seemed to comprehend the content of the work and its demands along the same lines. This is why it was relevant to analyse in greater depth a small number of the interviews from people who work at different levels in the organisational hierarchy.

Earlier analyses have focussed on the corporeality of call-centre work from the point of view of the customer service representatives, the relationship of female employees towards technology, the positive feelings and evaluations of the female customer service representatives towards their work, and of the formal and informal cultures in call centres (Koivunen, 2006; Korvajärvi ,2002a; 2004). In all these analyses, gendered practices are brought in. However, thus far gender as a particular resource in everyday interactive service work in call centres has not been a central focus when call-centre work has been analysed.

The interviews include facts, experiences of and thoughts about the conditions and practices of interactive service work in call centres. This analysis concentrates on how employees in three different positions in the call centre make sense of their work in the context of creating relationships with the customers that will generate profit for the company. The interviews provide information on how the employees make sense of their ways of using gender in interaction with the customers. The analysis was carried out by carefully reading, re-reading and relating the interviews to the conceptual frames of the interactional realms and styles of practising gender.

Smiling exchanges on the phone

All three informants discussed interaction during their interviews, and all of them, including the CEO, also described the concrete activities demanded in everyday work. Both the manager, Linda, and the customer service representative, Paula, spoke about their views within the call-centre firm, whereas Laura, the CEO of the firm, also outlined the significance of the interactive elements of call-centre work from the perspective of people outside the firm. They all stressed the importance of voice and its nuances as a tool in call-centre work.

Laura told us about her relationships with CEOs in other call-centre firms of a similar type, who have joined forces to improve the value, reputation and appreciation of call-centre work in Finland. The problem is, as she said, that 'people [in general] do not understand this concept and it is conceived of as something odd'. In addition, markets in Finland are so small that call-centre firms simultaneously both compete and co-operate with each other. If an outsourced activity is large, for example, it is common for one firm to subcontract parts of the contract to its competitors. Thus competitors have an interest in co-operating in their goals of promoting confidence in the services of the sector as a whole. Laura sees it as part of her job is to enhance the general image of the call-centre industry.

Laura also gave us her views on the concrete requirements of call-centre work. She saw the work of the customer service representatives on the phone as hard mental work, 'our people make our factory'. But she also described the work as being physically hard because of the constant need to use the personal voice. This CEO linked the relatively large number of male customer service representatives to the tasks dealing with technology because many inquiries concern technical matters. The other thing that she directly related to gender, and especially to women, was low pay.

A thirty-year-old, quite uneducated man usually tends to do physical work, whereas a thirty-year-old woman usually tends to get a job in a call centre where possible. I don't believe that women are better. On the contrary, I think that men are often much better than women. It is a question of personality ... It is a cultural thing: 'Switchboard Sallies' (telephone operators) have always been women and I feel that working on the phone is thought to be more suitable for women.

When Linda, the manager, analysed the requirements set for customer service, she stressed the point that customer service representatives need to have suitable voices. The importance of the voice is emphasised from the first moment when new employees are recruited to the firm. The first recruitment encounter – after the selection of the applications, which are sent to the firm electronically by filling out a form on its website – takes place on the phone. During the phone call, the candidates' voice, ways of using the voice and styles of speaking on the phone are checked and assessed, among other things.

Setting requirements for the customer service representatives is not only the employer's task in the call-centre firm. The client organisations also have their say in who is recruited. They suggest what kinds of people, voices, ages or gender they would like to have to represent their services or products to the customers. The client organisation sometimes even listens to the voices of candidates, and decides what kind of image of their firm is projected through certain voices to the customers. However, the client organisations choose from amongst employees who already have a job contract with the call-centre company. Thus the formal recruitment of employees was in the hands of the call-centre firm.

Linda said that very often there is demand for a 'youthful' and sporty voice. However, insurance companies prefer to have more mature adult voices, 'people who have life experience and knowledge to talk not only on a very superficial level'. Furthermore, 'a smiling voice, a joyful voice, a captivating voice' are all in demand. 'What we don't want is a phlegmatic, passive, reticent voice or a voice in which you can't hear the employee smiling. Smiling is extremely important.'

When the interviewer asked Linda about the gender aspects of the work, she ironically explained that very often for technically-related services clients wish to have men, 'they want to have civil engineers and we always laugh and think "how many civil engineers can we get hired for doing phone work here?"' She went on to say that undoubtedly civil engineers with their male voices are not eager to do 'phone work', which certainly in this context is seen as women's work, even though the tasks would include giving advice on technical issues.

In addition, Linda described how some products that are marketed and sold from the call centre are seen as women's issues. For example, incontinence, gynaecological problems and sanitary towels are issues which are regarded as 'private', and this is why the clients want to speak to a women about such matters. Thus gender is embedded as taken for granted in clients' wishes. More precisely, the clients link gender with their particular products and services.

Linda also compared the educational background of registered nurses and civil engineers, whose education is equally long in polytechnic colleges. She mentioned that the call centre does employ women whose educational background is in health-care or nursing, whereas male civil engineers were thought to be impossible to recruit. Thus in the case of male engineers the education is regarded as too high-level for call-centre work whereas in the case of female nurses the same length of education is seen as appropriate for discussing and selling products thought to belong to private life.

Gender is also present in the assumptions and experiences that have emerged from feedback from customers. Linda said that older ladies like a low male voice:

A harmonious low tone of voice certainly sounds plausible, safe, masculine, and great.
I don't know ... anyway, there is something in it. It may very easily happen that they would also like to speak about other things than only the matter in question.

She says that she has also noticed that male customers do not like a 'sexist voice'. According to Linda, they like somebody who does not read from the paper but speaks with a natural voice,

a soft, motherly, womanly ... an emotional, motherly voice is a voice that opens up something in the male customers and results in business deals.

However, a proper voice type is not the most important thing.

It is the branch and the task. For example, in the insurance policy campaigns, a youthful voice does not work at all.

In Linda's interview the stress is not only on the ways that employees and customers interact. She thinks that the interaction is not just determined by people – employees, client organisations and customers. The products or services and their gendered images also direct who, and which kind of voice, should be recruited for each different task.

The opinions of Paula, the experienced customer service representative, did not differ dramatically from the opinions of the manager. For her, gender means firstly the division between women and men in the labour market. When the interviewer asked, 'what is your opinion: why are there more women than men in these jobs?' The laconic reply was: 'the wages'. However, immediately after saying that, she started discussing the voices:

In many projects it would be good if there were men, good male voices. It is always convincing, you could even sell sand in the Sahara with a man's voice. If the male voice is good, if it articulates well, speaks slowly and the voice is cool, polite and convincing, it sells anything.

Paula thought that from the point of view of the firm it would be better if there were more men. However, the obstacle was the low wages.

We have had many really good men who have had really good voices. However, at some point they have left because of the wage.

She also emphasised that the voice is the only thing that can have an effect on the phone. 'We cannot use our body language the same way it can be used in "normal" selling.' Paula prefers to have men as her colleagues. In addition, according to her, men's voices are irresistible and superior compared with women's voices in customer service work. When the interviewer asked whether Paula uses different voices and whether she changes her voice, her answer did not concern the voice any more.

> *Firstly, you have to learn how to approach the customer. The most important thing is that you listen to the customers, what they say and know to ask the right question at the right moment. To listen to what the customer says is the most important thing. You have to somehow find such a kind of contact that the customer and I go onto the same wavelength so if the customers start to listen, they soon start to think that this offer would be fine for them.*

This is very much in line with what is called 'emotional work' (Hochschild, 1983) that aims to create a proper state of mind in other people. Paula explained further:

> *You need to speak up clearly and in an understandable way. The most horrible thing is if you say 'I don't know'. The customer service representative does not need to know everything but then she says [should say]. 'One moment please, I'll find out'.'*

Thus, successful interaction was not only about ways of using the voice but also ways of achieving a confidential relationship with the customer. Both a suitable voice and appropriate substantive replies to the customers, just in time, were, according to her experience, the ways through which a successful contact was possible. This has resonance with Bolton's and Boyd's (2002) suggestion that the term 'philanthropic emotional labour' is appropriate to describe the situation when the customer service representatives continuously calculate the customers' expectations. At the same time the employees are tightly controlled by the customers, as also suggested by Zapf, Isic, Bechtoldl and Blau (2003).

   In short, the CEO, manager and customer service representative were pretty unambiguous in their views on the work contents and work requirements in call centres. Accordingly, it seems that the employees in different hierarchical positions do not necessarily have opposing views on what the core aspects of work are. On the contrary, they seem to agree on certain aspects: the importance of how the voice is used, the significance of the superiority of men and masculinities in call-centre work and the gendering of products or services. It is this complexity to which I turn more closely in my concluding remarks.

Concluding discussion

Speaking with customers is located in the realm of pure relationships, especially according to the CEO and the manager in these interviews. From their points of view, phone calls are exchanges in which the customer service representatives have conscious and predictable aims. However, the ways in which they achieve these aims – of reaching a deal with the customer – are based on the performance of the customer service representatives through their voices. In contrast with the CEO and the manager, Paula, the customer service representative, stresses the coolness, politeness and careful listening to the customers which indicate that predictable styles of encounters are useful in the interaction with customers.

It is striking that all of the interviewees stress the superiority of men in call-centre work. For Laura, the CEO, men are often better at call-centre work because their personalities are more suited for the work. Also for Linda, the manager, men are desirable for call-centre work. In her opinion, men's education in engineering is more valuable than women's education in nursing. Further, Paula, the customer service representative, appreciates the voices of men as successful tools for selling anything. She would also like to have more male colleagues.

The views that an engineering education is more valuable than education in nursing and the desire to have more male colleagues reflect gendered discourses that are often used routinely. Finland has a reputation for promoting gender equality. However, at the same time, women and femininities are regarded as something negative in work. Male bodies, male voices and men are appreciated in female-dominated workplaces. Women's activities are not celebrated but, on the contrary, are hardly mentioned. However, at the same time, it is women who are considered as 'gender', whereas masculinities and men are silenced as gender (Korvajärvi, 2002b). Similar kinds of gender characteristics were also found in Italy in a study on women's entrance into supervisory or middle-management positions in male-dominated workplaces (Gherardi & Poggio, 2007).

The culture around call-centre work seems partly to repeat the characteristics that are familiar from other work contexts, as Kate Mulholland has also suggested (2002). Women's contributions are not particularly valued. However, these women interviewed at different levels of the call-centre hierarchy hold the striking shared view that men and masculinitiesconstitute the real resources in interactional work with customers. In contrast to other analyses, particularly in service work, men are reflectively appreciated in call-centre work.

However, women are also needed in the call centre. They are connected to certain products and services. Thus men are valued as individuals, as personalities or as good voices, whereas women's value is mediated through the products that have culturally acquired a female and private label. Men are also connected to certain technology-related services; it is preferred to have a masculine actor advising and speaking about the use of technology. Thus men and masculinities are understood as a resource in attracting customers as individuals in general and in relation to technology-related services in particular. Women are understood as resources by association with certain products, not as people. Thus women and femininities are embedded in the commodified products.

Customer attraction and persuasion requires a vision of what kinds of people the customers are. Sharon Bolton and Maeve Houlihan (2005) have studied customers as a third party in the relationships in call-centre work. They have suggested three different roles that customers play in the call-centre context. These are 'mythical sovereigns', 'functional transactants' and 'moral agents', which are overlapping categories. A 'mythical sovereign' represents the customer who is always right and whom the customer service representative needs to manage. A 'functional transactant' is a good customer. She or he is easy and likes to complete the discussions effectively and briefly. Customers as 'moral agents' are understood as ordinary human beings with socially meaningful activities.

The accounts of the informants in this study include an assumption of customers as mythical sovereigns. For them, customers are right and the task is to win their minds over to accepting the offers made by the call-centre employees. The CEO expects 'sporty and joyful' voices which seem not to include life experience. Whether the adult voices and age are combined with gender in these conceptions cannot be established on the basis of this direct empirical evidence. However, the described experience of how older women act as customers refers to the idea that men's voices are thought of as more convincing. At the same time the experience of motherly voices is thought of as something male customers find appealing. Yet, Paula's account suggests that customers are also seen as functional transactants and moral agents. In short, it seems that the view of the customer as difficult and as a person who is resisting the call-centre employees is exaggerated. Accordingly, the requirements to persuade only sovereign customers surpass the needs of the other customers who value brief effective contacts or who value good human relations.

It is a paradox that men are appreciated in call-centre work even though men do not seek call-centre jobs in the same ways that women do. However, the appreciation of men may be related to the wish and need to improve the status of call-centre work both in relation to the image and status of the work, and in relation to concrete ways of convincing and attracting people.

More fundamentally, the question is raised of how to create trust relations between the call-centre industry as a whole, the activities of call centres and their employees and the customers. More research is needed on how the two-way relationship between employees and customers is built up and what kind of a role gender practices play in these processes. In future research it will be necessary to link together practising gender and interactional relationships. Further study is particularly needed on the concrete ways in which the distance and closeness, or the styles of the encounters and pure relationships between the people in interaction, are contextually formed and on how practising gender imbues interaction in call-centre work. It is suggested here that the cultural gendered images of the products and services may imbue the styles of interaction.

This paper has indicated that these questions are also located beyond the employee-customer relationship. Gender segregation includes the unreflective preferences for women's and men's activities in work. These preferences are supported by the contractors and the cultural definitions of feminine and masculine products and services. Still, the missing male employees are celebrated in call-centre work and this is partly explained by a wish to achieve the missing equality between women and men. Thus the celebration of men may give space for women to develop ways of practising gender that go beyond the non-reflective repetition of the gendered division of labour in call centres.

© *Päivi Korvajärvir, 2009*

ACKNOWLEDGEMENTS

I highly appreciate the comments of Elisabeth Kelan for the earlier version of the paper. I am grateful to Laura Tohka for improving my English language.

REFERENCES

Adkins, L. (2002) *Revisions. Gender and Sexuality in Late Modernity*, Buckingham & Philadelphia: Open University Press

Adkins, L. (2005) 'The New Economy, Property and Personhood', *Theory, Culture & Society*, Vol 22, No 3:111-131

Cameron, D. (2000) *Good to Talk? Living and Working in a Communication Culture*, London: Sage

Casey, C. (1995) *Work, Self and Society*, London: Routledge

Frenkel, S.J., M. Korczynski, K.A. Shire & M. Tam (1999) *On the Front Line. Organization of Work in the Information Economy*, Ithaca: Cornell University Press

Gherardi, S. & B. Poggio (2007) *Gendertelling in Organizations*, Copenhagen: Copenhagen Business School Press

Gray, A. (2003) 'Enterprising Femininity. New Modes of Work and Subjectivity', *European Journal of Cultural Studies*, Vol 6, No 4:489-506

Hochschild, A.R. (1983/2003) *The Managed Heart. The Commercialization of Human Feeling*, Berkeley: University of California Press

Jackson, S. (2006) 'Gender, Sexuality and Heterosexuality. The Complexity (and Limits) of Heteronormativity', *Feminist Theory*, Vol 7, No 1:105-121

Koivunen, T (2006) Asiakastyön ruumiillisuus yhteyskeskuksissa [Corporeality of the customer work in call centres], Työelämän tutkimus-Arbetslivsforskning, Vol 4, No 1:1-11.

Korvajärvi, P. (2002a) Locating gender neutrality in formal and informal aspects of organizational cultures, *Culture and Organization*, Vol 8, No 2:101-115.

Korvajärvi, P. (2002b) 'Gender-neutral gender and denial of the difference' in B. Czarniawska & H. Höpfl (eds) *Casting the other: the production and maintenance of inequalities in work organizations*, Routledge: London:119-137.

Korvajärvi, P. (2004) 'Women and technological pleasure at work?' in T. Heiskanen and J. Hearn (eds) *Information society and the workplace: Spaces, boundaries and agency*,Routledge:London:125-142.

Martin, P.Y. (2006) 'Practising Gender at Work: Further Thoughts on Reflexivity', *Gender, Work & Organization*, Vol 13, No 3:254-276

McDowell, L. (1997) *Capital Culture*, Oxford: Blackwell

Misztal, B.A. (2000) *Informality. Social Theory and Contemporary Practice*, London: Routledge

Misztal, B.A. (2005) 'The New Importance of the Relationship between Formality and Informality', *Feminist Theory*, Vol 6, No 2:173-194

Taylor, P., G. Mulvey, J. Hyman & P. Bain (2002) 'Work Organization, Control and the Experience of Work in Call Centre', *Work, Employment and Society*, Vol 16, No 1:133-150

Warhust, C., D. Nickson, A. Witz, & A.M. Cullen (2000) 'Aestethic Labour in Interactive Service Work: Some Case Study Evidence from the "New" Glasgow', *The Services Industries Journal*, Vol 20, No 3:1-18

Webster, J. (2005) 'Women in IT Professions: Corporate Structures, Masculine Cultures', *Symposium on Gender & ICT: Working for Change*. Manchester. Accessed on February 1, 2005 from http://ict.open.ac.uk/gender/papers/.

Witz, A., C. Warhust & D. Nickson (2003) 'The Labour of Aesthetics and the Aesthetics of Organization', *Organization*, Vol 10, No 1:33-54

Employment in call centres in Bulgaria

Vassil Kirov and Kapka Mircheva

Vassil Kirov *is a research fellow in the Institute of Sociology at the Bulgarian Academy of Sciences in Sofia, Bulgaria.*
Kapka Mircheva *is a specialist in human resources management at Net Info.BG Ltd in Sofia, Bulgaria.*

ABSTRACT

In recent years, Bulgaria has become an important destination for call-centre outsourcing of client services from abroad. Thousands of new jobs in call centres have been created in the capital and the largest Bulgarian cities. This remarkable development has not yet been a subject of serious analysis. For this reason this article aims to present a summary of the development of the call-centre industry in Bulgaria, focusing on employment in the sector. In particular, the authors, focus on the characteristics of the workers who are sought, recruitment policies and training in call centres, working environments, remuneration practices and workplace representation of employees. The analysis makes it possible to draw some conclusions about the characteristics of employment in call centres in Bulgaria and how this compares with employment in the sector in other countries.

Introduction

It is not an exaggeration to claim that funtil recently call centres were virtually unheard of in Bulgaria. To the extent that such a person was known at all, the popular image of a call-centre worker was that of a not very polite lady from the national telecommunications company who made you wait for ten minutes only to inform you that she could not find the number you had asked for. The results from one international research project (TOSCA) in the early 2000s (Ialamov, T., 2002) confirms the hypothesis that jobs in call centres in the country were negligible in number at the time.

However, during the last five or six years there have been dramatic changes. A large number of multinational companies, such as IBM and Hewlett Packard, have moved existing call centres to Sofia or established new ones there[1]. Recent data provided by the Global Services Location Index (GSLI), a ranking of the most attractive offshoring destinations, confirm the increasing importance of Bulgaria as one of the most attractive offshoring destinations in Europe (ranked 9th in 2007 and 13th in 2008)[2]. During this period many local call centres have also started to offer their outsourcing

---

[1]   According to the Hungarian researcher Pellényi, 'Altogether, the role of Central and Eastern Europe is growing … Usually centres servicing Europe are relocated to and concentrated in the region, mainly by extra-European (US) multinationals. The most important attracting factors for these kinds of projects are the level of information technology infrastructure and use; the availability of skill base/(required) language knowledge; in certain cases FDI incentives, and finally, proximity/good geographic location. As the cost advantage of Central Europe has been gradually eroding, there is some upgrading while certain activities move further to cheaper Romania and Bulgaria' (Pellényi, 2007)

[2]   'Geography of Offshoring is Shifting, According to A.T. Kearney', 2009, Study http://www.atkearney.com/index.php/News-media/geography-of-offshoring-is-shifting.html (accessed on the 18th May, 2009)

services to companies interested in benefiting from Bulgaria's financial attractiveness, availability of skilled personnel and business-friendly environment. The reasons for the outsourcing and offshoring of such services are well known (Huws, et al. 2004[3]). What is not known is what kind of employment is developing in these newly-opened call centres. Is there an alignment with the employment features observed in other European contexts or might there be some Bulgarian specificity?

The objective of this paper is to present a brief overview of the call-centre industry in Bulgaria with several aims: first, to analyse how the labour force is recruited; second, to investigate how this labour force is managed; and third, to draw conclusions about the experience of call-centre work in Bulgaria in order to make comparisons with the results of internationally comparative projects.

There is very little literature about the development of the call-centre industry in Bulgaria and employment in this sector. This paper draws mainly on three sources of information. The first of these is an analysis of publicly available materials about call centres, mainly in the press, but also in Internet forums, including a discourse analysis by Kapka Mircheva studying employers' images of call centres operating in Bulgaria (Mircheva, 2008). The second source is a series of research exercises carried out by students at Sofia University under the supervision of Dr Vassil Kirov[4]. The third source is participant observation by one of the authors in the HR department of a call centre in Sofia[5].

This research interest in employment in new sectors such as call centres is embedded in other research by the authors on emerging forms of employment in Bulgaria. As well as playing an active part in the WORKS[6] project, a Bulgarian team from the Institute of Sociology in Sofia has also developed a networking and exchange project, financed by ASO, Austria[7] which has held a series of discussions on the impacts of the knowledge-based society (KBS) on national economies and employment in South-Eastern Europe. One of the hypotheses examined during these debates was that the KBS might have negative as well as positive effects. Might the pay levels in foreign-owned call centres contribute to deformations on the local labour market, limit

---

3   'The international migration of ICT service employment appears to be growing fast, both between EU Member States and globally. Within the EU, the UK has been the most important user of outsourced services, but there are signs that other Member States are rapidly adopting this practice. Former colonial powers have in the past turned first to their former colonies in seeking destinations but in the future they are increasingly likely to seek locations in eastern Europe. China is also predicted to grow rapidly as a supplier of offshore services'. (Huws and al., 2004:23)

4   Several papers have been produced by groups of students in the framework of the discipline 'Organisational diagnostics and consulting' of the Master's Degree Programme 'Labour markets and Human Resources Development' of Sofia University's 'Sv. Kliment Ohridski' in 2007-2008 and 2008-2009.

5   Between 2006 and 2008, Kapka Mirchevaworked as a recruiter in one of the biggest Bulgarian call centres, based in Sofia.

6   Work Organisation Restructuring in the Knowledge Society (WORKS) is an international research project investigating the impact of the restructuring of global value chains on organisations and individuals in Europe (http://www.worksproject.be), funded by the European Commission under its 6th Framework Programme.

7   The international project 'Reflecting the Knowledge-based Society in the Context of EU Enlargement: Research on labour market restructuring, employment change and skills acquisition in Austria, Bulgaria, Croatia and Macedonia' was co-ordinated by the Institute of Sociology of the Bulgarian Academy of Sciences (2005-2006). It was supported by funds from the Austrian Science Foundation and Research Liaison Offices with Ljubljana and Sofia (managed by the Centre for Social Innovation, Vienna) on behalf of the Federal Ministry of Science and Research of the Republic of Austria in the Framework of its Southeast Europe (SEE) Science Cooperation initiative.

innovation opportunities or inhibit career development? [8]. It was suggested that a deeper study of call centres in Bulgaria might shed light on such questions (Kirov & Stoilova, 2007). What kind of employment could be observed in Bulgarian call centres? What lies behind the generally positive image of these investments in the Bulgarian society? Are jobs occupied by low-skilled employees, as is the case in many countries? What training opportunities exist? How is the work organised? What forms of workplace representation exist? The answers to such questions could contribute to confirming or rejecting the hypothesis that a knowledge-based economy will have positive impacts on employment and the quality of work.

The call-centre industry in Bulgaria

The first call centres were opened in Bulgaria at the end of the 1990s. Most of them were branch offices of international companies. The motives for outsourcing to Bulgaria were the cheap labour, the relatively high educational level of the Bulgarians (comparable to India's workforce, for example) and the availability of a labour force speaking foreign languages[9] as well as the fact that the majority of foreign language speakers have good to excellent pronunciation. Additional attractions were the low cost of living in the country, tax advantages (with a 10% flat rate since 2007), fixed costs (rental fees, prices of consumables and services – cleaning companies for example), and per capita expenditure at the average level for Central Europe.

Already, by 2004, the press was announcing the success of some call centres[10]. A company located in the Sofia Business Park was dealing with queries relating to telecommunications services, natural gas, electricity and water for 120 million clients in Belgium, Germany and France[11]. 'City call Belgium', which operated only in Belgium up to 2003, offshored its office to Sofia in 2004 and is now called 'Imro Bulgaria'. In 2004 there were 425 employees in this company, but, according to statements made in interviews, they expected to hire about 1,000 in 2005.

The recently-privatised Bulgarian Telecommunications Company (BTC) also entered the call-centre industry in 2004, launching BTC Contact 12 and starting to provide outsourced services for MoneyGram. Between 2004 and 2008 (when BTC sold this company to Sofica), the call centre also worked for other international

---

8   The inspiration for this hypothesis was the text of the Indian researcher Sujata Gothoskar 'Content of and access to knowledge in the knowledge-based society: a view from the South', presented at the first WORKS conference, in Chania, in Greece, in 2006 on ' The transformation of work in a global knowledge economy: towards a conceptual framework', http://www.worksproject.be/documents/workschaniaconferencereportfinal. pdf (accessed on March 31st, 2009)

9   Unfortunately no statistics are available on the language abilities of the labour force in Bulgaria. However a recent survey of university students in Bulgaria ('Natzionalno prouchvane na profesionalnata orientazia I motivazia na studentite v Balgaria') provides data about the language skills of students: 59% of students in Sofia and 39% in the countryside know a foreign language (with respectively 43% and 26% speaking English).

10   In this year the Bulgarian government started to advertise the country as a good destination for investment in call centres

11   Stoilova, E., *Balgaria se prevrashta v magnit za kol tzentrove na svetovni kompanii*, (Bulgaria becomes very attractive for the call centres of world companies),31.03.2004, see http://www.dnevnik.bg/ bulgaria/2004/03/31/73352_bulgariia_se_prevrushta_v_magnit_za_kol_centrove_na/ (accessed on the 31.03.2009)

12   BTK Grup prodade na Sofica Grup AD mejdunarodnia si kontakt tzentar, http://computerworld. bg/21816 (accessed on the 31.03.2009) (BTK group sold to Sofica Group AD its international contact centre)

clients, including AIG, a British internet services provider, B Unlimited and an online system for hotel reservations called Hotelopia, a subsidiary of First Choice Holidays.

In 2006 and 2007, there was a development boom in call centres. The number of companies in the market increased rapidly as did the number of the people employed by them. Major international companies such as Hewlett-Packard (HP), Microsoft and IBM also started operations in the Bulgarian capital, Sofia, opening large call centres during this period. The HP call centre quickly grew to accommodate 1,000 workstations, with a commitment to adding an additional 250 in 2008. During 2007 some Bulgarian companies also started to use outsourcing in order to increase their efficiency and profitability.

These trends of continuous growth continued until the end of 2008. In the early days, the great majority of investment in call centres was in Sofia, but by 2007-2008 a high proportion was being redirected to other large Bulgarian towns and cities, some of them university centres. This choice of location was not accidental. One example of active collaboration by a university with call-centre companies is the University of Veliko Tarnovo which signed a business agreement with two Belgian companies. Under the terms of this agreement, the university provides office space of nearly 200 square metres and a company called Evrokor provides the necessary accommodation. The call centre offers around 80 part-time jobs to students and recent graduates. It is seen as a chance to start their careers and gain professional experience for the young people in this region. Veliko Tarnovo is a big town that is trying to prevent its young people from migrating to larger cities. The University of Veliko Tarnovo has a high reputation as one of the main language schools for Scandinavian languages in Bulgaria and is regarded as one of the best language academies for Western European languages. From the university's point of view, the call centre provided an opportunity for students to practice and develop their linguistic knowledge by working with native speakers[13].

BTC, which has been private since 2004, opened new call centres in the towns of Pleven and Bourgas, creating about 430 new jobs in the process[14]. The choice of these locations was made after a serious analysis which took account of the unemployment rate, the educational level of the population and other factors.

However, new centres continued to open in Sofia as well. In 2008, a company called 60K was established with British capital. This company advertised its ability to provide services in 17 different languages. Its first contract was for providing customer services for a producer of anti-virus software, AVG Technologies. 60K started with 225 employees and was expected to double this number by the first quarter of 2009, reaching 1,000 employees over the next two to three years[15].

---

13   See Milcheva, M., Universitet otdade teren i studenti za col tzentar, Dnevnik, see http://www.
dnevnik.bg/bulgaria/2007/12/05/404601_universitet_otdade_teren_i_studenti_za_kol-centur/ (accessed on the
31.03.2009) (University ensures infrastructure and students for call centre)
14   See '1 milion leva sa vlojeni v kol tzentara na BTK v Pleven', 11 2006, www.econ.bg , http://www.
econ.bg/news86025/paper75823.html (accessed on the 31.03.2009) (1 million leva are invested in the call centre
of BTK in Pleven)
15   See 'Kol tzentar na 60 K otkrivat v stolizata', http://news.sagabg.net/kol-centr-na-siksti-kej-otkrivat-
v-stolicata.html, (accessed on the 31.03.2009) (Call centre of 60K is inaugurated in the capital)

These examples illustrate the rapid growth of the industry, the different profiles of investors and the range of services provided. It should be noted that this development has been achieved without any special government support[16].

From the beginning of 2009, call centres in Bulgaria started to experience the effects of the world financial crisis. Bulgarian and international companies decreased their orders or postponed the implementation of agreements that were already signed. As a result, a process of 'optimisation of the teams' was set in train. In 2009, call centres started to lay off employees who were underperforming, reversing their previous policies under which such employees were seen as people that could not develop at the same speed as the majority and who therefore needed more time and help to acquire new knowledge and skills. New employees who were still in their probation periods also started to be laid off. The decreasing volume of orders seemed to be felt in all areas, including customer services, telemarketing and carrying out telephone surveys. Customer service and debt collection were the least strongly affected, because of their ongoing character. Surveys were the most severely affected, since these projects were typically one-off activities, paid for from budgets earmarked for marketing, which were among the first to be cut. At the time of writing, in early 2009, the Bulgarian call-centre business was preparing for the hard times that were expected, and reducing its expenditure as much as possible.

Before the start of the world financial crisis, opinion was unanimous that the future of the call-centre industry in Bulgaria would be one of continuing expansion. Even in 2009, some of the most influential forecasts remained optimistic[17]. The fact that a European country is able to offer services at a lower cost and better quality than some Asian providers has been interpreted as a strong indicator of further growth potential in the near future. The increasing numbers of companies and growth in investment substantiate such claims.

What comes next? Companies that are able to keep their key clients and survive the downturn will have the chance to continue working in an environment with low competition. One priority for them seems likely to be the optimisation of teams and the retention of productive and engaged employees. Although media statements from the industry acknowledge that a difficult period is still to come, there have been no bankruptcies or call-centre closures. The smaller players run the highest risk of closure. Meanwhile larger centres will need to plan ahead to ensure their long-term survival. Whether foreign-owned offshored centres in Bulgaria will benefit from job losses in more expensive locations remains to be seen. Bulgarian-owned centres have the chance to demonstrate their stability to their employees and clients. However it seems probable that, in the medium term, Bulgaria will retain its image as an attractive destination for call-centre investment and a location in which continuing growth in employment can be expected.

---

16   An advertisement featuring Bulgaria as an outsourcing destination funded by the State investment agency. was the only government support of any note for the industry There are no subsidies or other stimuli available for the investing companies.
17   A 2009 study by A.T. Kearney suggested that the crisis could benefit Bulgaria by increasing its comparative advantages. 'Geography of Offshoring is Shifting,', 2009, http://www.atkearney.com/index.php/News-media/geography-of-offshoring-is-shifting.html (accessed on the 18th of May 2009).

The labour force and employment relations

The results of a survey by the TOSCA project (Ialamov, 2002) suggest that, at the beginning of the millenium, the majority of call centres in Bulgaria employed fewer than five people, with a small number employing 10-20. The vast majority of these employees were women (87%), working mainly with clients in the travel industry. The most widely used working language during this period was Bulgarian, followed by English. According to these researchers, the full potential of new technologies was not exploited at this time. Call centres provided simple information services and were not used as tools for managing their clients' customer relations. The authors did, however, see an enormous potential for foreign investment in Bulgarian call centres.

As already noted, this situation changed very rapidly. There are no official data that provide a breakdown of employment in call centres in Bulgaria, but some hypotheses can be formulated on the basis of existing knowledge.

It is clear that several thousand people are now employed overall in call centres in Bulgaria. For example, Human Resources analysts Raikovska and Gueorguieva[18], estimated in 2008 that there were about 8,000 people employed in Sofia alone providing technical support to customers in call centres involved in Business Process Outsourcing (BPO) and that this number would increase to 12,000 in 2009. According to these experts, Bulgaria has the capacity to offer at least 3,000 suitably skilled new employees to companies in this sector over the next one or two years. Employees are mainly young (20-23 years of age) and the largest group are university students, followed by recent university graduates. It is unusual to find employees in their thirties or older in call centres. The bulk of the employment is in Sofia. The sector is characterised by very high turnover rates by Bulgarian national standards. Few call-centre jobs are specialised; however some jobs in the call centres of large IT multinationals require technical knowledge as well as communications skills. Most of the people working in call centres are providing customer services in relation to outsourced processes (mainly handling inbound calls). This is evidenced by the fact that many of the largest call centres in Sofia – for instance, IBM, 60K, Sofica and HP – are all involved in customer service, with the IBM centre handling both its own back office processes and those of its clients. Telemarketing seems to be losing strength and the proportion of workers supplying this function is declining.

To employees, the most attractive feature of these workplaces is the flexibility of the working hours they offer. Call centres offer both labour contracts and civil ones (contracts for short-term projects). Labour contracts may be permanent or temporary (depending on a variety of factors, including the wishes of the chosen applicant, an assessment of efficiency, the required investment in trainings, the induction period and the character of the project). Call centres offer opportunities for full-time or part-time employment. Both types of employment offer flexibility of working hours. Where possible, employers usually offer opportunities for personally-negotiated working schedules (for instance in telemarketing outbound call centres where workers are expected to achieve a set quantity of sales and reaching defined targets). Large

---

18   Bulwork, interview with Raikovska and Gueorguieva, 17 December 2008, http://jobs.bg/hc/analytics/295, accessed on March 31, 2009.

companies seem to adhere strictly to Bulgarian legislation requirements in order to keep their employees satisfied and stay on good terms with the relevant state institutions.

Recruitment

Because staff turnover is so high, the recruitment of personnel is a continuous process in most Bulgarian-based call centres and their personnel departments.

The main target groups are students at the beginning of their studies (searching for flexible working hours), recent graduates without professional experience, narrow specialists (philologists, for instance) who do not have easy opportunities for professional career development (for example, a graduate with a degree in Czech Philology with a high motivation to work with that language, but without any preference for any particular domain). An important role is played by the fact that call centres are reliable employers, offering good and stable employment conditions, payment and benefit packages (compared to other activities in the country – e.g. tourist agencies).

Some call centres in Bulgaria also try to promote diversity by employing foreigners. However this creates serious tensions when people from Western Europe are paid more than Bulgarians[19]. The reasons for hiring foreigners, despite their higher salaries, include the benefits gained from having native speakers in a team, both for the team itself and, by advertising its cosmopolitan workforce, to promote a positive image of the company both as an outsourcer and as an employer. Although they are larger than those offered to natives, the salaries paid to foreigners are of course not competitive when compared with Western European standards. Nevertheless, some foreign employees are attracted by the knowledge and experience that can be gained and the stimulation and broadening of horizons that comes from living abroad in a different environment and culture. Again, these are mainly young people, usually recently graduated, with little or no previous work experience. They are attracted to Bulgaria by the comparatively low cost of living, the pleasant climate and the rich social life. Small companies attract foreigners by offering career opportunities and flexibility in payment schemes (sometimes, for instance, offering lodging as part of the employment package).

The breadth of the target group for call-centre recruits makes it necessary for employers to be creative in their strategies to attract applicationsin order to ensure that procedures are not too time-consuming, and avoid losing good applicants because of postponed decisions. Where rare language skills are required, partnerships with local universities that offer courses in these languages may be used, like the one already mentioned at Veliko Tarnovo University. Attention is paid to establishing a positive and 'fun' image of companies, emphasising the youth of the team. Advertisements use language which is accessible to and recognisable by the target groups and a wide range of channels are used. These include recruitment websites, university careers advice centres, career forums, leaflets and brochures distributed among students, media advertisements, including on the radio and in national newspapers, corporate presentations and the use of job-search databases. Companies also hold open days, provide internship programmes, establish direct links with university professors who

---

19   Anecdotal evidence suggests that foreigners may be paid twice as much as Bulgarians for the same work.

can refer students and offer financial bonuses (sometimes equivalent to more than a month's salary) to employees who can recommend friends for vacant positions.

The recruitment process usually follows a conventional pattern. After scrutiny of the written job application, candidates are checked on their language knowledge and computer literacy and then interviewed, either by representatives of the HR department or by line managers or project managers, often by several of these.

Through articipant observation we were able to examine the recruitment criteria in some depth. A first prerequisite is good knowledge of a foreign language, with companies favouring candidates who have lived abroad and have practised the language on the spot. Candidates speaking two Western languages are preferred. The companies also look for a good educational level, rarely considering a candidate who is not a university student or a graduate. Well developed communication skills are also important, with preference given to candidates who already have some experience in working with clients. There is also a strong preference for candidates who are young, 'full of energy' and 'dynamic'. Finally, there is also a conscious effort to find candidates who are motivated to work with bonus systems based on personal results.

At the beginning of the expansion of call centres in Bulgaria it was relatively easy to find suitable candidates, but, since 2007, the competition in Sofia has been increasing constantly. This is the reason some call centres have established themselves outside the capital or established additional offices in these provincial locations.

These profiles demand considerable skill and knowledge from call-centre recruits, but, as we see below, it is questionable whether the jobs actually offer levels of achievement that match these: in many cases, the work can only be describes as routine.

Training of call-centre employees

Call centres are unusual among employers in Bulgaria in providing training for their staff[20]. Most centres with more than 100 employees have established their own internal training departments and the vast majority of call centres provide introductory training. This is normally carried out in groups (rarely individually) and includes presentations about the company, introducing its organisational structure and culture, projects and customers. An important part of this initial training relates to acquainting new recruits with the particular projects on which they will be working, including the specific requirements of the clients, the software, terminology and communication channels.

This initial training could last from a single day to over a week a week and is often supplemented by individual coaching. One reason that intensive coaching is needed is that the majority of recruits have no previous work experience. It is a frequent practice to start the training process with a group of shortlisted candidates and assess them closely during this process, only offering employment contracts to the highest achievers in the group. International companies also sometimes provide initial training for improving the language skills of their operators. In these cases they usually select candidates with basic or mid-level knowledge of the language and provide intensive courses with a duration of one to three months. After the final examination, students are ranked and those with the

---

20   According to the European CVT Survey, Bulgaria is among the countries with the lowest level of employer-provided training.

highest scores then start working with their newly-developed skills. This practice is found in contact centres that require knowledge of languages that have not been traditionally studied in Bulgaria. For instance, call centres operating in Belgian markets hire students with French language skills and offer them courses in Flemish.

International companies, especially those with in-house call centres, also invest in developing the so-called 'soft skills' that are crucial for the work of their employees. In order to improve the quality of their services, these companies have developed corporate training programmes on such topics as working with difficult clients, for conflict-resolution skills, successful telesales, etc. Most of these training courses are provided by internal trainers. It is rare in Bulgaria to invest in external training programmes for call-centre agents.

These training policies are greatly appreciated by young people who seize every opportunity to acquire new knowledge and improve their qualifications, in the belief that this will help them to advance their careers within the company find another job elsewhere.

This belief is justified. It seems to be the case that people who have worked in a call centre really are regarded as having developed interpersonal communication skills that are valued on the local labour market and are sought-after applicants for starting-level positions in sales, HR, banking, and a number of other fields. Their attitude to clients is usually developed to West European standards. These young people typically have experience of working with foreign clients in a variety of different spheres – IT support, accounting, hotel reservations, and debt collections. They are thus already 'trained' for the position of an entry-level employee in these fields. In the Bulgarian context, this know-how can thus be regarded not only as a 'privilege' for the call centre but for the call-centre operator as well.

In this perspective, call-centre work can be seen as providing initial working experience for young people that equips them with skills that can be used in a range of different employment settings in sectors that are exposed to the global economy.

Career development

An analysis of discussions in internet forums (Mircheva 2008), gives an insight into the operators' views. This study found that local call centres are regarded as offering better opportunities for promotion than international ones. This is attributed to the fact that their financial resources, when compared with those of international companies, do not allow them to compete in the open market for highly-qualified specialists and managers. They therefore try to develop their own employees and train their own specialists internally. The practice of using head-hunters to find experienced project managers is new in Bulgaria; the easiest way to ensure professional expertise in a team is to 'breed your own'.

In both foreign and local companies the main career development path is determined by the structure and operations of the company. The entry point is the call-centre agent who could become a supervisor and after that a project manager or become a trainer or HR professional. However career development requires patience and work experience in the company, perseverance and taking advantage of all opportunities to demonstrate one's personal qualities to the management. The high turnover and the routine nature of jobs in call centres mean that only a minority are able to progress in this way.

Here, there could be a contradiction between the high skill profile of the employees, their aspirations for career development in other spheres and the opportunities offered by call centres.

Employee relations and representation

There are no formal channels of representation for employees in Bulgarian call centres. In the post-1989 period, trade unions have not set up any sections in these recently established companies. Indeed it is questionable whether they have ever tried to unionise call-centre employees. In general trade-union density in Bulgaria has decreased significantly during the last decade and now probably stands at about 20% (EIRO, 2008). Although still strong in the public sector and some industries (Kirov, 2005), trade unions have an insignificant presence in private services. The average age of union members is increasing and they are finding it more and more difficult to attract young people. Many young people in Bulgaria seem to perceive the existing trade unions as retarded and behind times.

Even though, since 2006, the Bulgarian Labour code has made it possible to establish information and consultation bodies, such bodies do not exist in Bulgarian call centres. There is no evidence that employees have asked for such bodies. Neither is there any evidence that employers take seriously the right for a real representation of employees, which could allow them to demand improvements in their working conditions.

Hierarchical communication between management and employees is mainly formal, often carried out in a distanced manner. In general, it could be asserted that the working environment is characterised by a high degree of formalisation in the relations between management and call-centre agents. Here, the aim of management is to keep a distance between hierarchical levels and ensure a situation where managers are treated with respect. In some call centres in Bulgaria, everyday working discipline is subject to very strict regulation, for example with rules that stipulate precise times for coffee and lunch breaks, prohibitions on drinks at the workstation and bans on talking between colleagues during waiting times.

Such rules give rise to much discussion in the internet forums where call-centre employees exchange opinions. In some cases they have led to call centres being described as 'prisons' or 'concentration camps', but, in general, it is small local call centres that are described in this way. No such epithets were used in describing the big international companies. These companies typically come to Bulgaria and establish their branches either with the traditional hierarchy and culture, rules and values that have been established and proven for the region or according to the model used at their headquarters.

We can conclude that employees rarely have a significant 'voice' in call centres in Bulgaria. The hierarchy tends to be formal and strict in many cases and there seem to be few opportunities for employees to express their opinions or even make suggestions for improvements. But on the basis of the available evidence we cannot draw broad conclusions that working conditions are universally poor across the sector.

Employee strategies

Delving below the superficially attractive image of the companies that are creating so many new jobs in Bulgaria, we now turn to a discussion of the characteristics of employment in call centres and the individual strategies adopted by employees.

Compared with other forms of employment in the Bulgarian labour market, call centres offer several clear advantages. Pay levels are attractive, with monthly salaries of 1,000-1,500 Bulgarian leva (500 -750 Euros) for call-centre agents. These are higher than the salaries offered in the state administration and many private companies for junior positions for people with university degrees, and are significantly in excess of the average wage in the capital which, according to the National Statistics Institute, was only 300 euros in 2008. A second important advantage is the practice of offering flexi-schemes for working hours which is particularly attractive to university students, especially in an economy that has no tradition of offering flexible working time arrangements. The individually-tailored working schedules that are offered to telemarketing employees are an example of this. Under one such scheme an employee can agree a 'half working day' contract that covers a working week of between 20 and 22 hours with an individually-negotiated schedule of hours actually spent in the office. The freedom offered by this scheme makes it possible for a worker to handle two jobs at once or fit work in around the university teaching timetable. Companies that offer such flexible working arrangements usually have an attractive image on the labour market. Internet forum postings also suggest that some employees enter the industry in the belief that it will offer good opportunities for career advancement.

Most students prefer jobs in call centres to other service sector jobs, such as those in hotels or restaurants. In their view, call-centre work offers greater time flexibility, allowing them to attend lectures and seminars regularly. It also gives them a chance to gain experience with international clients and standards. Finally, an important advantage in a country where informal employment practices are widespread, they can be legitimately employed, with their social security contributions paid by the employer.

Nevertheless, after starting employment in the sector, many of these young workers find that the reality is markedly different from their expectations. They discover that the work is very stressful, with continuous pressure coming from the management (sometimes conflicting with other pressures coming from clients), monotonous work, lack of feedback and inaccessible targets. For the majority of call-centre employees career development inside these companies is not a motivating factor. They are cynical about the motives of colleagues who have reached the position of supervisors or team leader, referring to them as 'time-servers' or people 'who know which side their bread is buttered'. Even if they are not interested in a long-term stay in the call-centre industry, they still resent the rigidity with which they are managed and the way that their views are ignored. Over time, negative factors start to play stronger role, decreasing personal motivation for work and probably influencing the decision to quit this kind of job which is often made after a few months or a year of service.

Table 1. Characteristics of employment in call centres: comparison of international and Bulgarian findings

	GCC conclusions	Bulgaria
Selection	22% of call centres predominantly recruit people with college degrees, a relatively high proportion for what is considered to be a low skill job – but country variation is high.	Call centres recruit mainly university students and recent graduates.
Training	Newly hired workers typically receive 15 days of initial training, with somewhat less in coordinated countries (14 days) than in liberal countries (17 days).	International and national companies provide initial training in Bulgaria. In-house call centres offer deeper and richer initial training.
Staffing	29% of the workforce in call centres is part time or temporary, with coordinated economies making the greatest use of non-standard work arrangements.	Staff in call centres in Bulgaria are employed mainly part-time and employers prefer permanent contracts in order to assure a stable workforce.
Job discretion	Job discretion is generally low, but substantial differences exist across coordinated, liberal market, and recently industrialised economies.	No data available.
Performance monitoring	Frequency of performance monitoring (feedback on performance and call quality; call listening) varies internationally. Monitoring activities typically occur on a monthly basis in coordinated countries, on a fortnightly basis in liberal market countries, and on a weekly basis or more in industrialising countries.	Performance monitoring of agents is widespread. Supervisors spend 2-5 hours per week on quality control. In outsourced call centres this is specified in the contract with the client. The call centre is obliged to present its client with recorded conversations for quality checking.
Teams	Use of self-directed teams is low – 60% of centres make virtually no use of these work groups.	Use of self-directed teams is very rare in call centres in Bulgaria.
Collective representation	50% of call centres are covered by some form of collective representation, i.e., collective bargaining, works councils or both.	No collective representation of call-centre workers in Bulgaria.
Job quality	Job quality is highest in coordinated economies and lowest in industrialising economies. In coordinated economies, more call centres have high to very high quality jobs (41%) than low to very low quality jobs (24%). In contrast, in liberal and industrialising economies, more call centres have low to very low quality jobs (48% and 50%) than high to very high quality jobs (25% and 21%).	Co-existence of low quality jobs and high-quality jobs.

Sources: Holman et al, 2007 and the authors, 2009.

Comparison with call-centre employment in other countries

Researchers from the Global Call Centre (GCC) project, summarising the results of their large international survey, concluded that 'beyond these similarities, we find that call-centre workplaces take on the character of their own countries and regions, based on distinct laws, customs, institutions, and norms. The "globalisation" of call-centre activities has a remarkably national face' (Holman D. and al., 2007). We conclude this paper by summarising what is known about call centres in Bulgaria and comparing this situation with the results of the GCC analysis, which, in line with the typology developed in the 'varieties of capitalism' school, grouped other European national economies into 'co-ordinated market' and 'liberal' countries (Hall & Soskice, 2001). These are contrasted with a third category of 'industrialising' countries. This comparison, summarised in Table 1, is a first attempt to compare employment in call centres in Bulgaria with other European and international models. It shows that there are many similarities but at the same time there are significant differences, especially concerning workplace representation and the use of less formal and strict forms of work organisation.

Conclusion

Employment in call centres in Bulgaria has increased spectacularly in recent years. Both international and locally-owned call centres have built up their Bulgarian operations mainly by using the labour of university students or recent graduates. However the apparently attractive conditions of employment (good salaries, flexible working time, use of IT and languages, international experience and thorough training) are not sufficient to retain these employees for any length of time. Stress, rigid organisation and strong discipline make many young people quit.

The comparison of call-centre employment in Bulgaria with call-centre employment in other European countries could provide some elements of explanation of the paradox whereby these very well-paid young people working there (sometimes earning two or three times their parents' wages) are leaving these jobs relatively quickly. This draws attention to the fact that the new knowledge-based jobs in call centres in Bulgaria do not only bring positive effects. There is trade-off between the acceptance of routine work with little or no intrinsic interest on the one hand and good salaries and working time flexibility on the other.

This situation of high turnover suggests that call centres might do well to re-examine their long term recruitment and HR strategies. It is possible that more diversified recruitment, both in terms of profiles and geographical areas, and some changes in work organisation could be made in order to retain personnel for longer periods. It is still an open question to what extent jobs in call centres (or other forms of outsourced activities such as data processing) are beneficial for the long-term professional development of the Bulgarian labour force. In some cases, choices will have to be made between boring but well-paid jobs versus interesting jobs in innovative companies that pay lower salaries. At the same time, it must also be acknowledged that there are positive effects (from the point of view of employees) in the high salaries offered by the call centres compared to many other enterprises in the new or in the old economy. In some cases, these raised pay levels have actually obliged competing firms to raise their wage levels also, bringing a general benefit to workers on the local labour market.

There still remain many unanswered questions about the development of employment in call centres in Bulgaria and South-Eastern Europe in general. Further research is required and the authors of this paper plan to respond to this challenge by organising further in-depth studies.

© *Vassil Kirov and Kapka Mircheva, 2009*

REFERENCES

Gothoskar, S. (2006) 'Content of and access to knowledge in the knowledge-based society: a view from the South', *The transformation of work in a global knowledge economy: towards a conceptual framework*, Chania, Greece, 2006. Accessed on March 31, 2009 from http://www.worksproject. be/documents/workschaniaconferencereportfinal.pdf

Hall, P.A. & D. Soskice (2001) *Varieties of capitalism: the institutional foundations of comparative advantage,* Oxford: Oxford University Press

Holman, D, et al (2007) The global call center report: international perspectives on management and employment. A Report of the Global Call Center Research Network. Executive Summary

Huws, U., S. Dahlmann & J. Flecker (2004) Outsourcing of ICT and related services in the EU, European Foundation for the Improvement of Living and Working Conditions

Ialamov, T. (2002) Sravnitelno izsledvane na tzentrovete za obajdania, TOSCA project, see ppt at http://www-it.fmi.uni-sofia.bg/tosca-bg/ (Comparative survey of the call-centres)

Paul, J. & U. Huws (2002) 'How can we help? Good practices in call-centre employment', November 2002, Published by ETUC

Kirov, V. & R. Stoilova (eds) (2007) Changes of work and the knowledge based society, Special Issue of Sociological Problems

Kirov, V. (2005) 'Facing EU accession: Bulgarian trade unions at the crossroads' in D. Dimitrova & J. Vilokx (eds) *Trade Unions Strategies in Central and Easter Europe: Towards Decent Work*, Budapest: ILO:111-152

Mircheva, K. (2008) Polojitelen rabotodatelski imidj. Praktiki v razvitite darjavi i v Balgaria., Master Degree Thesis presented in the Sofia University 'Sv. Kliment Ohridski' (Positive Employer's Image. The practice in the Developed countries and in Bulgaria)

Pellényi, G. (2007) Magdolna Sass: Offshoring services: the case of NMS and Hungary, pp. 56 – 63, ICEG Conference Proceedings, Budapest

Access back issues of the journal

Institutions or individuals can subscribe online to **Work Organisation Labour and Globalisation** at http://analytica.metapress.com/content/121034/offerings. Or you can buy a print-only subscription from http://www.analyticapublications.com or order single copies from http://www.merlinpress.co.uk.

Volume 1 Number 1
The spark in the engine: creative workers in a global economy

ISBN 0-85036-582-1

A speeded-up, hyper-competitive global economy has an insatiable need for creative workers – to innovate, design new products and services, invent new processes, educate, inform and provide content for an ever-expanding range of new media. Policy-makers and employers insist that knowledge is essential for economic growth. Yet far from being nurtured, creative workers are subject to new forms of control. How do they experience 'knowledge management' from above? Do the rewards compensate for the stresses of long hours and precariousness? Is there an endless supply of geese to keeping laying the golden eggs? Or might some decide to flee the coop and imagine how to create a better world?

Includes contributions from Andrew Ross, Richard Shearmur, Sybille Reidl, Helene Schiffbänker,Hubert Eichmann, Simone Dahlmann, Ursula Huws, Bob Hughes, Bettina-Johanna Krings, Ashika Thanki, Steve Jefferys, Armando Fernández Steinko, Catherine McKercher, Vincent Mosco and Leif Schumacher.

Volume 1 Number 2
Defragmenting: towards a critical understanding of the new global division of labour

ISBN 1-4196-7774-8

New information and communications technologies can shift work seamlessly around the globe, opening up a bewildering range of new choices in who does what work, where, when and how. As value chains get ever longer and more elaborate, work becomes more fragmented and less stable and skills and processes are transformed. How can we make sense of these changes? And what are the implications for regions and workers around the world?

Includes contributions from Elmar Altvater, David Coates, Ursula Huws, Jörg Flecker, Peter Standen, Penny Gurstein, Chris Benner, Anita Weiss, Laura Schatz, Laura C. Johnson, Norene Pupo, Sujata Gothoskar, Marcia Leite, Andreas Boes and Tobias Kämpf.

Volume 2 Number 1
Break or weld? trade union responses to global value chain restructuring

ISBN 978-0-85036-610-5-9000

Most trade unions evolved to negotiate with single employers in a single country. Now, multiple sites around the world are linked to each other in complex value chains, and global employers are more likely to answer to their shareholders than to national institutions. In this new context, what is the future for traditional forms of organisation and representation? Does the defence of local jobs pit workers on different sites against each other? Or can new solidarities emerge that strengthen links along the value chain?

Includes contributions from Ronaldo Munck, Vincent Mosco, Pamela Meil, Jürgen Kädtler, Leonardo Mello e Silva, Marco Aurelio Santana, Michelle Rodino-Colocino, Monique Ramioul, Tom de Bryun, Marlea Clarke, Carolyn Bassett, Bruce Robinson, Patrick Develtere, An Huybrechs, Peter Waterman and Ursula Huws.

Volume 2 Number 2
The new gold rush: the new multinationals and the commodification of public sector work
ISBN 978-0-85036-689-1-9000

Over the past few years, a new breed of multinationals has arrived, almost unnoticed, on the scene. Like early capitalist adventurers, they have found a rich new source of wealth to exploit. But this seam of gold is to be found, not in the mountains of California or the depths of Africa but at the very heart of the welfare states of the developed world. This important collection of essays anatomises the emergence of the 'public services industry' and analyses the way in which government services have been commodified so that they can be privatised or outsourced. It charts the growth of the global companies that have sprung up to supply these services and documents the devastating impact on workers, including work intensification, casualisation, loss of union protection and erosion of occupational identities. It also explores the changing relationship between the state and the private sector and the implications for democracy of developments which transform citizens into shoppers.

Includes contributions from Stewart Player, Colin Leys, Judith Clifton, Daniel Díaz-Fuentes, Christoph Hermann, Torsten Brandt, Thorsten Schulten, Ruth Barton, Peter Fairbrother, Birgit Mahnkopf, Chris Dixon, Melanie Samson, Nils Böhlke, Annika Schönauer, Simone Dahlmann, Nicole Mayer-Ahuja, Patrick Feuerstein and Ursula Huws.

Lightning Source UK Ltd.
Milton Keynes UK
UKOW06f1131250416

272921UK00001B/109/P